Those names in parentheses beside the song title are often ignored and unheralded. Philip Self has provided a rare insight into the lives of those writers, and has given us a glimpse of their sacrifices, their memories, their humor and, more often than not, their humility. What an incredible bunch of characters.

Guitar Pull is a much needed contribution to the tradition of oral history, and is a loving and heartfelt tribute to these colorful and extraordinary artists.
—**Thad Tarleton, veteran music publisher**

It is fascinating to hear from the true originators of the music we cherish in a book that loves and respects songwriters as much as we do.
—**Mark Mason, BMI**

Guitar Pull is an intimate and fascinating book. I loved hearing the true history of Music Row and the early days of the country music business from these wonderful songwriters. It was fun to hear these inside stories told by people who don't pull any punches. They were so honest and candid about everything from substance abuse to who cheated while.

This is the real thing—no fluff, no spin. Philip Self is a wonderful interviewer who obviously knows the right questions to ask, and gets amazing answers.
—**Amy Kurland, Bluebird Café**

Reading *Guitar Pull* was like being in the room with all of my heroes.
—**Ralph Murphy, ASCAP**

I know of no book like *Guitar Pull*, devoted to our music's finest songwriters. In their own words we learn about the craft of songwriting, the business of song publishing, and the creative genesis of many of our favorite songs.

Philip Self captures a generation, really, of Music Row denizens the like of whom we will not see again.
—**Ronnie Pugh, Country Music Foundation**

I knew the songs. After reading *Guitar Pull*, I feel I know the songwriters.
—**Jeff Pennig, professional songwriter**

After reading this book, after not being able to put it down from the moment I picked it up until the moment I finished it, I was reminded once again that great songwriters have to be great storytellers. And that is what *Guitar Pull* is: a collection of compelling, colorful, and thoroughly entertaining stories told by fifteen guys and one gal who created, published, and produced some of the best and best known songs of the last half of the 20th century.
—**Sharon Pelton, television writer and producer**

A real insight into some of the people who wrote those great country songs.
—**Nick Shaffran, Sony Music Special Products**

GUITAR PULL

Also by Philip Self

Yogi Bare:
Naked Truth from America's Leading Yoga Teachers

GUITAR PULL

*Conversations with
Country Music's
Legendary Songwriters*

PHILIP SELF

Cypress Moon
NASHVILLE, TENNESSEE

Cypress Moon Press
P.O. Box 210925
Nashville, TN 37221
info@cypressmoon.com

The following grateful acknowledgments are made for permission to reprint excerpts from
previously published material:

"Outside The Nashville City Limits" by Joan Baez © Chandos Music (ASCAP)
"Good Ole Boys Like Me" by Bob McDill © Universal Polygram International Publishing Inc.
   (ASCAP)
"Gone Country" by Bob McDill © Universal Polygram International Publishing Inc.
   (ASCAP)/Ranger Bob Music (ASCAP)

Self, Philip, 1960-
         Guitar pull : conversations with country music's legendary
     songwriters / Philip Self. – 1st ed.
         p.   cm.
         Includes index.
         ISBN 0-9666894-1-0

         1. Country music – History and criticism.   2. Composers –
     United States – Interviews.   3. Country musicians – Interviews.
     4. Country music – Writing and publishing.   5. Music trade –
     United States.
     I. Title.

     ML3524.S45 2001   781.642'092'2
                                              QBI01-700171

First Cypress Moon Press trade paperback printing April 2002.

10 9 8 7 6 5 4 3 2 1

Cover photo of Tommy Collins by R.A. Andreas/Bear Family Records (www.bear-family.de).

Cover design by Hatch Show Print. Additional graphics by Guerrilla Design (www.guerrilladesign.com).

Typography and design by Roger A. DeLiso, Seattle, Washington.

Printed in the United States of America

To Mary

Old songwriters never die.
They just decompose.

—ROGER MILLER

Acknowledgments

Special thanks to the talented professionals who helped bring *Guitar Pull: Conversations with Country Music's Legendary Songwriters* to fruition: Roger DeLiso, typographer; Jim Sherraden and Jenny Gill, cover designers; Garrett Rittenberry, graphic artist; Nedra Lambert, proofreader and indexer; and Patricia Lockhart, transcriptionist.

Thanks to Jack Jackson, Kathy Scobey, Richard Weize, Mark Mason, Leslie Morgan, David Sanjek, Karen Willard, Lauren Buffert, Michelle Peay, Tresa Hardin, Clay Bradley, Mitchell Greenhill and Paul Brooks.

I am grateful to those who have allowed me to be gainfully employed in music publishing in the chronological order of their poor judgment: Tom Collins, Ree Guyer, Even Stevens and Betty Fowler.

I have been the recipient of the generosity of numerous songwriters over the years. Most notably, Jimmy Payne, Terry Thompson, the late Doodle Owens, J. Fred Knobloch, Jeff Pennig, Roger Murrah, Steve Dean, Michael Dulaney and Paul Dolman.

Finally, to the participants of *Guitar Pull*, my sincere appreciation for your willingness to so openly share your immense wit and wisdom. You are among the greatest songwriters to have ever graced Music Row. I am honored and privileged to have been in your presence.

Table of Contents

Introduction

JENNY HOWELL WAS MY FIRST MUSIC TEACHER. She wasn't a singer. She didn't play an instrument. She couldn't dance.

Now, in the Deep South where I come from, some folks can't dance because they're Southern Baptist. But Jenny was Episcopalian, so denominational doctrine wasn't the issue. She was born with spina bifida.

We may have never met if she hadn't been my best friend's big sister. Calven and I graduated from Miss Maple's Kiddy Kampus Kindergarten, Airline High School and Louisiana Tech University together. We were in each other's wedding. Our parents still live a stone's throw apart. Whoever dies first will be carried by the other.

In the '60s, Calven; his little brother, Michael; my big brother, Parker and I would play with Tinkertoys or jump on beds or build a fort with chairs and blankets to the strains of country music coming from Jenny's bedroom.

Jenny was a true fan. Not only did she possess an extensive collection of albums and 45s, but she subscribed to *Music City News* to boot. Jenny introduced me to Conway Twitty, Loretta Lynn, Buck Owens and Patsy Cline. She told us Patsy had died in a plane crash. When Bobby Goldsboro would finish singing "Honey," I would request it again. I imagined the lilting background vocals were angels and Patsy Cline had wings.

I learned the name in parenthesis on the record was the writer. I wondered why it was printed so small, and the person's first name had been reduced to an initial. Weren't the words and music the most important part? This seemed self-evident.

Over the years, I discovered I was a much more a fan of songs, than artists. "Marie Laveau," "Harper Valley PTA" and "Galveston" were the stars. Bobby Bare, Jeannie C. Riley and Glen Campbell were merely the fortunate ones lucky enough to sing songs with substance. Songs with heart. Songs Jenny played.

♩ ♩ ♩ ♩

When I was sixteen, I wrote my first song. Mama lied and said it was good. I performed it publicly. Ignorance is bliss.

♩ ♩ ♩ ♩

After college graduation, I had a hankering to spend some time in Nashville, Tennessee, intent on pursuing a songwriting career. But I was only staying for the summer, as I had an academic scholarship to Candler School of Theology at Emory University.

I packed my '77 Monte Carlo to the gills and set sail from Bossier City, Louisiana, to Music City, U.S.A. I arrived at sunset and headed straight to Music Row, where I walked up and down 16th Avenue in awe until darkness fell.

The next day I stayed so long at the Country Music Hall of Fame and Museum that I accidentally got locked inside. The cleaning lady who was vacuuming with her back to me nearly jumped out of her skin when I tapped her on the shoulder. I'm sure she thought the ghost of Hank Williams had come a-calling.

♩ ♩ ♩ ♩

With the help of the *Tennessean* classified section, I landed a job on the front desk at the Hall of Fame Motor Inn. The "Hall of Shame," as it was affectionately known, was quite a little happening in the summer of '82.

One evening, Boxcar Willie stopped by the front desk on his way to the Grand Ole Opry.

"Could you store this for me?" he nonchalantly asked, as he reached into his bib overalls and extracted a wad of cash that would have choked a mule.

"Yes, sir, Mr. Boxcar."

One afternoon, the manager asked me to park cars for a music business reception. Wayne Carson, who was riding high on the charts with Willie Nelson's version of "Always On My Mind," pulled up in his brand new red sports car. As he hopped out and I hopped in, he handed me two dollars. I looked at the stick shift and clutch, and suddenly remembered I didn't know how to drive a standard. Too embarrassed to admit my incompetence, I waited until the sliding glass doors shut behind Wayne and shook his automobile across

Division Street like it was having an epileptic seizure. I figured he could afford to fix his transmission with his next royalty check.

One day I was working the front desk, when George Jones and his entourage strolled into the bar for a snort while a warrant was out for his arrest in Baton Rouge, Louisiana, for failure to appear at a scheduled concert. This was during the Possum's "No Show" era.

"George Jones!" I thought. "Here's my lucky break!"

I abandoned the cash register and approached the spirited table.

"Hi, George. I'm Philip Self. I was wondering how a guy like me would get songs to a guy like you."

Without missing a beat, George reached into his shirt pocket and handed me a business card.

"Send them to my manager," he replied. "He listens for all my material."

"Wow! Thanks!" I exclaimed as I stumbled over myself leaving the table.

Laughter erupted in the background.

When I returned to my post, I discovered that George had given me the business card of the manager at a Gadsden, Alabama, bowling alley.

I'm sure the man was confused when he received three of my songs in the mail.

♩ ♩ ♩ ♩

Not long ago, a woman and her husband arrived at ASCAP, a performing rights society, on Music Row.

"I'm here for my meeting with George Jones," the lady songwriter announced to the receptionist.

"Excuse me?"

"We met George at a concert last week in Gadsden, Alabama, and he said to drop by his office at ASCAP next Thursday at two o'clock to play him some songs. So here we are."

The Possum is still up to his tricks.

I had to laugh.

♩ ♩ ♩ ♩

During my second year of graduate school I returned to Nashville for a weekend visit. My body left long enough to return to Atlanta and drop out of seminary. My heart stayed behind.

Ultimately, for me, the pulpit was too confining. Besides, hymnals don't have nearly enough drinking songs.

🎸 🎸 🎸 🎸

November 23, 1983, I moved to Music City for good. Two weeks later, I was carrying a tray at Rhett's Restaurant in the Opryland Hotel. I was a waiter, so I waited and waited and waited. Two-and-a-half years I waited. I broke a few dishes, but the big break never came.

One evening, I had picked up a shift for a co-worker. A man and his wife came into the restaurant with their young son and daughter to celebrate their wedding anniversary. I brought the children complimentary Shirley Temples and did my best to see that their special occasion was enjoyable. After all, my tip was incumbent upon it.

When the meal was completed and the check was presented, the gentleman handed me his credit card. As I processed the payment, I glanced at the name: Tom Collins. I had seen this same name on the back of Ronnie Milsap, Barbara Mandrell, Steve Wariner and Sylvia albums.

When I returned to the table I asked, "Are you Tom Collins the producer or Tom Collins the drink?"

His laughter earned me an invitation to his office where I was later hired at Tom Collins Music and began a fifteen-year love affair with music publishing.

What can I say? I'm a song junkie.

🎸 🎸 🎸 🎸

Nashville publishing houses are notorious for not accepting unsolicited material.

New to the business, I commiserated with those who could not get anyone to listen to their songs. So I started I.W.A.D.—Independent Writer Appreciation Day—at Tom Collins Music. Every Thursday morning from nine to noon, I would listen to unsigned writers thirty minutes apart. I soon understood the wisdom of the "unsolicited material not accepted" policy.

Teddy Heard, a former Houston debutante turned Music Row receptionist, was responsible for scheduling the appointments as word spread amongst novice writers that we were listening.

"I just got a call from Waco Joe Jones," Teddy informed me. "He'll be here this Thursday. He sounds like a live wire."

Sure enough, Thursday at 9:30 sharp, Waco Joe Jones graced us with his presence.

He wore a cowboy hat, boots and jeans, and a western shirt with a mustard stain. He carried an Airstream-looking silver briefcase.

"Is Bob Collins in?"

"It's Tom Collins. He's in a meeting, sir," Teddy replied, working the gatekeeper role to perfection.

"Well, I have a song that's perfect for Barbara Mandrell that I want him to hear."

"Hi, I'm Philip Self. Come on back and let's give it a listen."

We stepped into my office, I closed the door and Waco Joe sat across from me. He set his Airstream briefcase on my desk, shoved it forward so it would fit, and I tried in vain to catch cassette tapes and writer contracts as they spilled into my lap and onto the floor.

He had ridden the bus to Nashville with his wife and mother from Waco, Texas. He worked in a tire factory. His supervisor told him to keep on plugging. This he offered as I put his tape into the cassette player.

I pushed play and leaned back to give his song an honest listen, but Waco never stopped talking.

"That's my wife Lola Jean singing."

"Her cousin is singing the harmony part."

"The guitar player is a friend of mine."

On and on and on.

The song didn't sound too bad. That is, what parts I could hear over his constant high-volume chattering.

It suddenly became apparent I had to get this fruitcake out of the building without setting him off.

"So what do you think? Is it a hit for Barbara Mandrell?"

"It's a nice song, but I don't think it's right for her," I politely responded.

"Here's forty dollars. Put this in your pocket and play it for Bob Collins."

"That's not really necessary, Mr. Jones."

"Okay, make it a hundred."

Five crisp twenties stared at me from Waco Joe Jones's outstretched hand.

"Mr. Jones, the song has to be right for the artist."

"I'll tell you what. Lola Jean is a real good-looking woman. Why don't you drop by the hotel room, if you know what I mean."

"I'm sorry, Mr. Jones, but that's not how we do business around here."

And I handed him back his tape.

He placed it in his opened Airstream and I feared a gun was coming out. I was relieved when he closed the lid.

After our meeting he went and sat in a wingback leather chair right outside of Tom's office. A few minutes later, unable to meet with Tom, Waco Joe Jones stormed out of the building nearly slamming the door off its hinges.

A week later the staff and writers had all gathered in Tom's office before our annual Christmas luncheon.

I looked out the window and here came Waco Joe Jones with Lola Jean in tow. Toilet paper hung out the back of her jeans.

"Oh, God!" I announced. "He's back!"

Husband and wife stormed Tom's office.

"Mr. Collins, I'm sorry to barge in like this, but I have a song that I want you to listen to for Barbara Mandrell."

"Well," Tom calmly replied as I looked for an escape route, "we're about to have our Christmas party, so I can only listen to one song."

Tom put the tape in his cassette player and pressed play.

I was expecting to hear the song from our meeting a week ago.

Instead I heard my own voice saying, "I'm sorry Mr. Jones, but that's not how we do business around here."

The room, present company included, fell out laughing.

Waco Joe's real name was Eddie Lunn. He was Tom Collins' former next-door neighbor.

My initiation into the music business was complete.

🎸 🎸 🎸 🎸

Guitar Pull is my second interview book.

The first, *Yogi Bare*, featured America's leading yoga teachers. Country music and yoga may not appear to belong in the same breath, but participants in both art forms include recent converts the Dixie Chicks and longtime practitioner Willie Nelson.

I was struck by several parallels between the two books:

In *Yogi Bare*, I sat riveted as Julie Lawrence spoke of losing her husband in the Vietnam War. Marijohn Wilkin experienced the same profound loss and emotions when her husband was killed in World War II. Both are yoga enthusiasts, with Marijohn practicing headstand into her late seventies.

Also, Martin Pierce and Tommy Collins each shared their collective wisdom concerning argument. In *Yogi Bare*, Martin stated, "Argument is not a very effective way of changing people for the better." Tommy added, "You can't win by arguing."

Two different journeys; same destination. Truth is like that.

Martin and Tommy were the first participants from each book to pass away. They died several months apart. Both possessed a unique and authentic spirituality.

I am humbled, and strangely honored, to have been the last person to interview Tommy Collins.

Leonard was truly loveable.

Jenny Howell died July 2, 1989, from complications related to spina bifida. Her thirty-six years on earth well outdistanced the life expectancy predictions of the most optimistic attending physicians at her birth. I like to think country music helped sustain her during her journey through this world in a wheelchair, as well as improve her quality of life.

I've lived in Nashville seventeen years now. It's home. I can relate to Bill Anderson when he speaks of Commerce, Georgia: "I didn't grow up there, but I did a lot of growing up there."

I recently celebrated my fortieth birthday. My wife, Mary, cooked Cajun cuisine consisting of chicken and sausage gumbo, red beans and rice, and bread pudding.

After supper as friends and family sat around the living room, Chuck Jones played and sang "Your Love Amazes Me." The Gibson was passed and suddenly a guitar pull had broken out. After the six-string had circled the room and I cradled the wood and wires, it suddenly occurred to me—Jenny's on the dance floor tonight.

I bet Tommy Collins asked her to dance.

Photo courtesy of BMI Archives

Tommy Collins

If you need it, we have an indoor bathroom. I also got an outhouse. That's all we had on the farm in Oklahoma.

My dad grew up with outdoor plumbing in Belcher, Louisiana. Now he has a two-holer. I was at the Hall of Fame dinner when Dallas Frazier introduced you before you were inducted. I thought there was an amazing amount of grace in the way you started your acceptance speech. You quoted something I heard on a bootleg tape in 1985.

"The Pissed Off Pastor."

"The Pissed Off Pastor." And when you started, the whole room roared. That routine is legendary, though never commercially recorded.

I had a second wife and her name was Bobbie. We didn't get along because of my drinking. And I don't blame anybody for telling a man, "Look, it's either the bottle or me. Either get yourself some help, or I can't stand it anymore." We rented a little old place up the Cumberland River.

Anyway, I was in the house by myself on a reel-to-reel. I didn't get drunk, but I had a couple of cans of beer. I was functional. And I just thought that I would write this thing called "The Pissed Off Pastor." You have a copy of it?

Of course I do.

Good. Good. It's amazing how popular that thing got.

"Good morning, congregation. My, it's good to look out and see a nice crowd this morning. Your clothes look so nice. It's good to see you on this Easter Sunday morning. I'm going to get right into the message. I'm not going to smooth anybody's fur. I heard that 'Amen.' I will preach on. I'm going to tell it like it is, as they say."

What year did you record "The Pissed Off Preacher"?

1978. I took it up to Mel Tillis's office because I had already made a deal with him. I was getting a little salary every week. It was enough to get by on. I think I asked for a hundred-and-fifty a week. I worked for him for a year. So I played it for the staff down there, and they liked to cracked up.

Jimmy Darrell was in charge of Mel Tillis's publishing company. Jimmy Darrell called yesterday. He and his wife are Christian people. And they come out about every Sunday afternoon. They might miss one once in a while. I think he says they're going to come out Sunday. Jimmy said years ago, he said, "I personally have made at least five hundred copies of the 'The Pissed Off Pastor.'"

I used to live in Hendersonville. I shared an apartment there with a guy. Close to Ferlin Husky and close to Johnny Russell's place. Ferlin invited Russell and I to come over for a Christmas dinner and visit some. So I went over there. Ferlin Husky has a son named Terry. He wasn't but about fifteen, sixteen years old. He said, "Did you write that pastor thing?" I said, "Yeah." He said, "Did you know kids at school have a copy of it? They're making me a copy." That's how it's mushroomed.

The R.I.A.A. should probably certify it gold. How were you named Tommy Collins?

My born name is Leonard Sipes. Ken Nelson of Capitol Records was going to sign me, but he thought Leonard Sipes would be too hard to remember.

At the time I was living with Ferlin Husky for about a year. And so did Dallas Frazier, who's an outstanding songwriter.

Ferlin, under the name of Terry Preston at the time, was recording one of my songs in Los Angeles. I wasn't on that session, so at the break the group asked me if I'd go next door and buy them sandwiches. One fellow wanted a Tom Collins. And Ferlin Husky said, "That's your name: Tom Collins. Except we're going to call you Tommy Collins."

Were you happy with the name Tommy Collins?

Well, I wanted to be on Capitol Records so bad. I don't know if my mother ever understood that I changed my name. You either got a simple name, or they wouldn't sign you. But after that along comes Efrem Zimbalist, Jr. and Englebert Humperdink.

But name changes were not unusual for Hollywood.

That's right. Roy Rogers's name is a lot like mine: Leonard Sly. John Wayne was Marion Morrison.

That was the thing to do, and so I accepted it.

A lot of people credit you for the Bakersfield sound.

I'm just so proud to have been part of the Bakersfield sound. I'm going to be perfectly honest with you. Making records—when Capitol did get its tower on Vine Street—was one of the big deals in my life.

And things were so simple then, Philip, when it came to making records. In those days, my guitar rhythm was coming through the same microphone I sang into. That's how unsophisticated it was. And I fell in love with the Fender Telecaster guitar and the treble sound that Buck Owens was playing. That wasn't coming out of Nashville at all.

On my first record "You Got To Have A License," Ferlin Husky said, "I'm going to play some Missouri hillbilly lead on that." And he did an old song called "Cripple Creek." Outside of that, Buck Owens played lead guitar on my records.

Did Buck Owens tour with you?

He didn't tour much with me, but he did play guitar behind me on the Grand Ole Opry. We were both scared to death.

Carl Smith told me backstage, "I just wanted to tell you, the first time you're on the Opry, they boo you. I don't know why, but they do that." He really scared me. But as it happened, the audience gave me a lot of attention when I went out. When I finished, the applause was good. And Carl said, "Well, I guess you changed the policy." He was quite a trickster.

I got the invitation to be at the old Ryman Auditorium because I had "You Got To Have A License" and "You Better Not Do That" on record. I was making payments on a 1953 Buick. I didn't own that Buick yet. So I called Buck, he came over to the house and we went down to Los Angeles from Bakersfield and picked up Ken Nelson and drove all the way to Nashville.

Ken said, "Tommy, the back tires look a little slick. Let's put on two new tires." I said, "Ken, I don't have the money." He said, "Capitol Records will take care of that." That amazed me because I wasn't used to people doing things like that for me. Capitol Records bought the gasoline. When we stopped to eat, Ken Nelson paid for everything. He said, "You're on Capitol Records. You shouldn't be spending that money. You've got a family."

Ken Nelson took care of all the phone bills and everything. "Call your folks. Make some calls. Put it on this number." So I did.

I don't imagine Ken Nelson pointed out that Capitol Records was charging you back for the tires, gasoline, meals and phone calls.

Well, he didn't. But, you know, hindsight is better than foresight. Ken and I are friends. I hear from him once in a while. He'll send me a card or I'll send him something.

The Opry paid me two hundred dollars. I cashed it while I was in Nashville. Paid Buck fifty dollars. Ken Nelson flew back to Los Angeles to his home.

Buck and I drove my '53 Roadmaster Buick back to Bakersfield. We both agreed we didn't want to see each other for a while. It was a common understanding between us. I mean, we put the pedal to the metal, too. But can you imagine why I was so happy to be offered to be a member of the Grand Ole Opry. I lived two thousand miles away, and you had to be at the Opry twenty-six Saturdays a year.

At two hundred bucks a pop.

Can't do it. Can't make that.

I just worked one show, but I thanked them graciously for inviting me to be a member. I might be booked in Portland, Oregon, on a Thursday and I'd have to fly back to Nashville to make two hundred dollars. Pay my own ticket. Get my own motel room. Doesn't make sense, does it?

No, sir.

I thanked them, but I said, "My roots, my family are in Bakersfield." Paying two hundred dollars, the Opry lost some people. They lost Webb Pierce, I think.

They did.

I heard that Grandpa Jones was going to quit, too, and then they gave him a paid-up National Life policy.

The Opry owned the artists back then, because they were such a powerful broadcast.

Oh, yeah, the National Life and Casualty.

I got to Nashville about the time the Gaylord's bought the Opry.

E. K. Gaylord, the original Gaylord that I know, had a dairy farm in Oklahoma. He owned both newspapers—*Daily Oklahoman* and *Oklahoma City Times*. And he was very instrumental in moving the capital of Oklahoma from Guthrie to Oklahoma City. He had the bucks.

I thrashed on his property. My uncle had a thrashing machine that would make a straw stack. I had never heard of a combine. Never operated one. I go way back to the thrashing machine called a separator. And I worked for Mr. E. K. Gaylord. I saw him out there. He was just another farmer. I didn't know he was that well-to-do, see. But his sons and grandsons come up here and paid all these millions for Opryland and the Grand Ole Opry itself.

Were you on the California Hayride?

No, I worked with Cliffie Stone, Tennessee Ernie Ford's manager, at a place called Hometown Jamboree in Los Angeles.

I was writing songs for Central Songs, which was owned by Cliffie Stone. I was signed as a writer with no front money from Central Songs. Nobody told me that I could get a draw.

Cliffie was instrumental in the founding of the Academy of Country Music.

Could have been.

How did you get to Bakersfield from Oklahoma?

I was going with Wanda Jackson at the time in Oklahoma City. We were on a little radio station, KLPR. Pretty Miss Norma Jean, as Porter Wagoner named her, was on there, too. Wanda and her parents had lived in Bakersfield. She was an only child of Tom and Nellie Jackson. They invited me to go to Bakersfield. So Wanda and I rode in the back seat and went to Bakersfield. And that was a new world to me. I didn't have a place to stay, so I stayed with one of Wanda's aunts who was widowed. I just did favors for her—cleaned up around the house and went to the store for her.

Then I met a fiddle player by the name of Oscar Whittington. I said, "I'm looking for a job." He said, "A man named Terry Preston"—that's Ferlin Husky—"has a band out here at the Rainbow Gardens every Saturday night. Why don't you meet me and I'll introduce you to him."

After I'd met him, Ferlin said, "Are you good?" I said, "Well, I guess I'm okay." He said, "Now, you've got to have confidence in yourself." I said, "Well, I think I'm pretty good." He said, "You're hired. Why don't you come live with me and my wife?" So I moved out from the widow woman and moved in with Ferlin Husky. Just a matter of weeks after that, Dallas Frazier moved in there, too. And that's his picture there with Tennessee Ernie, Jean Shepherd and me. That's Dallas on the left.

Dallas was pretty young then.

Yeah, he was. He was on television with a program called "The Hitchin' Post." And a guy named Herb Henson—Cousin Herb—had that show. Capitol Records did a show at the Civic Center in Bakersfield in honor of Cousin Herb Henson's ten years on local television there. Others tried having shows, but they never were as successful as Herb's. But on that show was—I'll name myself first because I might forget me—there was Tommy Collins, Buck Owens, Jean Shepard, Glen Campbell, Rose Maddux, Joe and Rose Maphus, Roy Clark. A big lineup of talent.

Ferlin Husky's a great entertainer.

Oh, wonderful. People used to say, "I'd rather follow anybody as Ferlin Husky on stage."

Hank Williams died on January 1, 1953, and I was working for an oil company. And Ferlin said, "I want you to help me write some songs as near like Hank Williams as you can." So he had several records with Capitol where he was trying to sing like Hank Williams with the break in his voice like he thought Hank did, but it never really worked.

For Hank it was authentic and for Ferlin it wasn't.

Yeah, that's right.

But once Ferlin got to where it was authentic for him, then things worked.

He's one of those type fellows that has a winning way.

You left the music business for the ministry.

I was in the ministry for seven years. I went to seminary two years in Berkeley and pastored a couple of Baptist churches in California. I wanted to broaden my ministry. I just wanted to tell people about Christ and what He'd done for me.

And as it happened, I kind of just slowly got away from the ministry. I went back to Capitol Records, but I had matured somewhat, and Ken Nelson and I agreed that we should call it quits on Capitol Records.

Johnny Cash lived in a place called Casitas Springs with his first wife. They had about four daughters. He invited me to come over, so I drove from Bakersfield. Of course, he's a big name.

There was a pay phone at the bottom of the hill where his place was. All I had to do was find Casitas Springs. He said, "Call me from a pay phone and I'll direct you right to the house." So I called him and he answered. I said, "This is Tommy Collins, Johnny. You invited me to come over." He said, "Sure. Just come right on up the hill, you can't miss it. If you don't mind seeing a guy with some teeth knocked out. I ran into a tree." And sure enough, he had some missing. He had a luxurious home. It looked like so nice, you shouldn't walk in it.

Johnny was on Columbia Records. He said, "Don Law likes your singing." And I told him Ken Nelson and I decided to call it quits this time.

I had met a guy named Johnny Bond, who was just recently inducted into the Country Music Hall of Fame. And he published some songs that I wrote. So he spoke to Don Law for me. I called Don Law, who was what they called an A&R man, on the phone from Bakersfield. I said, "Mr. Law, this is Tommy Collins. I've talked to Johnny Cash and Johnny Bond." He said, "Lad, do you want to be on Columbia Records?" And I said, "Yes, I do." He said, "Consider yourself on."

So we set up a time for the first session in Nashville.

I flew into Nashville and I got a room at a hotel that doesn't exist anymore—the Andrew Jackson Hotel. When I went to bed that night, I picked up a *Reader's Digest*. I used to read those little quips at the bottom. And one said, "If you can't bite, don't growl." So I wrote that song that night before my session the next day on Columbia Records. And the first crack out of the box, "If You Can't Bite, Don't Growl" got to number seven in the nation.

But Nashville, then, just seemed to have such an ego that it was disturbing to me. I had been used to such freedom and such enjoyment. For example, Grady Martin had already been chosen to be the leader of the session. He played wonderful guitar. Later played for Willie Nelson on the road. But I was used to the treble guitars. And so I asked Grady Martin, I said, "Can you play some treble?" He said, "No, I can't." He was a man of few words. There was a whole lot of false pride about the Nashville way of doing things that I didn't like. I said, "Well, Grady, I need some licks here that kind of go along with my image." He said, "What image?" That's rude, see.

Buck Owens would say, "Tommy, if that's not what you want, I'll make it right." He was so humble on those sessions. But all of a sudden, I'm with a bunch of people that tell you what to do. And I, frankly, didn't like it. I don't like it to this day. Just look how long it took them to induct Buck Owens into the Country Music Hall of Fame.

Before I went to the first session I had heard that if Grady Martin didn't like your songs, he might just put his guitar in the case and walk out. I had a little bit of gall about me, but I got the impression you can't whip a big machine like that. It was so cold, Philip.

When I was cutting my second album for Columbia Records, I said, "I want somebody on the session that plays a Fender Telecaster." Don Law said, "Well, Grady's a genius on a guitar." And I said, "Mr. Law, I'm going to decide some things, or we can't go on." Because then I could always go to some other label, see. I had some clout of my own. He said, "I know a man who plays a Telecaster—Fred Carter, Jr." So I used him one time. You could tell Grady didn't like it. But I'm sorry about that.

No need to be sorry, it was your record.

That's right. Exactly. And it was my life. It was my living. I had a wife and children in Bakersfield. And so we used Fred Carter, Jr., on that session. And, boy, he played some good stuff.

When did you go to seminary?

In '57 and '58. It was a three-year course, but I didn't graduate. I wanted to pastor.

So when you came to Nashville and recorded for Columbia, you were getting back into the music business?

Yeah, I was. For a while I wouldn't work clubs and I sold Kirby vacuum cleaners. I wanted shows. The package shows were wonderful. You would go out and do your thing in twenty, twenty-five minutes. That's all there is to it.

When did you make your acquaintance with Merle Haggard?

A minister friend—Carlton Ellis was his name—and I were pulling into a drive-in to get us some Mexican food sent out to the car. He passed away. I don't mean to sound religious here, but he pastored the church then where he and I both were saved, where we accepted Christ.

And I heard "Sing Me A Sad Song" by Merle Haggard on the radio. And I said, "Who in the world is this with a voice like that?" I had been up north going to the seminary and pastoring in two different places, Gold Flat and Lincoln, California, see.

I said, "I've got to meet that guy." I kept asking around and found out where Merle lived, and drove over to the house. I met Merle's first wife. Leona Hobbs was her name. She was the mother of two boys and two girls. Noel, the youngest one, was just in diapers.

Leona Hobbs is not Leona Williams?

No. There have been two Leonas in Merle's life.

This Leona comes from a family named Hobbs. That's her maiden name. There was Dana, Marty, Kelly and Noel. They lived real close to a little old church in just a make-do house. That's all he could afford then. And he didn't have his pardon yet from San Quentin. He'd been in prison two years and nine months and said he sang some of my songs when he was in prison.

We got acquainted fishing. He loved to fish. He said, "You know, I can't drive an automobile. Do you mind to drive?" And I said, "No." So Merle Haggard and I actually got acquainted fishing on the Kern River. When Merle got his pardon from Governor Reagan, he was so proud of it he had it framed.

The first time I sat down in Bonnie Owens's living room in Oildale, Merle sang some songs and I couldn't believe how he could sound like other artists. He said, "Turn your head a minute. Who is this?" And he sounded just like Marty Robbins. I've seen him on stage impersonate three or four artists, and if you turned your head you would think they were singing.

Is Merle as good at imitating singers as Del Reeves?

I knew Del Reeves when they called him Curly. But Merle covered more territory, with all due respect to Del Reeves, because he could do Roy Acuff. Del gets him to a "tee." And, of course, what's his name. He might have had one called "Old Rivers." I'd like to think of his name.

When you think of it at four in the morning, don't call me.

Walter Brennan. And there are others that Del Reeves does real good.

Every time I'd have a single out, I'd have a suit made in Van Nuys, California. So I had this black lamé suit made with rhinestones on it. And Merle said, "I'm going to impersonate Buck Owens tonight. Can I use your jacket?" I said, "Yeah." That's the last I ever saw of that jacket. He didn't steal it. He took it off and threw it to somebody and it was gone. Merle can imitate Buck Owens and Ernest Tubb. I've never heard anybody equal him, with all due respect to Del.

I never can get this straight. Was Bonnie Owens married to Merle and then Buck?

No. Buck and then Merle. Buck and Bonnie had two sons, Buddy and Mike, so she kept the name Owens.

But when they divorced, she continued to sing with Merle.

I know it. Now, as far as I know, after Leona, Bonnie Owens was next.

Leona Hobbs.

Leona Hobbs.

We're not to Williams yet.

Hobbs. That's right. We're not to Williams yet.

But Merle called me and he said, "Tommy, I'm in love." I said, "Well, that's good." He said, "I've asked her to marry me." I said, "Who is it?" He said, "Bonnie Owens." See, Merle's lifelong career-wise producer and manager has been Fuzzy Owen with no "s." O-w-e-n. Charles "Fuzzy" Owen. And he still is managing Merle. Still living in Bakersfield.

At that time, Fuzzy played a steel guitar, but he wasn't one of these session players. He played upright bass on my records and I told him, "You learned to play bass on my records." Well, Fuzzy had been going with Bonnie Owens.

Boy, I'm bringing out some stuff here, ain't I? Fuzzy Owen and his wife, Phyllis, were temporarily separated. And he was going with Bonnie Owens.

There were three main nightclubs in Bakersfield at that time—The Blackboard, The Lucky Spot, and The Clover Club. Bonnie was a waitress at The Clover Club. She'd wait on the customers there, and she'd get up and sing a song or two. She had married Buck Owens and they were divorced.

So Roy Nichols, who played lead guitar on some of my records—wonderful guitar player—told me that when Merle told Fuzzy he was going to marry Bonnie, Fuzzy said, "Well, give me two weeks." Now, Fuzzy is an amazing person. But Roy said, "I think it's going to take him a little longer than that." Because Merle and Bonnie were pretty thick, see.

So Bonnie and Merle got married. And Merle started making money then. They lived in some nice places. He built a nice house right on the Kern River. He had palm trees brought in. He had his own farm and fish out there. And Bonnie Owens had a lot to do with raising his children.

Since Merle wrote "Leonard" about you, I guess you're at liberty to talk about him.

Merle and I decided to go fishing. And he said, "Tommy, I have to share something with you. I've grossed a million dollars." I said, "That's good. Do something with your money." Because Merle's the type, if he saw something he wanted, he'd buy it. Like a pair of snake boots one time. We was just walking down the streets of Bakersfield past a place called the Emporium. He said, "Let's go in here a minute." We went in there. I knew he didn't have too much money. He said, "How much you want for those boots there?" The guy told him. He tried them on and said, "I'll take them."

Now I really got to go back three or four years behind this million-dollar year. Merle called me one time and says, "I got a chance to fly to Phoenix and make a hundred and fifty dollars. And they'll pay my plane ticket, but I don't have the money. Will you loan me a hundred and fifty dollars?" I said, "Sure." So I drove up to the Bakersfield airport and his mother had already come out there with the hundred and fifty dollars. What we often call an overnight success, actually that took some years in preparation. The dues paying time.

Remember that Merle was in prison for two years and nine months. He and another guy were getting in cars, wiring them up, and taking off into some other state. One night they were going to break into this restaurant from the alley. The lights were off and they thought, "Well, nobody's here." They were working on the chain and the owner was inside. He called the cops and they put him in jail in Bakersfield.

It came Christmastime and Merle asked the jailer, "I'd like to get out and see my mother for Christmas. She lives here." Flossie was her name. That's the way Merle put it to me. Merle is about as truthful as they come. He may forget some things, like he'd want you to fly out there, you'd get out there and he'd be gone somewhere.

I'll file that away for future reference.

Well, I'm not the only one that knows that about Merle. He doesn't mean it personally. He gets so preoccupied.

When did Leona Williams come into the picture?

Merle and Bonnie had divorced. And he says, "I'm going to get married again." I got a letter of invitation to the wedding in Gardnerville, Nevada. He's going to marry Leona Williams. Who is the bridesmaid? Bonnie Owens.

You've got to be kidding.

I had never heard anything like that in my life. Bonnie will sing with him to this day. But can you imagine that? Bonnie Owens being the bridesmaid.

Here's the one's that I know: Leona Hobbs, Bonnie Owens, Leona Williams, there's one called Debbie and Theresa. That's five. I married Merle and Theresa.

Is he still married to Theresa?

Yeah.

That might be the one that sticks. You might have had the touch.
We have a couple of parallels in our lives. I started out working in the music business at Tom Collins Music. So we kind of got our start with a Tom Collins.

How about that?

The other thing is, we're both seminary dropouts.

Where was yours?

I went to Candler School of Theology at Emory University in Atlanta. It was United Methodist. I spent a year and a half there. It was a three-year program.

Methodists do good work for the Lord.

Yes, they do. I was raised in that tradition. But I was torn between music and ministry.

Yeah.

What led you to the ministry?

Well, I was married to a woman named Wanda. It was my first marriage.

Wanda Jackson?

Not Wanda Jackson, no. Wanda Jackson and I just went to the picture shows.

My wife had been going to Central Baptist Church in Bakersfield and I hadn't. I had dropped out of the whole thing. I had been selling Kirby vacuum cleaners. Merle Haggard said, "You can make five hundred dollars a night. What are you doing selling those machines?" I said, "I want to stay out of nightclubs." Anyway, Wanda asked me if I'd go to her baptism. Baptists do it right there in the baptistery. So I did.

At that time I had a brand new '55 Cadillac. And I was so twisted in my mind that I was proud of that Cadillac. It wasn't a Coup de Ville, but a beautiful car. That thing cost a little over five thousand dollars. I'd park it close to the church, you know. I'm not proud of that feeling.

I sat toward the back a little bit and she was baptized that night. There was a preacher there from Springfield, Missouri. Just good solid preaching. And I got interested. I got under a conviction. You follow me?

Yes, sir.

Of course, you do. And I suddenly believed that Christ died for me. And, Philip, it was like the lifting of the whole weight of the whole world. That's the only way I look at it. Oh, I walked out of that building and I felt so clean.

I'm not going to be a Bible thumper here. And Jesus said, "No man comes to the Son unless the Father draws him." So, God has to accept us, too. And He'll let us know when the time comes. That's why a person—especially a kid—should never be pushed into making a decision for the Lord, because God has to be in it. It's not authentic. It's just going through the motion. Nothing eternal happens.

So, my belief is that the Bible teaches that once you're born again, nothing will change that situation. And now I'm preaching, aren't I?

Preach on, Brother Tommy.

My mother was a Methodist. She loved the Lord and believed in Christ. And on my dad's side, the Church of Christ.

You can flip my parents and you've got the same thing. Mom was Church of Christ. Dad was Methodist. His grandfather was a Methodist minister.

How about that? Another parallel in our lives.

There you go.

Now, my aunts and uncles would say, "Oh, Leonard, didn't you listen to your dad? Don't you know the Church of Christ is the only one? The only church that's valid?" I said, "Well, let me put it this way: If I could get the assurance that I have gotten from the Holy Spirit of what you're talking about, I'd just jump at it."

But I don't believe there's only one church. In fact, I don't believe there'll be any denominations in heaven. I tried to tell my aunts and uncles this. Why they were so fanatic. And probably Christians. I'm not the judge. But a lot of those old died-in-the-wool Church of Christ people believe that's the only religion. The only one.

My Paw Paw and Granny are right there with them. You became a Baptist minister.

Yeah, I did. Those are my roots. My oldest brother, Aubrey Cletus, is eighty-three, and he took me to a Baptist church from a very young age. That was my exposure to Sunday school and to preaching.

I went with a Methodist girl, Nancy Jessup, for a while. And I'd go to the Methodist church with her. We'd sit there and secretly hold hands.

But I like to say it this way: Yes, I go to the Baptist church. It's a little "b" for Baptist and a big "c" for Christ. So any church, any gathering, any assembly that preaches Christ as the Son of God and preaches that he died for our sins, I say, "Power to them."

Do you think there will be Hindus and Muslims and other good hearts from other world religions in heaven?

No. Not at all. Sincerity doesn't get it done. I'm sorry. They don't believe in Christ.

Jesus said, "I am the way, the truth and the life." He didn't say, "One of the ways." And if we can come by the cross and not take advantage of it, we go to perdition. That's what I believe. You can believe what you want to.

I used to argue with Jehovah's Witnesses. I'd get out my Bible. I quit arguing with them, because you can't win by arguing. It's not an intellectual matter. So twice now, the Jehovah's Witnesses have come to my door. And I said, "I'm so glad you came. I'm not interested in your magazine. Come on in. I want to tell you what Jesus did for me." "Well, I can't now. There's this lady waiting in the car."

In Merle Haggard's musical tribute to you entitled "Leonard," he indicates you left the music business for the ministry. However, preaching didn't work out, so you returned to music. He speaks of the toll this took on your personal life, including divorce, alcoholism and drug addiction. He expresses concern for your life during this period, but alludes to the fact that you turned it all around through Jesus.

So after you left the ministry and went back into music, that was when things took a downturn in terms of your personal life.

Yeah, right.

See, I didn't just quit the ministry. I wanted to be more of an evangelist. And a part of the ministry I didn't care for, like visiting in hospitals. I did things that I should have had somebody help me do—taking church members to the grocery store. I wanted to broaden my ministry. But little by little, I got away. I got involved with bennies, downers, to stay awake, and then alcohol. I stayed on that for several years.

Merle Haggard had Bob Wills and his whole band out at his place. And I wanted to go out there so bad. But I was getting the reputation for drinking. So I called Roy Nichols, who was playing the guitar for Merle, and I said, "Roy, I'd like to see Bob Wills. I've met him before, but I'd like to come out there." And he said, "Well, it might be all right if you come with me." See, I didn't realize what a separation I had caused between me and my friends.

December 14, 1982, was my sober date. Outside of a little toddy—and then just very little—I don't drink.

I was going to double date with this married friend of mine, Tommy Willis. He and his wife and her sister and I were going out to a place called Chaffin's Barn to see a live show. It's close to the Loveless Café.

I live just a stone's throw from there.

You live close to there?

Five minutes.

Well, I'll be dern. That Loveless Café is supposed to be such a good restaurant. I've been in there a time or two, but I was drunk. And I don't have to go into all detail about this because you see me sober now.

Absolutely.

But God helped me with that.

Anyway, somewhere in my book was Merle Haggard's phone number in California. And I had an apartment then that I had inherited from a guy I had been somewhat in business with in Louisville, Kentucky. I took over the payments of the apartment and moved in. Anyway, never mind that. I'm chasing rabbits. A guy said, "I've been running amuck all day long, I don't know why I keep doing that. Never have caught one." A muck.

So Merle's phone number was somewhere in my book and this friend of mine, Tommy Willis, must have called Merle, because I didn't. I got on the phone and Merle said, "Tommy, do what you have to do." And I said, "Well, they're talking to me about going to a treatment center." He said, "Go ahead." I said, "I'll do it for you." Merle said, "No. Do it for yourself. I'll take care of it."

I had never heard of Cumberland Heights. An old timer named Cherry and Tommy Willis took me out there.

We're not too far from it here.

No. It's up River Road. So they dropped me off there. It took me three or four days to sober up. They said I entertained. Said I really did some good performing. That's what they told me. I remember how they laughed. They weren't laughing at me, because I had enough sense about me to do good material. I write comedy things. I sang them a few of my hit songs. I stayed out there thirty days.

It cost three thousand dollars to go to Cumberland Heights in 1982. I saw the check from Merle Haggard. Three thousand dollars. That's pretty good, isn't it?

Yes, indeed.

And so once again, I felt that sense of belonging to the world, belonging to life again. I could have a life one more time. I lived by myself, but I started praying for a woman.

Well, Hazel and I met in '86. I'd go up and visit with her in Missouri on my way to Oklahoma. Her husband had died of a heart attack. And so I just prayed for a wife. But I realized after church one morning that I might as well have mentioned her name because that's the one I wanted. I even called Hazel from my sister's place in Oklahoma. I said, "I love you. Will you marry me?" She said, "We'll talk about it." I sent her a letter to Cape Girardeau, Missouri, and I wrote, "I want you to be my wife. If you are agreeable, call me back when you get this letter." She called me.

Hazel said, "Do you want me?" I said, "Yes, I do." She had a job then in marketing and she was a hair stylist. She cut my hair yesterday. We're trying to look nice for you today.

You're a handsome devil.

I'm not.

I said, "Yes, I do want you." She said, "Will Tuesday be too soon?" Wow. I was getting excited.

I ran to the jewelry store, bought her an engagement ring. Went to the florist, bought this nice bouquet of roses and had them on the dresser in my back bedroom.

I handed her that little ring holder. She opened it up and said, "I've already accepted. Why don't you put it on my finger?" I did. That was a wonderful thing. I'm proud of my woman.

We were married August 8th, 1998.

You're newlyweds. I feel like Bob Eubanks.

Yeah.

There's a lot of beauty we miss using alcohol and drugs. Eventually, it'll kill you—a wreck, you mess with somebody else's woman and her husband kills you, heart attack, cirrhosis.

If your time comes tomorrow, are you ready to go?

Yes, I am.

Why?

Because of what Christ has done. It's not the way I've lived. It's because I've put faith in Christ and trusted him as my personal savior. See, Jesus had no sin. Why would he be dying on the cross? Not for his sins, he didn't have any. So he paid the ransom. God demands perfection. Not from us. But He got that perfection in His Son. His Son satisfied Him and His distaste for sin. John 3:16 says, "God so loved the world that He gave His only begotten Son and whosoever believes in Him shall not perish but shall have everlasting life."

You're going to believe that or not. That's the question put to us. I'm not asking you or anybody else. There's a scripture in Ephesians that says, "We are sealed by the Holy Spirit." What kind of hope is it to hope you've done something good enough to get to heaven? What kind of hope is that? There's no hope in good works.

Being saved is not a judgment on our lives. There'll be a judgment day, but for Christians it's only for rewards. It's already determined where you and I are going by our choice. As George Jones says, "Choices."

Do we choose Christ or do we choose our own way of looking at things? That's self-righteousness. We don't have any righteousness of our own. Now we are saved to serve and we usually become a better quality person after we're saved. But we'd all be surprised to learn the people who have not made a public profession of Christ. And the scriptures say, "If you're ashamed of me, I'll be ashamed of you." An innocent man had the power to call down legions of angels and deliver him from that cross, but he endured it. Before he went to the cross, he went to the Garden of Gethsemene and prayed to this effect. Prayed this way: "Father, if there's any other way, let this cup pass from me."

What he's saying is, and I don't mean to sound authoritative. I'm not authoritative. The Bible is the only authority there is. "If there's any other way to save man from the consequences of his sins, I'd rather not have to die on the cross. Nevertheless, not my will, but Thine be done."

I'm preaching, but I have a license to preach. Our hope is in Christ.

Marijohn Wilkin

When were you bit by the writing bug?

I was teaching school in Tulsa when I knew I had to write.

You were teaching music.

Yes.

To what grades?

First through the sixth grade.

We had an extremely advanced school system that was copied from Dallas. Even that long ago, in the '50s, the children were coming to their music teacher, they were coming to their art teacher. So I had a gazillion children, as you can imagine.

And the mother of one.

Ronnie of Ronnie and the Daytonas, who did "G.T.O." He wrote it and recorded it.

Did you publish it through Buckhorn Music?

We opened the company with it. And that was really, really neat. Just a few weeks ago, he took his copyrights and had a vinyl released of "G.T.O." He

Photo courtesy of BMI Archives

started his own company with "G.T.O." and I started the company with "G.T.O." back in the '60s. Isn't that neat?

That is.

So that worked out good.

If you had stayed in Tulsa, taught school, raised your son, and never have come to Nashville and written songs and been involved in music publishing, would that have been sufficient?

No. I would have written. I just came to where the writing was, because I was starting to write in Tulsa. I got my first song recorded while I was still teaching school. That's kind of unheard of. But I use the word "appointed" to write. I had to write.

Who appointed you?

I suppose the finger of destiny, or if you believe in God, God did. That's what I had to do.

Did you have spiritual musings from your youth?

I was raised in an extremely religious family. So I suppose I did and didn't even know what it was. It was a way of life with me. I never really thought about God pulling me. I didn't realize that until much later. As I have come to find out through the years, I could watch the new writers coming in and I could tell the ones that were appointed to write and those that were self-appointed to write. And it's much more difficult for those who are self-appointed as opposed to destiny-appointed. It's just a harder road to climb.

Would you say most are self-appointed?

No. Not those that stay. Not those that we know about.

It's just that you have to push so hard. It sounds almost as though it were predestined, and I don't actually mean that. But I can tell even by the writing of those who are appointed to write, their mission in life is to give music to the world. Regardless of what kind of music it is, because we have to have music. And some of us are blessed with the talent.

If you had your first song recorded when you were in Tulsa as a schoolteacher, it doesn't sound like the road was too difficult.

For me it was amazingly not difficult. It was almost frighteningly easy. Which is why I knew it was meant to be. I just couldn't have opened the doors that have been opened for me throughout all these years. But you don't see that right at the time. You just think, "Wow, that's great!"

My only difficulties were personal. I've never had any career difficulties.

What was the nature of the personal difficulties?

They were my own private dealings, my own private life. I began to drink too much, not realizing that I was an alcoholic. Hank Williams did it that way, so it seemed like the way to do it. He hadn't been gone long when I got here.

You segued from an extremely religious family to piano bar on Printer's Alley.

It was all pretty weird. It was even weird for me to be playing, but see, all I could do was music. It's pretty ridiculous be able to play and sing as easily as I could, and not do that for a living. I'd never even been in a piano bar. I didn't even know what they were until I got to Springfield. That was the year that I paid my dues. We about starved to death that first year.

"We" being?

My husband and my son.

There was an Italian family-owned restaurant in Springfield, which was a lovely place to eat and just a really nice place to be. The owner had a piano in there, so I introduced myself to him and I said, "How would you like to have some dinner music?" That's the way I offered my services.

I started playing the piano through the dinner hour. I played from six to ten. And Lucky Nola, who was a booker working in Springfield, saw my potential, because I would play the songs that I had written. So when Lucky moved to Nashville, he said, "You ought to be in Nashville. If you're going to shoot tigers, don't just sit and wait for one to come by." So Lucky got me a job in the Alley playing piano bar for Happy Hour from five to ten at the Voodoo where Skull was.

Skull Schulman was murdered.

He was one of my dearest friends and one of my longest acquaintances in Nashville, as he was to so many people who had worked in the Alley at one time or another.

They were very, very good to their employees. Very good. And it was really a neat, safe place to perform. I hate using the word *perform*. I feel like a trained seal when I use that word. The piano was up behind the bar and the patrons couldn't get to us.

Kind of like at Pat O'Brien's on Bourbon Street?

Exactly.

And you would have a few Hurricanes.

Yes. Not anymore. Not in about seventeen, eighteen years, in fact. Card carrying. But it's a really nice way of life.

Anyway, I had a very nice few months. Then I realized I was no closer to country music or to being a songwriter by working at that piano bar. I could have been anywhere working in a piano bar. So this ain't going to get it, because I was constantly learning the new songs to keep up—Broadway music and very little country, because Nashville was not a country town. Not at all. So I did pop and I did Broadway and I did the old classics. And that was the year that "Old Lonesome Me" by Don Gibson was such a tremendous hit. I remember one night I did it twelve times in a row because the whole bar was singing along with me.

Did you enjoy entertaining people?

Well, again, I did it so easily. I'd been playing and singing since I was five years old. I played piano bar just like I taught school, because I discovered that playing for a bunch of inebriated guys was like dealing with children.

Both prone to wet their pants.

You don't argue; you just smile. I didn't drink on the job and they were constantly wanting to send a drink to the piano player. So we worked up something called an Orange Surprise. It had no alcohol in it. Honestly, I had the most vitamin C of any piano player in town. Orange juice rolled down the piano.

I *never* drank on the job. I discovered that alcohol is a tranquilizer, and so it would tranquilize my vocal chords to the point that I couldn't sing on pitch. And I had enough sense to realize that. I wasn't in total control of my voice pitch if I ever had a drink, so I never drank.

You began singing with the Jordonaires.

I worked with the Jordonaires a lot when I took a tremendous leap of faith to stop working at the piano bar. I had a nice salary, and I had nice tips, and I had all day off. But, as I said, I wasn't any closer to writing than I would be in any town. Then Cedarwood offered me a position. They paid me fifty dollars a week to plug their songs and write and make their lead sheets. It was not an advance. It was actually a salary. I was one of the few who worked for a salary, because most worked for an advance unless you were the secretary.

And this gave you an opportunity to learn the publishing business.

You betcha. Six years I stayed there.

How would you plug a song back in 1960?

It was much easier, I'm sure. What we have to realize is there were only about three or four producers in Nashville.

That hasn't changed much.

And the rest of them came in from L.A. and from New York.

Same as today.

I'm just ignoring that.

But, really, we had more producers coming in from out of town, so it was a big deal. And they would let us know when they were coming in. They would come in and spend a whole day listening to Acuff-Rose songs, a whole day listening to Cedarwood songs, a whole day listening to Tree songs.

Were songs played live or were they played on tape?

Played on tape. When we knew they were coming in, we'd have our new demo session. I would pitch right there in the office. They would come in for a week, and we knew which hotel they were going to be in and who they were going to record.

They really needed the writer when they came to town.

Oh, yeah, they had to have the songs. They came in without any music. They came in from the West Coast or they came in from New York where they didn't have country music available to them. So it was much easier.

Were you pitching guitar/vocal demos or were they full-blown demos?

They were band demos. Except for "The Long Black Veil." Danny Dill and I wrote that. I put the music to his lyrics that morning, sang it a cappella to Mr. Don Law, taught it to Lefty Frizzell that afternoon and cut it that night. I played piano on the session. So Cedarwood never had a demo on it, and that's one of their very best copyrights.

Were band demos unusual at that time?

No. The "A" players did it all. The "A" string players did everything. And we would book the "A" string players when they weren't playing a regular session until they got too big for it. Then we had to find some "B" string players to start doing our demos.

But that was a great era to live through. Kristofferson came six years after I did. He compares it to the Hemingway and friends era. And that sounds right, because it was definitely a happening. It will never happen again. It was the beginning of the beautiful Nashville sound.

How did you happen upon Kris Kristofferson?

Kris was stationed in Germany with my second cousin.

The way it always happens.

Donny had told him that he had an elderly relative who lived in Nashville. I wasn't elderly at the time. I thought it was comical. Kris thought it was real comical when he got here. And of course being the silver-tongued devil that he is, when he walked in and saw me he said, "You can't be Donny's elderly relative."

Somebody asked me the other day if I had a desire to write. And I said, "The word *desire* is not strong enough." And again, I understand that in people. Kris had to write. He *had* to write. I think his obsession was even worse than mine, because he also needed to be a star. I didn't. I didn't need stardom. And he wanted to sing worse than anybody I ever heard. He wanted to sing in my vocal group. "You can't sing in my vocal group."

Because you can't sing.

You can't sing. And he's still singing. The man has to sing. And he had to write.

He sent me a song from Germany. I wish I had kept the tape. It was a long, rambling, something about an eagle flying, but it was poetic and I couldn't turn him down. I just couldn't turn him down. It scared me to death for him to be here, because he wasn't a country singer. But I said, "You're going to be a writer, and that's all there is to it. So I'll give you the chance. I can't say no."

But if he hadn't come to Nashville—he was being mustered out at the time of the service—his next assignment was to teach literature at West Point. I suggested to him that he take a part-time professorship somewhere. I said, "You're too brilliant, Kris, to stop everything just to write country music. You're just too brilliant." "That's what I want to do." So he got a job as the janitor at Columbia. And I felt so sorry for his wife. She came here a captain's wife and ended up a janitor's wife. The spouses don't understand that we don't have a choice. And of course, his didn't end up too happily either, but he's still doing what he had to do.

And the silver-tongued devil ended up on the silver screen.

He's really expanded on it. I believe that Kris will finally be a great novelist, because he's brilliant. So educated. So well-traveled.

He's in his early sixties.

He is.

James Michener wrote late in life.

I think Kris will.

Have you expressed that to him?

I don't suppose so.

You ever speak to him?

It's been about six months ago, I guess. And I had a real nice visit over the phone. He's such a likable person. Just extremely likable. So I'm always glad to hear from him. I get the color photo of the family every Christmas. A few years back, he and I did a Tootsie show. He helped me sing "One Day At A Time."

Which he helped co-write.

Right. But that was several years after he had written for Buckhorn. He just happened to be in town.

How long did he write for Buckhorn?

Three years.

And then he went to Combine.

Yes. When he wrote for Buckhorn, he was unknown and learned the craft. That's what we all have to do, really. We come here as potential writers, but it takes a while to learn the craft. I was fortunate when I first came in that I co-wrote. That way I could learn faster, because I was writing with such writers as John D. Loudermilk and Mel Tillis and Wayne Walker and Danny Dill. All five of us, as well as Kris, are in the Songwriters Hall of Fame. Kris always wrote alone, and so it took him longer without having a co-writer to guide him. But what he wrote was what he had done the night before.

He must have been fairly busy.

He was awfully busy. I just shake my head.

Why did he leave Buckhorn?

Well, I couldn't carry him any longer. He hadn't had a hit. And he wanted to be an artist. He wanted to sing. I had produced one single on Kris that he wrote called "The Golden Idol," and Billy Sherrill took it and put it on Columbia. But as Billy says, "I still don't know what the song was about." It was about this girl that we both knew who wore too much makeup.

I read where you "embarked on a long spiritual journey overseas in 1968."

I didn't realize that was what I was doing at the time. I can just remember that I needed to read something a little bit deeper than *Billboard* or a Mickey Spillane book. I almost had a culture shock when I came out of the schoolroom from all highly educated people around me to country music. I changed my way of talking. I dropped all my g's. I had been a schoolteacher for seven or eight years and the whole thing was a tremendous shock. So I hadn't grown in the way that I was accustomed to growing.

I had learned a lot. I really had. And it was great experience. I joined the National Publishers Association. I went to publisher's meetings in New York City. I learned the trade. And that was good, but that was all I learned for years. I had to grow in all ways.

When Kris left the company, the company itself was in one of those slumps. I had a partner by the name of Hubert Long. Hubert had a lot of other companies that were solvent and doing real well, and so it was no trouble to leave the file cabinet with Hubert and just close up for a while.

My husband had been killed in a strafing battle as a prisoner of war of the Italians in the Mediterranean. Well, to a young war bride in Texas, where was Algiers? Goodness, I didn't know where it was on the map. I couldn't imagine it. So I took a ship from Naples through and over the Mediterranean for several days. I knew where the battle had been within hours and where they went down. That's actually what I went for: to cross through the Mediterranean where he was killed, to get a sense of where it was, that it really was a place on earth and that you really could be there.

He was headed for Naples, and so I went to Naples and just stayed for a while. I felt like I was getting so ignorant that I had considered going to school in Heidelberg, Germany. But after I went through this experience, I didn't need to stay over there.

Your sojourn was over twenty-five years after the event.

It doesn't matter. If you lose someone somewhere, if it's fifty years ago, you still want to go where it happened. And today I know that even the airlines take those who are left to the site of a plane crash, because if you never see the site, if you never know the site, there's absolutely no closure. There's just none. "I really don't believe this."

Was being at the site a metaphysical experience?

Yeah. And I knew it. The Mediterranean is usually as smooth as glass. It was just rolling that ship. You had to hold on to walk.

As well as was transformational?

Tremendously. Although I never thought of it as being a spiritual trip.

While I was in Rome, I was only a couple hours flight time from Jerusalem. And having been raised as religiously as I was I thought, "I'll just arrange a tour from Rome to Tel Aviv." And Cooks, which is the big tour company in Europe, arranged a few days in Israel. Now remember I'm doing all this by myself. I don't know if I had no brains or if I had no fear. I had to speak another language. But I discovered that a smile was the same in any language. And they loved nice luggage, and at that time, for a traveler to be well-dressed. So I got along fine in all countries.

You had good luggage and a good wardrobe, so you were okay.

I was okay. The only place I was even the least bit afraid was in Spain, because Franco was still in power. I had a layover in Spain and I had made the mistake of wearing trousers. At that time, Spain frowned upon women in trousers. I was so uncomfortable that I went to the American Embassy and spent the day. I asked the men there, "Why am I being whistled at, stared at, and cab drivers won't stop and get me?" They said, "Because you have on pants." That was the only time on the entire trip that I was the least bit uncomfortable.

What happened when you returned to Nashville?

I just fell back in the music business. Johnny Cash had cut "The Long Black Veil" on the *Folsom Prison Blues* album and it was soaring up the charts. Kris's song "For The Good Times" was about to be a hit. So boom! I just walked back into a full-blown business.

That's when I made my last marital mistake. I came back kind of cleansed and I married again. And that one didn't work out. At all.

Joan Baez cut "The Long Black Veil" on the *Blessed Are* album. She had also written a song on that album called "Outside The Nashville City Limits." And it was written about the farm in Fairview where this last husband and I lived. In the song she had quoted my husband as saying, "And there's just me and Marijohn and now I think we're home." It kept me married an extra year just because of that line in the song. I kept listening to it and thinking, "Well, maybe we are."

Anyway, Hubert Long died, my mother died and my marriage was just really rough. Too much drinking. Too much drinking.

Both parties?

Yes. It just wasn't going to work. And that's when I wrote "One Day At A Time." That was just a cry for help. I really didn't know what else to do. I just didn't know what else to do.

I went to a preacher and he asked me what kind of problems I had. I said, "A lot." It was really the soul. It was a matter of a lifestyle that I wasn't comfortable with. I used to watch the people in Nashville and think, "Why can't I be as comfortable getting drunk as they are?" But I couldn't be. There was always this eating at me. "This is not what you're supposed to be doing." And I realized it was my insides that were bothering me, nothing really outside.

I get the feeling you're not talking about your liver.

My soul.

Was not at peace.

Not at peace. It just wasn't at peace.

And what brought "the peace that surpasses all understanding"?

A spiritual awakening.

"One Day At A Time" was actually a prayer. I had gone to this minister and he said a strange thing. In fact, doctrinally he got it wrong, but I didn't know the difference so it was all right. It worked out to my advantage. He said, "Thank the Lord for your problems." Well, that's not what you're supposed to do. It's "in everything, be thankful unto the Lord." Not for your problems. And I was driving all the way back to the farm in Fairview saying, "Thank you, Lord, I think. My mother's dead; my partner's dead."

Man, I was backed up against a wall. I was just in a mess. I was going to buy the other half of Buckhorn from Hubert's estate. Dottie West had bought a house from me and I had taken a second mortgage. She was way behind on that. And I knew if she didn't get that paid up, then I was going to have a house in town on my hands and a farm and a boat sitting in the river, and I ain't going to be able to do it. I was really scared. I was up to here with problems. They seem very minute, I'm sure, of some people's problems. But it was a big problem.

And so that's how the song came out: Do it one day at a time, dummy. It wasn't about Alcoholics Anonymous. It was about doing it one day at a time. It was unraveling this thing that I was in. To know I was going to get a divorce and buy the other half of Buckhorn and be in business by myself for the first time ever with my partner just dead and my mother just dead and sell the farm in Fairview and get a house back in town. And with this song came peace. I couldn't even to this day tell you how I worked all those things out. But I did. Got rid of the farm. Got a divorce. Dottie got "Country Sunshine" with the Coca-Cola Company, so she got an advance. She paid me for the house over on Shys Hill and I took a house in town as a trade on the farm. I got a loan from the bank to buy out Hubert's half of Buckhorn. And I went on Word Records. All within a year. And that's not even normal to live through something like that.

This was your second recording career.

Well, my first one didn't amount to anything, really. I just put out an album on Columbia. I put out four albums for Word and then they did a book. But, again, I didn't come here to be an artist. I came here to be a writer.

You moved to Nashville with your second husband.

At least.

There was a short-lived relationship after the first marriage?

They've all been short-lived. I just should never have remarried because my first husband was my soul mate. And I was supposed to write.

Harlan Howard made the statement that all of his wives knew that his writing came first.

I wonder if that was in the pre-nuptial agreement.
So your third husband moved to Nashville with you. What did he do while you were writing?

I'm not real sure.

You weren't keeping real close tabs at this point.

No. He's the one I should have stayed with.

So you stopped at three.

No.

Can we get a head count?

Four. I have been single since the '70s and handling it very well. Once I quit drinking, I was okay.

You did an album called The Blue and The Gray *for Columbia Records to commemorate the 100th Anniversary of the Civil War.*

Mr. Don Law suggested it. See, I never was a country singer. I was actually a folk singer. And he recognized that. So he asked me if I would like to put out an authentic album. And that was one of the neatest things that I got to do in the music business, because I studied all these old Civil War books and got the songs. The Jordonaires came over and we rehearsed before we got to the studio. It was a real neat experience.

I was singing about the Civil War, but in my heart, I was singing of the travesty of World War II. So it came out very realistic.

You understood the price.

You better believe it. A cannonball don't pay no mind. And it was cathartic for me to do it.

What was your first husband's name?

His name was Bedford Russell.

Bedford Russell.

He went in December and he was killed in January. I mean, boom! He just went over there and was killed. No dog tags, no nothing. We were married only three years.

It was real weird. It was an international happening. He was shot down over north Africa and picked up by the Italians. And we were still enemies with the Italians that early in the war. He was chasing Rommel. The British, Canadian and American flyers and their crew were fighting the Germans in the desert.

He was on a submarine being taken to Naples to an Italian prisoner of war camp. And for some reason or another, they didn't have a Red Cross flag on the submarine. And the British strafed them. Today it's called friendly fire, which is a very irritating phrase to me, but that's what it's called.

Your husband was killed by the British, who were the allies?

Right. All the more senseless.

You wrote a huge hit called "Waterloo," which is in reference to Napoleon Bonaparte's famous defeat. It was recorded by Stonewall Jackson, who is a descendent of a revered Confederate general by the same name. You lost a husband in World War II. You recorded an album of Civil War songs. Your life seems karmically tied to war.

It's karmically tied in with war. That's right. But I didn't even read the articles from the paper until about ten years ago. My world tilted. And it didn't get back on its axis until just a few years ago. I'm serious. And finally through the help of AA, I listened to people come out with their pain. What I tried to do was act as though it had never happened. But if you put away the hurtful memories, then you don't have any memories.

You threw out the baby with the bath water.

Exactly. Remember, I'm from an era when we didn't go to psychiatrists. And besides, what was my pain when one mother had lost five sons? The pain was relative.

But it was your pain.

But it still couldn't match a mother's pain of losing five boys. We kept our pain to ourselves. And I could never write about it. I could never write about it in my songs.

When I first came here, nobody even knew I'd had a husband killed in the war. I just didn't talk about it. I never mentioned it. Because, remember, we were on the third husband by then. Get over it. But I *never* got over it.

I did better single. I got more peace when I was single, because then I wasn't having to live some kind of a pretentious life. So all these self-inflicted things that I have gone through, that's part of the growth process.

Does it feel resolved for you?

I don't think you ever resolve it. You just learn to live with it. Or live without it, I should say. But now it's okay to talk about and to say, "Hey, that was a part of what I did."

What are your thoughts on the hereafter?

I think it consists of spiritualization—a learning and a growing process to become more and more spiritual. Regardless of how spiritual we are, we're still animalistic. And I think it's a forever training process.

Will you still be writing songs in the hereafter?

Oh, yes. Absolutely. But they'll be in color.

But not reincarnated as a songwriter.

No.

The first thing that goes is the earthly pain and ache. And then I believe we get to do whatever we did here, if that's what we want to do. But the whole point is to glorify God. It's not to glorify ourselves. And I'm quite sure I'll be a songwriter.

You've been a songwriter, a song plugger.

A backup singer.

Prepared lead sheets, an artist, a pianist, a producer.

And a publisher.

Did I miss anything?

That's it.

Sometimes I just wonder, "Why did you do all that? Why did you try to do so much? What is the point?" But I'm so thankful to have been able to make a living out of music, which, to me, was a hobby. It was never the end to me. And even singing was not an end. It was a means to an end. I have made a living now for forty some odd years in the music business. And that's pretty phenomenal.

Anything in the music business that you didn't get a chance to do that you would like to do?

Not really. If one part of my musical life wasn't making a living for me at that time, then I could go to another part of it. I'd get out and hustle up some sessions to sing backup if I needed some quick money. That was the only thing that scared me when I got older: I couldn't moonlight.

I have been fortunate. It hasn't been all luck, I know that. A lot of it's been luck. A lot of it's been being at the right place at the right time. And again, this is what I was supposed to be doing. And I'm still writing. The neat thing is no matter how old you are, if you're still writing, fine. Nobody can stop you.

You practiced yoga in the '60s for peace of mind.

Right. I had been reading about it and I still hadn't had my spiritual awakening, and so I thought, "I'll try this." Actually I became addicted to it, as you can, which was great. I gave about an hour a day to it. Taught myself. And I did learn to still my thoughts. It wasn't the answer for what *I* needed at the time, because I needed a spiritual awakening. But it helped me and it helped my movements. It gave me a sureness. Even today, doctors and nurses will notice that I have more agility than most old people my age, and they will ask me what I have done. I say, "Yoga. For years."

I asked my doctor about yoga just a few months ago, because I have osteoporosis now and I was kind of afraid I would twist myself around and break something. She told me to go ahead and do it. So I still do yoga. I do it before I get up in the morning. Yoga taught me to watch the animals. They always stretch before they get up. They don't jump up like people do and take off. One of the greatest things that I learned is to watch the animals and do like they do. The older you get the more you really, really need it. But now I am afraid to stand on my head. I truly am.

When was the last time you did a headstand?

Oh, it's been several years.

But you were doing it into your seventies?

Right. But I'm afraid now that I have osteoporosis that I would take a chance on breaking something. I'm thinking about getting one of those machines that stands you on your head.

Being inverted is magical.

It's magical. We need that. Part of an old person's circulation problem is because we're not on our heads.

How long would you stay in headstand in your seventies?

Oh, I would stay at least fifteen, twenty minutes. And you can just feel things going on. I was leaning against the wall. I never did learn to just do a plain old headstand.

Do you meditate?

I don't meditate, per se. I stay in a form of prayer most of the time. Someone told me the other day that they believed that I had one foot in heaven and one in the earth right now. And I can believe that, because I'm very detached at this time from the world.

I can be in a different zone when I write. Totally different zone. In fact, I want to be in a different zone, because I don't want to be contriving songs. I want to be inspired. I want to hear my songs being given to me in my head.

I spend some time every day at the piano. I'm either writing something new or playing gospel songs that I've written through the years. It's a whole lot easier life now than it was. I still have a few demons, but they're easier to overcome.

In a few days, you reach a milestone. And in a few weeks, I reach a milestone. I'll be turning forty. You'll be turning forty times two.

It's tiresome. It's really tiring. Eighty is too old. And the feeling that I'm going to have to live more is what I'm afraid of.

You're going to have to live more?

Yeah. I don't know why, but I just have a feeling that I have to be here quite a bit longer.

Do you feel young at heart?

No. Not really.

Eighty's eighty.

Eighty's eighty. I remember being at a BMI dinner about four or five years ago, and Mae Axton had just turned eighty. And I was complaining about being old and she said, "You don't know what old is till you turn eighty." And she didn't live long after that. But she was really complaining. I have a friend that I taught school with and she's really complaining. There's a certain entrapment going on.

What do you mean by "entrapment"?

I'm the same as I was at forty, but I'm trapped in an eighty-year-old body. And that's the entrapment. And that's really difficult. But then, of course, I'm not the same that I was at forty. I still see myself, or think of myself, as somewhere in my fifties. But I can't do what I did at fifty. Aging is a difficult thing. It's really difficult.

Are the difficulties mostly physical?

It's physical. I kind of got it figured out, though, as far as the time thing. There is no time. Things have to be in sequence for us, because we'd explode. We couldn't live it all at once.

But if we're twenty, we're remembering and we're living twenty years. All the time. At the snap of a finger we remember eating watermelon on the back porch when we were six. So think of all I'm remembering.

I don't imagine it would all fit in that filing cabinet you left with Hubert Long.

And it's all in the computer. So I'm living eighty years now every minute. Every minute.

Is that fascinating?

It's tiring. God, it's tiring.

And your perception of time?

Oh, you cannot believe how fast it goes. Can't believe how fast it goes.

Someone once explained the perception of time to me: If you are two, then the time it takes to get to three represents 50 percent of the time you have lived. But if you are fifty, then the time it takes to get to fifty-one represents 2 percent of the time you have lived. They are both 365 days, but the perception has changed. Do you agree with that?

Yeah. And I wouldn't go back for nothing. Nothing.

Do the aches and pains of the physical body encourage us to let go of this life and experience what is on the other side?

I'm sure that's a motivation. Of course, my motivation is that pilot that's waiting over there. That has been my motivation for all these years. He's my soul mate.

But you're not ready to join that pilot yet.

Oh, yes, I am. I was in the hospital last summer and because I made the statement "that's okay, I'm ready to go," they thought I was suicidal. And I tried to make them understand the difference in being suicidal and ready to go.

Your spiritual bags are packed.

Yeah. This friend of mine called the other day and she was a little scared. And I said, "Think of it as going on a trip and we don't have to take clothes."

R.C.A. Victor Records   HANK COCHRAN   Hal Smith
                                                     Aritsts Productions
                                                     119 Two Mile Pike
                                                     Goodlettsville, Tenn.
                                                     859-1343

Photo courtesy of BMI Archives

Hank Cochran

Who named you Hank?

Everybody called me Tex, because I had worked in the oil fields when I was about thirteen, fourteen years old for a couple years. I got to wearing cowboy boots in Hobbs, New Mexico. I went from Hobbs to California. And by then I was playing guitar. They had amateur shows out there, so I entered the Squeakin' Deakon Show at the Riverside Rancho in '51. It's not there anymore, but the stars came out from Nashville at that time. This guy who professed to manage me said, "You don't want to be called Tex." I said, "Well, my name is Garland. You want me to go by Garland?" He said, "No." So he come up with Hank and called me Hank Perry.

Perry is your middle name.

Yeah.

So I tried to drop the Hank when I moved to Nashville. But it stuck for some damn reason. I was Hank Cochran. And it just stayed. I never could get back to Garland, so I just had it legally changed to Hank Cochran. My wife, Susie, said I was a different person when I was Garland.

The evil twin.

Yeah, he would come out and she said he wasn't very nice. I said, "Well, he is gone for good. I have had him legally took away." And I got tired of signing Garland Perry Cochran on everything that was legal wise. After a while, I just said, "That's ridiculous. Nobody even knows my name is Garland." So I just had it legally changed to Hank Cochran.

Was your first aspiration to be a recording artist?

No. I wanted to be a writer.

Before I came to Nashville, me and Eddie Cochran recorded together. I lived in a place called Bell Gardens, California. I was working in that area at seventeen. I wasn't supposed to, but I put a little band together.

You grew up pretty young.

I don't remember growing up. Since I was about nine years old, I've been on my own. I just took care of myself. Me and my uncle hitchhiked away from Mississippi when I was twelve, thirteen years old. That's how I wound up in Hobbs, New Mexico.

This was the late '40s?

Yeah. So me and my uncle went in this service station in Hobbs. He was a little bit older than I was. He played a little guitar. I went in this service station and asked this guy did he know where I could do a couple days' work to get something to eat. He said, "Well, I know the people across the street who own that little café." So I went across the street and got a job in that café. The woman who owned that café had a house, and me and my uncle moved in that house. I worked at that café for I don't know how long. And one day, me and this kid got to be friends. I knew his family and all of that. And he called me one day and he said, "My daddy needs a person on the roustabout crew, because they had a blowout."

Time to call Red Adair.

Yeah. Only he hadn't got there yet. So I said, "Hell, yeah!" So I went to work roustabouting. Lefty Frizzell told me that during that time his dad worked fifty miles from where I was in the oil fields.

We would leave Hobbs and most of the work we done was in Texas. Drilling and all that. Forty or fifty miles was a long way then. I worked the graveyard shift, which is eleven to seven.

Did you have communication with your folks after you left?

Yeah, off and on. Me and my dad didn't get along at all, because I went through some bad times every time I was around him. So me and him just completely didn't see each other at all.

You were put in an orphanage at age ten.

I was supposed to go stay with my dad after him and my mother had separated, and he had remarried. But then he put me in the Saint Peter's Orphanage in Memphis. And I left the orphanage. Then he got a house and farmed what you call sharecropping. I was just an inch above a slave. Just working and plowing until dark, and then taking mules in and undoing them, and gathering wood and water. Then get up before daylight and go get the mules and harness them all up and everything. By the time I got back to the house, what little there was to eat was cold. Like biscuits and gravy. We're talking about rough old days back then. It was hell.

What was orphanage life like?

It was really bleak. It was a Catholic orphan home, and I had never been in anything like that before. My grandfather was a preacher, so I didn't know anything about these nuns wearing all this stuff. I accidentally knocked off one of them wimples. She slapped me clean across the room. I mean, she hit me like a man. But it looked like her head was shaved.

I've heard if you went to Catholic school, you would go to heaven, because you had the hell knocked out of you.

Boy, that's the truth. I've got it made.

So you went to California for music.

Yeah. I just went to California. And I was already playing and singing. And just got more into it, because there was more happening out there. It was more open.

A good bit of country music was going on.

Oh, yeah. Buck and Hag and Tommy Collins and a bunch of others were out there in Bakersfield. I knew Glen Campbell back in the '50s. Harlan Howard would send songs back to Nashville to Pamper Music.

You wrote a number of hits for Pamper Music. How did Pamper get started?

Claude Cavendar was recording his wife, but she was a horrible singer. Ralph Mooney said, "Why don't you start a publishing company and put some songs in it, so when you record her you'd get some of your money back if they play it anywhere." So Claude went in the bathroom and there's Pamper Shampoo. He said, "I'll just call it Pamper Music. What do I do now?" So he started the BMI company. He said, "Has anybody got any songs?" Ralph Mooney was one of the writers of "Crazy Arms." He said, "Me and Chuck Seals have a song called 'Crazy Arms.' It's a little different, but we sure think it's a hit." And he cut it with his wife.

Ray Price was somewhere in Florida, and a disk jockey caught his attention and said, "There's a record come in here and it's the worst single that you ever heard. I played it on the air one time and the people just went crazy about the song." And Ray's got one of the best ears in the business. He said, "What's the name of it?" The disc jockey said, "Crazy Arms." Ray said, "Let's hear it." He played it for Ray. Ray come back to Nashville and made a deal with Hal Smith and Claude Cavendar, and incorporated Pamper Music accidentally through Florida.

Did you find it more fun back then when the music business was sort of shooting from the hip?

Oh, yeah.

When you hear something on the radio today, the next record after it sounds just the same. They all look alike. They all wear a hat.

Used to when you heard it, you knew that was Hag, or you knew that was Price, or you knew that was Loretta. And Johnny Cash especially.

And they lost that identity. Greed got into it. When you got into that much money that was being made, and that many stations had went country, then greed really gets in. The big New York corporations come in.

A real good song ultimately is the answer.

You did well during the Urban Cowboy era. Was that part of the changing of the guard?

Well, that was one of them. It's done this before. It'll change. Now they're working on an artist more to get an identity for that artist. The sales have went to hell, because it was spread out so much. And the radio don't tell the artist or the song, and so people don't know what the hell to buy.

Radio stations wanted to charge record companies to announce who they were playing.

The record companies are raising hell. And they have no reason to raise hell. They're sending the radio stations that stuff. How can you raise hell for something that you're doing? They're just flooding them radio stations with the same stuff. When something a little different is sent and somebody ventures out enough to start playing it, that's when things will change. And it will always be that way. Somebody has to kick the damn door down.

Patsy Cline kicked some doors down.

Absolutely.

LeAnn Rimes kicked some doors down.

Yeah. Every label now has got a thirteen-year-old.

The copycat syndrome. And claiming it isn't because another one was selling multi-platinum.

Absolutely.

Back when I was writing my first hits, the writer got a penny and the publisher got a penny. So the publisher didn't want you writing with anybody other than the writers that was with your own company. They wasn't having no million sellers like they are now. And you had to sell a million records to make ten thousand dollars.

And there weren't as many country radio stations.

No. There was three hundred.

Describe your arrival to Nashville.

When I first got here, I was living over at Mama Upchurch's. She was an older woman. It was a room in a house and that was it. Ten dollars a week.

A lot of music people?

All of them. Just nothing but. And she would take them in. Hank Williams stayed there.

It was a boarding house.

It was.

I stayed there for the week when I was here in October. And then I called her in January when I came here on the bus to stay. And it was snow everywhere. There wasn't anybody to pick me up at the bus station. I called her and I asked her could I come over and stay. She said, "Well, son, everybody over here has got the croup." I said, "Well, Mama, if I stay out here in this snow, I'm going to die anyway." And she said, "Oh, son, that's right. Have you got any money, because you can catch a cab over here to 423 Boscobel. If you don't have any money, just catch a cab over here and I'll pay and you can give it back to me later. I don't want you to be out there in the cold." But she said, "I'm full up and you'll have to sleep in somebody else's bed until they get back from the road. And by then, somebody else will be on the road." So I bed hopped until somebody was making enough money to move out and get their own place.

Were there any shenanigans going on at Mama Upchurch's? Drinking and so forth?

Naw. Ain't supposed to. Didn't do it. We went down to Tootsie's. Well, it wasn't Tootsie's then. It was Mom's, and then it turned into Tootsie's Orchid Lounge.

You minded your manners around Mama.

That's right.

Mama Upchurch was an older woman, and she just took care of so many people right up to her death. She'd charge ten dollars a week for us to stay there. When I went to Mama Upchurch's to stay, Shorty Lavender was there, who worked for Ray Price at the time. Played fiddle. He wound up owning a big agency before he died. Johnny Paycheck was there. He was going by Donny Young. Darrell McCall was there. He was Darrell Young. And him and Donny were supposed to be brothers, but they wasn't.

You can't imagine how many people stayed there when they first came to Nashville—The Carters, Carl Smith, Stonewall Jackson. They signed Stonewall to the Opry before he ever got a recording deal.

Really?

That's how they were doing it back then. And now, I just read in the paper, today's paper as a matter of fact, that they're firing some people that have been on the Opry as musicians for forty years. They are firing them and hiring younger people that can't even hold a candle to these guys. Vince Gill said so in the paper.

There's no better drummer than Buddy Harman, and they're firing him from the Opry. Leon Rhodes, who plays guitar, used to work with Ernest Tubb. And there ain't no better guitar player than him. It don't make sense. Don't fix it if it ain't broke.

The big stars that belong to the Opry don't have a deal where they have to work twenty-six Saturdays a year. Ernest Tubb and them guys had to come in from tour and work on Saturday, and then go back out. They took the best day of the week out away from them to be a member of the Opry. They don't do that now. The big stars that do belong to the Opry don't work it. They just work it when there's a big TV show or a special.

When I worked the Opry, when I first came here, it was ten dollars for the first spot and three dollars for the next spot after it. I played rhythm guitar with Justin Tubb. Pamper Music also had a booking agency, and some of the artists that they booked was members of the Opry. I got to know all of them real close. They let me play rhythm guitar, so I could make that extra three dollars.

That was in the Ryman hothouse before they moved it to Opryland. The stars come out there in those suits with sweat running down off of them. Everybody in the crowd, which was twenty-two hundred people, had those little fans. There was two air conditioners and one of them was in Roy Acuff's dressing room, which everybody just swarmed when he walked out of the door.

How did you become acquainted with Patsy Cline?

Darrell McCall was playing bass for Patsy Cline every now and then. He was real close friends with Patsy. So Darrell introduced me to Patsy. And we got to be friends, because she liked songwriters. We'd all go over there and sing songs and everything. But she was signed at that time to Four Star Music and Records, and she couldn't cut anything except Four Star songs. They were releasing them on Decca. They was the distributor.

Patsy's contract came up in 1960 and she had her first session where Owen Bradley could find songs and produce her. I got to meet Owen Bradley. Mr. Bradley. And we became friends. Me and Harlan had this song called "I Fall To Pieces" started and was working on it. I went over to Harlan's and we finished it. My job at Pamper was pitching songs, so I sang it for Owen. I didn't even have a copy of it. We hadn't even demoed yet. I sang it for Owen and he said, "That's a hit. I'll cut that with somebody, if you'll bring me a dub of it."

The office was in Goodlettsville and there was no freeway. I had to drive all the way into town to play everybody a song on a seven-and-a-half, on a little Wallensac. Every song plugger in town had a little old Wallensac. If they liked it, they'd say, "Yeah, bring me a dub of it." Then I had to drive all the way back to Goodlettsville, go in this little house that's sitting right out there that I had brought over here a few years ago when Hal Smith sold the property, and cut a dub of the song off of a seven-and-a-half tape. I had pitched "I Fall To Pieces" to practically everybody, and Owen had pitched it to people on the label to cut.

Patsy didn't really like the song. Owen finally put his foot down and he just said, "We're cutting this song. And we're cutting it this way." And he cut it that way. And then he cut another thing of mine that she really liked called "These Shoes Don't Fit Me Anymore." And then she cut another song of Freddie Hart's. It wound up on the back of "I Fall To Pieces."

A guy was at the session that knew Owen real well and he was a big songwriter at the time. He had wrote a couple Brenda Lee hits. He talked me into leaving the session and going and getting a beer when they started on Freddie Hart's song. I said, "Well, I got this new song that she's going to cut also." He said, "They're going to be on Freddie's song at least thirty minutes. We can run right there to that little old market."

It's now called Kim's Market.

That's it. We went down there to get a beer. And in the time we were doing that, they couldn't get the Freddie Hart song. They decided to cut the thing of mine, but Patsy couldn't find it. So they went back to the Freddie Hart thing. By the time I got back, they got it recorded, or I would have had every song on the session. Which, who knows what would have happened?

That was an expensive beer.

You ain't kidding. Turned out to be very expensive. And every year it turns out to be more expensive.

But "I Fall To Pieces" has bought you a case or two.

Pamper had two promotion men, and we worked on "I Fall To Pieces" diligently for six months before we got it to break. I talked to Owen and said, "Can we get some help with this?" Patsy hadn't had anything which was a monster hit since "Walking After Midnight" years before. He said, "Sell me five thousand records somewhere and I'll get Decca to help you."

So we told our promotion man, Pat Nelson, who lived in Cleveland, Ohio, "Take Patsy with you and go up there where you live, where you know everybody, and break this record. Sell us five thousand copies." He went up there and took Patsy with him and they worked that whole area. Then he talked this one guy that he really knew on this big pop station into putting Patsy's record on. He said he would play it all week if Patsy would stay over and do a sock hop.

So she stayed and he played it. The first order out of the distributor up there was five thousand records. Owen called and said, "You got it." And

Decca went to work and it broke open. Just as it started, Patsy had a wreck and was put in the hospital. They thought she was going to die.

I would sneak in the hospital on a Sunday, because we got the chart on Sunday for what "I Fall To Pieces" was going to be the next week. She was all bandaged up and couldn't even see me. I went in there one day and she said, "What's it doing?" And I said, "Patsy, we're in the pop chart." She said, "Aw, hoss, you're kidding." I said, "No, we got a damn pop smash!" She said, "Lord, have mercy, and I'm laying here dying." I said, "You ain't going to die. We're going to make some money. You're going to be a star." That was my first hit.

What if "I Fall To Pieces" had not gone up the chart?

I wouldn't have said a thing. I just would have told her how much I loved her, and I didn't know what was happening, because I hadn't heard anything. But I wouldn't have put in negative thoughts.

She recovered from the car wreck and than her plane crashed.

Yeah. (*Tears.*)

How did Patsy Cline's unexpected death affect you?

Well, it really tore me all to pieces, because we really got to be close friends.

Why do you think her music has endured the test of time?

I think the originality of it.

I was supposed to be on the plane, and I went over to tell Patsy that I couldn't go the next morning. She played me "Faded Love." She was really proud of it, because she was able to sing it without modulating.

Me and Susie went and bought LeAnn Rimes's new album. We put it in the car and listened to it on the way home. And she did "Faded Love" that way.

I imagine that was like stepping back in time thirty-five years.

That's exactly what it was. (*Tears.*) Excuse me.

So I hadn't listened to it since. I want to write LeAnn a letter and tell her I thought she done me and Patsy proud.

Loretta Lynn took some of Patsy's music back to the charts.

She cut an album called *I Remember Patsy*. The first single was "She's Got You," which went to number one. The next single was "Why Can't He Be You," which got in the top five and won a BMI award.

When record companies started into the album sales, they would only put out maybe one single. They hardly ever put out two singles on an album. They'd put out one single and then fill the rest up if it was a big hit. And they'd sell a bunch of singles. Ray Price was selling 250,000 singles.

When Ray did "Night Life," he did a *Night Life* album. He tried to concentrate on that type of song for that album. He was one of the first that was doing a concept-type thing. I had a song called "If She Could See Me Now," and he said, "Well, Hank, this don't really fit." But by the time of the session, it did fit.

Ray Price was my boss. He was one of the owners of Pamper Music. So he was actually my boss. My job was to show Ray Price the best songs that I could find. I would take him to the session and then bring him home. We would stop on the way, and he'd pick up two quarts of Wild Turkey, which is a hundred and one proof whiskey. He is still doing it, and he is singing just as good, or better, than he ever sung.

I recently went in with him and produced three sides. I've been with Ray for forty years. I'd say, "Ray, I think we've got it all set and everything. You ready? Want to give it a shot?" He'd say, "Come here, Hank." We'd walk out to his brand new $600,000 bus. And he would take a double shot of whatever he was drinking. It would either be that real high-dollar tequila or high-dollar whiskey that he was drinking.

To keep his pipes from getting corroded.

Yeah. And go right back in there and that one cut was it every time. He was doing it then and he's still doing it. And he's seventy-something years old.

I saw Ray Price two years ago at the South By Southwest Music Festival in Austin, Texas. He had about eight fiddles in the band. The same keyboard player has been with him over thirty years. You must be good to your players for them to stay with you that long.

Well, he is.

We was just up in Gatlinburg. And I saw the guy that runs the Palace. He come out to the house. We got to talking about Ray Price, and he said Ray had just played there. Forty dollars was the cheapest ticket and he filled it. Packed it. That ain't bad, is it?

No, it's not. When I was a kid, I just loved Burl Ives.

Oh, he was a wonderful person. When I was a kid—and this is the truth—when I was a kid picking olives in California, one of my favorite artists was Burl Ives. And then I come here and get to meet him and get to be friends with him and write one of the biggest hits he ever had.

"Little Bitty Tear" had been cut twice before Burl Ives recorded it. They cut it like they cut "Waterloo." And I told both producers, I said, "Man, you're missing the whole song." But they still went ahead and did it that way.

Owen Bradley's assistant at Decca, Silverstein was his name, loved "Little Bitty Tear." The song. And he pitched it to everybody that come in. Well, Burl Ives come to town, and he pitched it to Burl and he cut it. I'd never even met him when it came out, because they wouldn't let me come to the session.

Wayne Walker came down to Tootsie's after the session and said, "If there's a hit on the session, you've probably got it." The album come out and Decca put out two singles. Nothing happened to either one of them. And Owen said, "We'll be lucky to sell twelve thousand."

Well, Burl Ives hired this guy in California, and he went to work on that record out there and he broke "Little Bitty Tear." It wasn't a month later that Owen was calling us for an ad in *Billboard*, which was about eight hundred dollars. I knew what had happened in California, but I said, "Mr. Bradley, I don't know how we could afford an eight-hundred-dollar ad with only twelve thousand sales."

When I was in college I went to see Honeysuckle Rose *at the drive-in with this girl I was dating. It was the second movie of a double feature. It followed* Take This Job And Shove It. *Anyway, you can get distracted at a drive-in, so I think I missed your performance.*

You probably did because it's at the end. I had another song in there and it ended up on the cutting floor. But it wound up in the album, and that was my main objective. I had three songs in that album, and it's triple platinum. It's around here somewhere on the wall.

Was Honeysuckle Rose *your big screen debut?*

That was it.

And that's just Willie's life story. Slim Pickens was Garland, which is my name. He was Buck Bonam's right-hand person. He's playing my part, because in real life, that's what I did. I signed Willie in 1960 when nobody else would. I got him on record and got all of these songs of his recorded. "Crazy" is one of them.

You and Willie Nelson met forty years ago.

Yeah. We're just as close.

How many songs have you and Willie co-written?

I counted them here a while back. It was about fifteen or sixteen.

So your friendship is based on something other than writing music together.

We're friends because we're friends. He's always been there if I needed him, and I've always been there if he needed me.

What do y'all do when you get together that we can print?

We just BS and talk about the old days and what's happening and so forth. That's about it. Sometimes we get together for a day or two and not even say a word to each other. It's just that vibe there between us. He's trying to get me back on that bus to go hang out with him.

He played Jackson, Mississippi, and I went down there to see him. And, man, I don't know how he does it. He does no less than two hours on stage. I sat on the bus after the show while he signed autographs and talked to all these people for two more hours. There's four hours before we could even sit down and talk and visit. And then he said, "Are you going to New Orleans with me?" That was the next day. I said, "Well, I come down here to tell you I love you and just hug you."

He plays about two hundred dates a year.

At least. It's the derndest thing I ever seen.

When I was working in the royalty department of a major music publisher, we got a levy from the I.R.S. concerning Willie Nelson that had a lot of zeros on it. And I have often wondered, how could someone who has contributed so much to American music and culture, and who has given so generously to help others with Farm Aid and a host of other benefits, be treated so bad?

The government came in and took everything and auctioned it off. His awards and stuff like that. And Willie is well loved. So people completely monopolized the auction and bought everything that they auctioned off and give it back to Willie.

All that went down right after Willie was campaigning for a guy who was running for governor in Kentucky and his stand was on legalizing marijuana. And I would bet money that's what happened. The guy didn't get elected, but he will run next time. And Willie's going to campaign again.

Willie's been very vocal about the legalization of marijuana.

Well, it's ridiculous. The government would make so much more money legalizing it. And have you ever seen anybody in a fight on marijuana?

They might hold a truckload of Twinkies hostage.

Yeah. That's right.

I've seen how drinking destroys people's lives. I ain't never seen nobody destroyed on marijuana. I don't even smoke marijuana. I have tried, but I can't smoke it. It just puts me to sleep.

In fact, I was supposed to be in that one movie he did with Robert Redford.

Electric Horseman.

Yeah. I was supposed to be in that. He talked me into taking a couple puffs, and I went to sleep and missed my scene. Him and Redford just left me asleep there in the room.

Right is right and wrong is wrong. And to me, I don't see anything wrong with smoking marijuana.

It's unbelievable how many people are in jail on simple possession of marijuana. Increasingly, our prisons are privately run and publicly traded. Well, what does it take to make a profitable and growing prison business? Prisoners.

That's right. And so there's people going to jail for a roach. Now, that ain't right.

There's a man in Canada who shipped in several tons of hemp seed for birds to a U.S. buyer. And it had an almost undetectable amount of THC, which is the hallu-cinogenic property of marijuana. You could eat a whole boxcar load of this birdseed and not get high. And our government has it impounded.

I saw a book by the guy that ran for governor of Kentucky where he talked about hemp. Willie was helping him the last time he ran. He's got a car that will run on hemp oil. That could be made out of hemp.

That's what Henry Ford wanted to do.

There's so many farmers that's going to go under that could be making a fantastic living growing hemp. It will do almost anything, and it ain't even the kind you smoke.

Sure. Clothing. Paper. Lip balm. Soap. It made the rope on the Mayflower.

Gas.

And consider this, one acre of hemp will generate as much paper as two acres of timber, and you can harvest it again the next year. I've dibbled loblolly pines in north Louisiana. That ain't a lot of fun.

And how long will it take for those trees to come back. It's ridiculous.

"Guv'ment," as Roger Miller would say.

Yeah, guv'ment.

Did you hang out much with Roger Miller?

Yeah. Sure did. Hung out with Roger before he had a hit. We was over at his house one time and Roger said, "Boy, wouldn't it be something if we'd be sitting around here and one of our songs was playing on the TV." I said, "Well, it'll happen one of these days."

That was eleven Grammys ago for Roger.

Me and Ray and Willie were in Texas and they were fixing to cut the *San Antonio Rose* album. We were going over songs, and I was writing it down and was going to come back to Nashville and hunt them up. And Willie said, "I'm going to run down to the office for a minute and I'll be right back." Ray said, "Would you bring me a half a chicken on your way back?" Willie looked over at me and said, "He thinks we still work for him." I said, "Don't we? What am I doing? I'm hunting up songs for you all and I don't even have anything on the session so far. You're running and getting him a half a chicken, and you're going in and cutting an album with him. What does that tell you?"

It's still that way. Ray will call me and say, "Hank, would you mind doing something?" And I say, "No, sir, Mr. Price. You know, I still work for you." We kid about it. It's the same way with him and Willie. But it's been great. Forty years of it, it's been great.

There's been some real sad, bad things that have happened. We've lost a bunch of good people. The only bad thing about getting older is you lose so many friends. In the last few years, I keep thinking about who all have died. Like Roger Miller. One year, I saw Roger at the BMI awards and the next year he was dead.

You said you were looking for songs for the San Antonio Rose *album and you didn't have a thing on it. I've heard that you were one of the best song pluggers this town has ever seen.*

Well, I had two on it before it was over.

You wore them down.

Yeah.

What's the secret to being a good song plugger?

You got to have a song.

And beyond that.

Well, I just wouldn't quit. I pitched Mel Tillis a song and he said he liked it. About a week before the session, I said, "You going to cut that song?" He said, "Well, I'm thinking about it." I went down there and moved in with him. He said, "What the hell you doing out here?" I said, "I'm going to stay with you until you cut that song of mine, then I'll move."

At least he knew he could get rid of you in a week.

Yeah. So I stayed with him. He cut the song. And then he wrote another one with the same damn title and cut it with Roy Clark.

I used to go on the road with Jan Howard, Harlan's wife then, and play rhythm guitar. She was recording and making good records and pretty big records. And I would stay up with Ernest Tubb and drink beer with him all the way back. Me and him and the bus driver were all that was up. And we'd stop, because we didn't have a refrigerator on the bus, and get a six pack. Then we would drink that for however long it took, and then we would stop again and get another six-pack. The driver didn't drink.

But you didn't want Ernest drinking alone.

That's right. And Ernest told me, he said, "Son, you're doing a good job over there at the office pitching songs. I've been noticing you. And I want to tell you. If you got the song, whatever it takes to get it recorded, do that. If you have to go down the chimney like Santa Claus, go down the chimney. But get the song cut. If it's a good song, stay with it and do what you have to do." And I did that.

Let me quote the great Hank Cochran: "Make up your mind what you want to be and what you want to do, then take every path that might lead in that direction. Let everyone know what you want so they can help you. And they will. Be definite and determined."

That's right.

After a while, they see that you are determined and you're going to do it, and they will help you because they want to be part of it.

Is that the best advice you could give to a songwriter?

That's the only. Stay with it. I told Emmitt Rider, "Just because one person don't like your song, or I don't like it, that don't mean it ain't a hit. If you like it and you believe in it, stay with it."

You have had hits that were not hits the first time they were released.

Not the first or the second time. "Don't You Ever Get Tired Of Hurting Me" was in the Top Ten twice. Once with Ray Price and once with Ray Price and Willie Nelson as a duet. But it didn't hit big. And other artists cut it.

Ronnie Milsap called me and said, "I'm going to cut a country album, would you come over here?" I said, "Yes, sir." I went over there and he said, "Would you sing me your favorite song that you wrote?" So I picked up a guitar and sung "Don't You Ever Get Tired Of Hurting Me" as close as I could get to it. He said, "I'll cut that."

And he cut it. He flat cut it.

You once said, "I have a theory that somebody besides me must write my songs, because half the time I don't have the slightest idea where they come from." That's the inspiration side of the coin. But the other side is the craft. How does a writer balance inspiration with craft?

It hasn't been an issue for me so far. There has been times that I feel like I'm burnt out. And I have taken two or three turns when that would happen.

In 1975 I went to California and bought a yacht, a fifty-foot Grand Banks, and was on the ocean for a year. It took us a year to get from San Diego to here. Then we turned around and took it to the Bahamas and stayed on it for about six years.

When did you fall in love with the water?

I can't remember. I lived part of my life in Greenville, Mississippi, which is on the Mississippi River. Even then, I was going over to that levy and watching that water. My grandfather on my mother's side fished for a living. I went with him. He would make nets and catch gar and catfish. Anything that would hit it. And then later in California, being right there on the ocean and going over to Catalina Island. It's just been a part of me since I was born.

You didn't write during your yacht hiatus.

No. I didn't even write nothing.

Did that disturb you?

It didn't seem to bother me. I felt like I had to get all that out, and it was just taking its time.

Willie said, "If you don't get off that damn boat and come back to work, we're going to quit talking about you and cutting your songs."

So I come back and went back to work.

It took someone like Willie to put the proverbial boot to your butt.

Yeah, you might say.

But that's what friends are for.

Absolutely. And thank God that I have friends like that and could step right back in where I left off.

I'm just very happy and very proud to be here. I worked very hard at doing my best by everybody. I think you will be rewarded for all you do for others. The Good Lord has been awful good to me.

BILL ANDERSON
Recording Artist

Photo courtesy of BMI Archives

Bill Anderson

You're music career started in Commerce, Georgia, not too far from my mama's stompin' grounds of Trion.

I went there to work with a radio station. I didn't grow up there, but I did a lot of my growing up there. That's where I began to work as a disc jockey and where I really began to formulate whatever it was I was going to bring to Nashville.

You got your first cut in college. That's an early start.

Yeah. I think I got my first song cut in either '56 or '57, so I would have been eighteen or nineteen years old. It was pretty bad, but it was the first one. I remember how upset I was. They only put "Anderson" on the label. And I thought, "You could have at least put 'B.' You didn't have to put 'Bill,' but at least put 'B. Anderson.'"

I know how you feel. I had forty-five seconds of a song I co-wrote in the Jack Nicholson independent film, Blood and Wine. *And when the credits rolled they had put two "ll's" in Philip. The other three people in the theater didn't notice it, but I sure did.*

It's the little things that are important.

When did you start writing songs? And what made you say, "This is the career for me"?

Well, I've always loved country music. My mom and dad tell me I could find hillbillies on the radio a long time before I could tie my shoelaces. And

I've always loved to write. When I was in school and the English teacher would say, "Write a paper and bring it to class tomorrow," everybody would go "ugh" and I would go "yeah!" I've just always liked words.

The story songs attracted me to country music first, because I love words that paint pictures. And I love the simplistic melodies of country music, which in my early days were somewhere between what we would call bluegrass music today and the old-time church hymns with a little black music thrown in.

You grew up in church.

Yeah. My grandfather was a Methodist minister.

Did you hear him preach?

Not a whole lot, because he very rarely preached in the same town where we lived. But he did towards the end of his ministry. I don't know if it was hearing him preach, as much as it was getting what my mom absorbed from him as his daughter. That kind of filtered down to me. It was just a part of the fabric of life where I grew up.

My father's grandfather was a Methodist minister as well. I see that same influence in him. It really shaped the fabric of his life.

I think that's what it is more than necessarily going to church and listening to the sermons every Sunday.

My grandfather said something to me just before he died that has had a very profound effect on me. Some of his sermons were on the radio in the various small towns where he preached. He preached in the days before mass media. He lived to be eighty-eight years old and he preached almost right up until the end. This man preached a lot of sermons.

I went up to see him on his deathbed two weeks before he died, and he said something to me that I've never forgotten. He said, "Billy, I don't know much about this business that you're in. But I do know this: You're in a position to reach more people with one song than I've reached with every sermon I've ever preached in my life."

And boy, what a responsibility comes with that. He wasn't trying to load me down with guilt, but he was right. I'm sure one night of playing and singing on national television or making a record that gets played on the radio reaches more people than he ever reached with every sermon he ever preached.

Part of the beauty of country music is the moral fabric of a lot of great songs. And even in the songs where the person is doing the wrong thing, it really serves as a vital lesson of how not to live your life. That's just as valid. Is there any memorable feedback you've had from fans that your music has touched?

Well, I could sit here and tell you all kinds of things fans have said. I've had people get on me for writing things they didn't necessarily agree with.

I wrote a song back in the mid-'70s that was a big hit called "The Lord Knows I'm Drinkin'." And the idea of the song was that this guy is drinking with a woman who is not his wife. This lady comes in and is berating him. And he basically says, "Look, lady, I don't have to answer to you. I've got to answer to somebody a whole lot bigger than you."

I certainly didn't intend it to be anything that was going to ruffle anybody's feathers. I actually thought it was kind of funny, but some people are humor impaired. The song actually was drawn from a real experience. My wife at the time and I were having dinner in a little restaurant across the street from the church we attended. We had ordered a glass of wine with our meal and some of the deacons and people from the church came walking in. And I said, "Do you think we ought to slide the wine glasses over there behind the menu?" And my wife said, "Why? The Lord knows I'm drinking."

Country music will hit you head-on. Or it used to, anyway.

Did you consider the ministry?

No, I considered being a baseball player. The three loves of my life have always been writing, country music, and sports. I had it in my head that the entertainment business was something that other people did. I never thought it was something I could do.

Once I discovered I wasn't good enough to play baseball at the next level, I got into sports writing. During my last couple years in high school, I was the sports editor of a little weekly newspaper in my hometown. And I did some stringer work for the *Atlanta Constitution*. I had my own byline on the sports page in the Atlanta papers for a couple of years.

If I had not gotten in the music business, I would have done something with mass communications or public relations. The ministry—I don't think so. I didn't ever feel like I was cut out for that.

Do you feel like music has been your ministry?

That's an interesting thought. Maybe in a way. If not a ministry, maybe a witness of some kind.

I've certainly made a lot of mistakes in my life and I've done a lot of things wrong. But I try to conduct myself in public and around the fans and with my songs and shows that I do in such a way that nobody would be embarrassed. You can bring the kids or you can bring Grandmama. It's not going to be offensive. They may not like it, but it's not going to be because the material is vulgar or off color, or because we're on the stage drunk or doped up.

I'm sure you saw your share of that on the road.

Yeah. I never put anybody else down for doing it. It's just that I didn't choose to do it that way.

You've got your Atlanta Braves cap on today. I started going to Braves games in '67, when we would travel to Georgia from Louisiana on Highway 80 to visit my grandparents. I've seen a lot of rotten baseball over the years.

If you're still a Braves fan, you've been to the depths as well as the mountaintop.

I used to go to spring training with them back in the '70s. A good friend of mine named Dave Bristol managed the Braves for a while. Dave and I were very close. I'd go down and they'd let me put on a uniform, get out there and run around. A couple of years the Braves were so bad I thought if I had really tried, I probably could have made the team. That's pretty bad.

Maybe Garth could have played for them. My mom's sister taught Rick Camp how to pitch, which explains a great deal about his career.

That's where I've heard of Trion before. That's Rick Camp's hometown. I got to know Rick fairly well.

In five decades of writing you've amassed over fifty BMI awards.

No wonder I'm so tired.

Billboard ranks you as the No. 27th country artist of all time.

Well, I've slipped a couple notches. I was 24th the last time I looked.

That's still high cotton.

That's a nice compliment.

When you started in the music business, did you have a burning desire to record, or was your main focus songwriting?

It was both.

I formed a little band when I was in high school. And I guess the dye was cast the first time I ever went on a stage. Three of my classmates and I entered a talent show my sophomore year in high school. I don't remember all the songs that we did. I know we played the "Orange Blossom Special," because it was about the only song a little fiddle player could play. But I had written a song and I sang it. And that was the one that caused us to win the show. So from the very beginning, without me even realizing it, the two were hand in hand.

Who had the van?

It was a '48 Studebaker.

Describe your experience of working with some of the younger talent in town, like Gary Nicholson and Steve Wariner. Though they're no spring chickens.

This co-writing thing that I've gotten into in the last four or five years has given me a whole new perspective on songwriting. I always thought songwriting was this thing that you did late at night—two or three o'clock in the morning—with the curtains pulled and the lights turned down low. You closed the door and saw how miserable you could get and wrote a song.

I'm exaggerating in a way, but I'm not in a way either. Songwriting was a lonely thing. It was a lot of introspection. It was a lot of getting off in that quiet place by yourself.

I'm finding out today that songwriting can be "Hey, let's get together with a couple of our buddies, and let's sit around and pick and see what we can come up with." That's been a real eye-opening thing for me. I never thought I could do it. I had this prejudice in my mind that you can't punch a time clock and write a song. And I think to a certain degree there's some validity to that.

I thought nobody in the world ever wrote the second verse of a song first or wrote the chorus first. I've come to find out we all do. And everybody who writes has the same doubts and insecurities and feelings and emotions that I have. The biggest revelation in writing with these young artists is finding out that you can do it in the broad daylight with the sun shining in the windows. You just sit there and let the creative process happen.

Did Steve Wariner's re-recording of "The Tips of My Fingers" re-open a lot of doors for you?

That's when I decided that I'd been missing out on a lot. I went for about ten years without writing at all.

Country music started changing in the early '80s, and I had a couple of negative experiences with my songwriting. I kind of tucked my tail between my legs and thought, "Okay, the music has changed and maybe I don't know how to change with it, so I'll go on to some other things." That's when I got very heavily involved in doing the game shows and the soap operas.

But when Steve cut "Tips of My Fingers" in '92, then all of a sudden I realized, "Hey, man, that's a song you wrote thirty-two years ago and it's speaking to the people that are listening to country music today. You got a whole closet full of those things at home. And if you could write that then, you can write that now."

It set off a little lightbulb in my mind. The first thing I did in trying to get back into songwriting was to take a lot of my old songs and update the demos. Rework them and make them a little more contemporary. And I've had some luck with those.

Would "Walk Out Backwards" be an example?

That's right. That was the first step I took.

No pun intended.

And then I thought, "Well, I'll just take the plunge and go knock on some doors and see if anybody will write with me." Heck, I didn't know if they would laugh me off Music Row. When a guy's been around since dirt, some people think, "What can he contribute?" But some of them were very nice.

I think what legitimized the whole thing was when Vince Gill wrote with me. We got together and wrote a couple of songs. He cut one of them and it was a hit.

When I heard Vince's recording of "Which Bridge To Cross, Which Bridge To Burn," it knocked me out. It was one of those truly powerful songs where the emotions were so real. And it was a fresh way of writing an old idea.

Vince and I wrote two different days. We wrote "Which Bridge To Cross, Which Bridge To Burn" the second day. I thought the song we wrote the first day, "The Cold Gray Light Of Gone," was the better of the two.

I left and went on a cruise for a couple of weeks. When I came back, I asked him, "Did you record our song?" He said, "Yeah, I sure did." I said, "Great!"

It wasn't until later I realized he recorded "Which Bridge To Cross." He's tried to cut "The Cold Gray Light Of Gone" a couple times, and he just never has been able to get it the way he wants it.

Where did the hook come from for "Which Bridge to Cross"?

I was listening to a gospel radio station one day, and I heard that line buried down somewhere in the verse of a song. I don't even know who the artist was, what the song title was, or anything. That line just jumped out and hit me right between the eyeballs. You find song titles buried in other songs. I've had people take a line in a song of mine and turn it into a title.

Did you write your book, Hope You're Living As High On the Hog, *when you took the songwriting hiatus?*

Yeah. The book came out in '93. Also, I did my autobiography during that time.

I went through a pretty rough time in the mid to late '80s. My wife was in a real bad automobile accident and we went through a long, drawn out legal fight. Then I had some misfortune with the Po' Folks restaurant.

I might have started writing songs again sooner if I hadn't had so much on my mind. I was just totally bogged down.

How is the book writing process different from the songwriting process, and what did you enjoy about it?

When you write a song, you have got to condense it. You're writing inside very defined parameters. You've got three minutes. Get to the point quick. When you write prose, it's exactly the opposite. Embellish it.

When I first started writing my autobiography, my editor said, "Don't just say you fried the onions, make the reader smell the onions."

I would think in songwriting, you've got to make the onion bring a tear to their eye.

That's a good analysis. That's right. In prose, you make them smell the onion and in song, you make the onion bring a tear to their eye. That's good. I'm going to use that. I'm glad I thought of it.

In writing the *High on the Hog* book, I learned that there's a tremendous difference between spoken humor and written humor. Some things are funny when you say them, but when you write them, they fall flat on the page. And vice versa.

And that was trial and error?

Trial and error, absolutely. But I felt a lot of growth because it caused me to do something I had never done before.

It probably was a real catharsis for you.

It was. And I love that kind of thing. I love a challenge. I would really love to write a novel. And who knows, some day I may go hole up on top of a mountain in Gatlinburg and take a shot at it.

To be a successful songwriter you've had to learn the art of re-writing.

Oh, yeah. And I don't mind re-writing. In fact, I welcome the challenge to re-write. Steve Wariner and I re-wrote the last verse of "Two Teardrops" about three times before we got it just the way that everybody wanted it. And I have no problem with re-writing. I'm not stubborn on that kind of stuff.

How much re-writing did you experience in your career at the request of your publisher?

Not much. I worked very closely with Buddy Killen the first three years I was in Nashville. And he would make little suggestions. He'd say, "I think maybe you could do that part a little bit better." Or, "What did you mean by that? It's not real clear." But I've always been my own best editor. If I live with it long enough, usually I can spot what's wrong with it.

I ate a lot of times at the Po' Folks restaurant.

I did, too.

Best milk gravy this side of the Mississippi. I hated seeing them go. What was your role in Po' Folks?

I was not involved at all in the very beginning. People think that I founded the company, which is not true. I got involved when they came and opened their first restaurant in Nashville. They had already opened about fifteen or twenty throughout the Southeast before they came here. I was so closely associated with the name Po' Folks because of my song "Po' Folks." I called my band the "Po' Boys" and then the "Po' Folks" when I added girls to the band.

The name was just so synonymous with me, particularly in Nashville, that people started coming up to me and saying, "When did you go in the restaurant business?" I found out later people were going in the restaurant and saying, "Where's Bill Anderson?" They finally instructed the waitresses to tell people that I was back in the kitchen, because so many people were wanting to know what my connection was.

One day the owner of Po' Folks asked me if I'd like to be the national spokesman for the restaurant chain. At the time, I thought, "Heck, yeah. This is pretty good." He gave me some stock in the company and paid me well for what I was doing. That part of it was fine.

The part that I shouldn't have ever gotten involved in was the franchises. A lot of us did—Buddy Killen, Burt Reynolds, Conway Twitty, Barbara Mandrell. All of us wished to different degrees that we had never done that. I thought a restaurant was a place to go to eat. I never knew it was a business. I found out the hard way.

Did friendships survive the investments?

Oh, yeah. Our friendships survived. I can't say I'm friends with some of the people that I was in business with.

You all were probably a country store away from being the Cracker Barrel.

We were at about the same point at one time. The difference was Cracker Barrel stayed in-house and grew slower. They didn't franchise their restaurants. You don't have as much control over it when you franchise, as you do when you own and operate it. You could write a book on how not to be in the restaurant business and all you got to do is tell the story of Po' Folks.

But it was good vittles.

The food never was the problem. There were a lot of other problems, but that was not one of them.

I am very grateful for the opportunity I had to meet Roy Acuff and Cousin Minnie Pearl—the King and Queen of Country Music. What are your thoughts on some of the pioneers of country music?

Oh, Lord, I loved Roy Acuff. He and I recorded one song, "I Wonder If God Likes Country Music," which was, if not the last, certainly one of the last times he was ever in the recording studio. I'm pretty sure it was the only video he ever did. I got to know Roy in a very special way, and I loved him a lot. The same with Minnie. I toured with her and picked up a lot of wisdom from her.

My teachers were Faron Young, Ferlin Husky, George Morgan, Johnny Cash and so many of the people that I toured with early in my career. This was in the days of the old package shows. I would go out and do my part, and then I would go to the side of the stage and watch them perform, because I felt like I was going to school. I was learning from them. And that was very important to me. The young performers don't have the opportunity to do that today like we did back then. And they should.

George Strait is one of the top grossing concert performers.

George Strait is not an entertainer. George Strait is a good singer and George Strait has got a certain charisma about him that makes him successful. But George Strait is not an entertainer. Very few of these young performers are entertainers. They go out on stage and sing their hits. But entertaining is a whole different thing. When I came along, you had to entertain.

Ferlin Husky would go on stage after you performed and imitate you, which you initially mistook as making fun of you. What did you learn from that experience?

Well, I learned not to jump to conclusions. I took it as a very negative thing. I took it as, "Hey, I was on that same stage thirty minutes ago doing what I do, and the people were cheering for me. Now he's out there imitating me and they're laughing at me." And it bothered me.

But Ferlin was so great. He came to me after he picked up on my sensitivity to it and said, "I just want you to know two things. Number one, if you weren't different, there wouldn't be anything to imitate. Number two, if I didn't like you, I wouldn't give you the publicity." That changed my whole way of looking at it. I love it when people imitate me now.

One of the best concerts I ever saw was at the Christy Lane Theater in Branson, Missouri, with Ferlin Husky.

He's a fabulous entertainer.

Absolutely.

Entertainer. That's what I'm talking about. There's a difference between a singer and an entertainer. And I learned to be an entertainer from watching Ferlin Husky and Faron Young and the ones that knew how to entertain people.

Of course, we've lost "The Singing Sheriff," but what makes them special?

Well, the fact that they can just totally extract any emotion from the audience. Ferlin Husky would have you on the floor laughing, and then before he got through singing "Little Tom," he'd have you crying. Faron Young could do the same thing. George Morgan could do the same thing. And audiences always left there feeling they had been entertained.

I knew from the beginning that I didn't have the kind of a singing voice that I could just stand on stage for an hour and mesmerize an audience. I knew I had to learn to do other things. And watching them, I learned how to entertain, learned how to be less inhibited on the stage.

I'll tell you one thing—you're a great host.

Thank you.

I learned about hosting from watching Roy Acuff. To me, Roy Acuff was the consummate host. He did two things that I picked up on. Number one, Roy Acuff never hogged the spotlight. He shared the spotlight with all the people that were around him on that stage. If it was Bashful Brother Oswald's time to shine, or Jimmy Riddle's, or Howdy Forester's, Roy realized that and that came cross to the audience. And number two, Roy Acuff never acted like he was the star at the Grand Ole Opry. The Grand Ole Opry was the star. And, to me, the Grand Ole Opry is still the star. The show is the star. We're all just little pieces and parts of it.

I love being a host. I have no problem in introducing somebody else and letting the spotlight shine on them. I enjoy the challenge of keeping something moving like the backstage TV show that I work on. If you enjoy what you do, I think people pick up on that.

Describe your experience of working with Owen Bradley.

I was so fortunate. I was among the first artists that Owen Bradley signed when he took over at Decca. My first meeting with Owen was amazing.

This is a great illustration of how things have changed in this town. Buddy Killen had brought me to Nashville. And he knew that I wanted to do more than just write. He knew that I really wanted to record. So Buddy called Owen on the phone and said, "I got this kid in town from down in Georgia. He's kind of different, kind of unique. He writes some real good songs, and I'd like for you to hear him." And Owen said, "Okay, what time you want me to come over?" It was almost like an old doctor making house calls.

I just can't imagine that happening today. Can you imagine a producer saying, "What time do you want me to come?" Owen Bradley left wherever he was and he came to Buddy Killen's office. Today, you've got to go through forty-seven secretaries and knock down twenty-six walls just to see a record producer or the head of a record label.

Owen and I hit it off from the very beginning. He was very honest with me the first day. After I sang two or three songs for him, he said, "Well, you ain't the greatest singer I ever heard. But you really got some good songs and you're different. Nobody sounds like you. If you'd like to try to make some records, I would, too." And that was exactly what we did.

Owen kind of became a father figure to me. After I got over being nervous and intimidated around him, I always felt like I could go to Owen with any problem that I had. I could talk to him about anything that was going on in my life, and he would give me the benefit of his years, his wisdom, and his advice.

I had the pleasure of spending an afternoon with Mr. Bradley out at The Barn. He was a grandfather figure at that point.

Well, I guarantee you, if you listened, you learned, because he was just that kind. He was a wonderful man. I owe so much to him.

Not long before he died I told him, "Owen, I'd rather you turn down a song of mine than somebody else accept it." He would tell you why: I don't like this, or I don't like that, or this is not right for this person. It was an achievement just to get him to critique a song.

Owen and I built up a trust with each other. I took him a song in the late '60s called "Wild Weekend." I had recorded songs like "Mama Sang A Song" and "Five Little Fingers." A lot of these mom, home and apple pie songs.

So I walked in with a song called "Gonna Have A Wild Weekend." And I sang him the first verse about this guy going to get away with a little blonde-haired, blue-eyed darling for a wild weekend. He said, "You can't cut that. What else you got?" I said, "Wait a minute, wait a minute. Let me sing you the next verse. You hadn't heard it all yet." "Well, you can't record it." I said, "Well, listen to the next verse." When I got through, he said, "I'm telling you, you can't cut that." I said, "One more." At the end of the song, the guy's actually singing about his wife. And Owen slammed his fist on the desk and said, "God dang, that's great! Let's cut it!"

From that moment on, I felt like Owen and I had a real trust with each other. That was the defining moment in our relationship. Because he trusted me enough to let me sing him the rest of that song, and then he realized that I hadn't steered him wrong. I had so much respect for him, and I think at that point he gained a little respect for me.

Owen virtually told me how to write "Still." I had done "Mama Sang A Song" with the recitation. We went number one in the country charts and got in the pop charts with it. He said, "I think the thing that hurt us from really,

really having a big pop record was the fact that the song was religious in nature. You take that same format—you sing a little, you talk a little—and you make it a love song, then I think we can take it all the way to the top." But I didn't just write "Still." I wrote "Still" and then Owen came in and made "Still" into a great record.

To do a recitation successfully, it has to go beyond lyric to become prose. And I think "Still" does that as well as any.

Well, I never would have written "Still" if Owen hadn't of pointed me in that direction. He said, "I think we found the formula. Now we've got to find the right song to put into the formula." And Lord knows he was right, as he was most of the time.

Other than Dolly Parton's "I Will Always Love You," I can't think of a song that has charted more than "The Tips of My Fingers." What do you think is the reason for its longevity?

If I knew the answer to that, I'd do it every time I wrote one. I think it's just the right combination of whatever the ingredients are. The song's got a lot of range in it, but basically it's a very simple song.

One of Owen Bradley's favorite expressions was, "Boys, Howard Johnson's makes twenty-eight flavors of ice cream and vanilla still outsells them all." And I think that's part of the success of "Tips of My Fingers."

I'll never get this straight as long as I live. Is it "tips" or "tip"? What was it originally and what is it now?

It "tips" now. I wrote it as "Tip Of My Fingers," which I thought was the right way. For some reason, "tip" sounds wrong now and "tips" sounds right. I did it as "tip." Roy Clark cut is as "tips." Eddie Arnold went back and did it as the "tip." Steve Wariner did it as the "tips."

Bill Anderson and the Tips. I'm still confused.

Ralph Emery and I used to get into some violent arguments about that. He always felt that it should be "tips," and I yielded.

Speaking of Ralph Emery, that brings us to TNN. How long have you been associated with Opry Backstage?

I did a show called *Backstage at the Grand Ole Opry* in syndication before TNN ever signed on. TNN didn't come along until 1983. So *Backstage* is in about it's fifth or sixth incarnation, and I've been associated with it off and on for twenty years.

How important was TNN to the growth of country music?

Well, they certainly paralleled each other. I think TNN put a face with country music, and I think that was very necessary at the time.

When I came along, people would hear your songs, but they wouldn't know who you were. They didn't put the face with the song. It took a long time for that whole process to assimilate. With one video, somebody can become known, whereas it took us years to get known. That's why I was so fortunate to be on TV early in my career. I had a syndicated show starting in '65, and I had only been in the business about five or six years. It really enabled the whole package to get put together and that's what TNN has brought to the table.

As an artist, do you miss the fact that you didn't get to make videos on most of your hits? And taking that a little farther, now that you've had current hits by new artists, what are your thoughts about the video process?

I would have enjoyed making videos on my hits, although I have a face for radio.

I've made a few videos. I made the one with Roy Acuff. Then I made a couple others back in the '80s. I think videos are both good and bad, just like everybody else does. I think they enhance some songs; I think they limit some songs. For the vast majority in the middle, it really probably doesn't make a whole lot of difference.

Obviously, they couldn't do a video on "Wish You Were Here." How are they going to show a plane crash? On some songs, you're better off letting your mind make its own video. They didn't play it on many of the airline in-flight programs either.

Growing up in the days of radio as I did when you listened to dramatic shows and comedies, you had to use your imagination. I think TV has made us lazy in a lot of respects.

I've noticed that in a lot of really great songs, the first line is an important clue to what the song is about. For example, using the word "terminal" in the first line of "Wish You Were Here."

When Debbie Moore, Skip Ewing and I were writing the song, that very thing came up. We kicked that around, because of the old joke, "The first thing you see when you get to the airport is a big sign that says 'Terminal.'"

I had a very interesting experience with "Wish You Were Here." The first time I heard it, I was preparing to fly to Los Angeles. Several people had uncharacteristically hugged me throughout the day. I was on the plane with Billy Ray Cyrus's wife, Tish, and she had an uneasy feeling as well. I started thinking, "Have I been getting clues and I should have been heeding them?" But at 35,000 feet, it was too late to change my mind.

Mark Wills told me that when the record came out, he was really scared to get on a plane for a while.

Also, the song has a little mystery, in that the guy doesn't get to his destination to mail the postcard, and yet his beloved receives it.

I know it. Skip Ewing and I went around and around writing that. I said, "We're not explaining it." And Skip kept saying, "We don't have to explain it."

The original title of the song was "Postcard From Heaven." That was Debbie Moore's title. She brought it to me. It wasn't until Skip got involved and said, "Let's call it 'Wish You Were Here,'" that it all really came into focus. But the postcard, that was the key to the whole thing from the beginning.

Somebody sent me a postcard last week with an aerial view of the Michigan State Penitentiary in Jackson, Michigan. And printed on the front of the postcard was "Wish You Were Here."

Part of the greatness of country music over the years has been the instant vocal identity of the singer. When it was Willie, you knew it. Waylon, you knew it. Cash, Conway, Loretta, Dolly, you knew it. That seems to be missing today.

I miss that more than anything. When I came here, if you weren't different, you might as well go home. If you sounded like Ernest Tubb, there was already one of those. Today it is just the opposite. If you don't fit into this little preconceived mold of what you're supposed to sound and look like, you might as well go home. John Anderson is a great stylist. He's so distinctive, you immediately know who he is, and he can't get arrested.

John Conley is another example.

John Conley. That's right.

There's a whole new set of rules out there. Just when I learned the answers, they changed the questions.

Have these become corporate rules?

I don't know that you can go to a record company and say, "Let me see your handbook of rules. Hey, you've got to wear tight jeans and have a cute butt and a black hat."

Everybody says give me something different. But then the minute you give them something different, they say, "Oh, no, not that different." And then they run back to the safe thing.

It's not only country music. I saw this happen in the game show business when I was in California. Because I hosted a show at ABC, I got a pilot to host a show at NBC, and it came within a hair of getting on the air.

They would call me and say, "Come out here. We want you to do a pilot for this show because you're really different. We really want somebody different." And I'd go out there and do the pilot. Then they would say, "Gee, Bill Anderson does a pretty good job hosting a show, but he's not like all these others. He's different from Monty Hall, Bert Convy and Alex Trebec." I would bust my butt, and they would turn around and hire whoever they were secure with.

A song of yours that is not as well known by the public, but probably one you really had to write, is "Forgiveness."

Yeah. Yeah, I did.

It didn't make any difference to me whether that ever got recorded or not. It was just something I felt like I really wanted to write. There's no way to go down the road of life without stepping on somebody's toes, even though you don't mean to. If you live long enough, you'll make enough mistakes that you would like to ask forgiveness from anybody whose toes you might have stepped on along the way.

But it's hardest when it's someone you love.

Yeah. I starred in that movie, too.

What makes this industry so hard on a relationship?

Well, it may be that this industry attracts people who would have a hard time with a relationship, whether they were in this industry or whether they were pumping gas. I don't know that our business attracts "normal" people. I don't know that creative people are "normal" people. You could get into a real chicken and egg thing with that real easy. Are we crazy because we're in the music business? Or are we in the music business because we're crazy?

Is "Forgiveness" the most honest song you've written?

Possibly.

I think country music could use a little more honesty, and not quite so much political and social correctness. John Jarrard and I were talking about the old drinking and cheating songs. And I said, "People still drink and they still cheat, they just don't do it on the radio."

I'm all for singing songs of love and compassion and making the world a better place. But let's don't just sweep the other stuff under the rug and pretend it doesn't exist, because it does exist. And if we're going to sing about life, then life's got a lot of different colors. Why just sing about the reds and the greens when there's all the other colors out there, too.

The album Fine Wine *is a wonderful culmination of your career. How is it different from other albums? What was fun about it?*

Well, working with Steve Wariner was fun. Recording it without any pressure to cut a number one record was a lot of fun.

There are a lot of honest songs on the album. "The Paper" is a very honest song. Hal Ketchum and I were both going through a divorce, although he didn't know I was going through one and I didn't know he was going through one when we wrote that song. "Twenty Years" has got a lot of honesty in it, in that when I go back to my hometown, it's changed so much. And I wrote about some real people in that song.

I think the best thing about this album was the fact that we were doing it totally for the fun and the love of doing it. Steve was at a point in his career where he had the time to devote to this. And Steve is so creative in the studio. It was such a pleasure to work with him. There was nobody standing over us saying, "Oh goodness, you can't do this or you can't do that," so we just did what we wanted to do.

And bringing in Eddy Arnold, Jean Shepard, Steve Wariner, and Roy Clark on "Tips Of My Fingers." God, that was so much fun. The first time I heard Eddy Arnold's voice in there, I thought I was just going to die. I used to go out and buy his records. It was really special to have him on the album.

Are you going to do another album?

Yep. I don't know that I'm going to do one for Warner Brothers, because *Fine Wine* has not been all that successful from a commercial standpoint.

I'm going to probably do an even more intimate or personal album. I'm going to do one even more close to the bone.

You have been writing songs for over forty years. To what do you attribute your enthusiasm?

I don't know. There's just always been a fire in my belly for it. What the heck else would I do? I can go fishing for about twenty minutes, and then I'm totally bored. I can play golf for about two holes, and then I realize I ain't a very good golfer, it's hot, the mosquitoes are buzzing, and I would just as soon get out of there.

This is just something I really enjoy. And as long as I do, and as long as the Good Lord blesses me with good health and the ability to do it, then what else? And I don't think I'm a workaholic. I take time. I enjoy things. I don't do this twenty-four hours a day. But I enjoy it.

I think a lot of people get into the music business thinking it's all play or it's a get rich quick scheme. I don't think the general public grasps what a work ethic this requires.

It's two words—*music* and *business*. But people don't stop to realize it's two words. And I'm not saying that every creative person has to put on a three-piece suit and be a businessman. But I think you've got to treat it with a certain respect, especially if you want to be in it for a long time. I really wanted to make it my life's work.

I never got into the business for the money. It just never was one of my concerns. I love it so much I would do it for free if I could afford to. I just can't afford to.

After the songwriting layoff, were there doubts if you could make a comeback?

Well, number one, the down period was only as a writer. I was busy as the dickens with all the other things. I never felt at the time that I was in any down time at all.

Songwriting is an art and a craft. I was still doing the art part of it. I was still writing. I would still get ideas. I would jot down two or three lines on the back of an airline ticket flying to California to do a game show. Or I would start a verse and half of a chorus in a motel room late at night. But the crafting—the discipline of sitting down and turning that into a song—that's what I didn't do. I just didn't have the burning desire at that point.

During that period, did you feel like the rules had changed?

I felt like the music had changed. During the '80s, a lot of pop music was being passed off as country. Today there's some rock and roll stuff being passed off as country.

Also, I had one thing that happened that kind of drove the nail in the coffin for a while. During the tail end of the Urban Cowboy thing, I had written a female song. I felt like there had never really been a definitive female Urban Cowboy-type song. Everything had been pretty much from the male perspective. And I was real excited about it.

I made an appointment with a publisher/producer in town to play it for him. When I walked in his office, there were eight or ten people sitting around, and I wasn't real comfortable with that. He said, "What is it you've got?" I said, "Well, I think I've really got something. It's a female song to give a woman a voice in this Urban Cowboy thing." And in front of all these people he said to me, "Who do you want me to pitch it to, Kitty Wells?" I said, "No. I don't want you to pitch it to anybody." And I turned around and walked out of the room.

And I thought to myself, "Okay. It's come to this. It's changed this much." I felt like he was totally saying, "Your time has come and gone." And I thought, "Well, okay, if it has, then I'll go do some other things." And that's when I went and did some other things.

When "Tips of My Fingers" hit, I realized that I had said something thirty years ago that could still speak to people. I felt I could do it again. And I had some doubts. But I knew if people would take time to listen to something that had a little substance to it, that I could do it.

Looking back, what has been the highlight of your songwriting career?

I'm living the high point right now, because I'm enjoying what I'm doing more than I ever have. And with co-writing, I'm sharing it with other people.

Do you feel like a mentor?

I feel part mentor, part student. I feel like I'm learning, too. The people that are writing today had a lot more influences than I had coming along. I had Hank Williams, Eddy Arnold, Ernest Tubb, Roy Acuff, Bill Monroe, gospel music and some black music. But today they've got all the influences from the rock and roll era that I didn't really have. I didn't grow up with that. I was already eighteen years old when Elvis hit.

These writers grew up with the Beatles, the Rolling Stones, Ray Charles, B.B. King and Aretha Franklin. So I can learn from people like this. Sure, I can be the mentor, but at the same time, I'm not too old to learn new tricks.

Do you have a desire to produce?

Not really. Not the day-to-day producing thing. Not the real intricate, minute-to-minute, punch in this guitar lick. I got better things to do with my time. I don't have the patience for it.

I've always had an eye out for talent ever since I brought Connie Smith here in the '60s. I've always enjoyed watching young people develop. I never would want to be a manager. I never would want to be a producer.

What advice would you give to a beginning songwriter?

We're not like a novelist that can go write about an old man chasing a whale or the millions of things that prose writers could write about. We're somewhat limited in what we can write about. So I think your greatest challenge is to find a different slant.

"Which Bridge To Cross" is another version of "Torn Between Two Lovers," which is another version of "One Has My Name, The Other Has My Heart." But you have to say it in a way that it hasn't been said before. That's why I was so proud of "Two Teardrops," because everybody said to me, "I've never heard it written that way before." That's what you strive for—to be original.

If a guy comes up to me and says, "I can sing just like Johnny Cash," I would say, "Well, good. Go home and learn to sing like yourself and come back. There's already a Johnny Cash." I feel that way about writing. Be original.

What challenge is still out there that you would like to achieve?

That great novel I've never written.

I believe it's in you.

I would like to see if it's in me. I would like to see if I can get it out. And I think at some point I will. There's only twenty-four hours in a day and seven days in a week. Right now I'm doing other things, and I don't want to clutter my mind with too much. But there will come a time, and it will probably come in the next few years.

Every day is a challenge to me. I wrote this in my autobiography relating it to baseball. In this business, you can have a zero batting average. You can be zero for life, and you can wake up one morning and hit a home run. And that is the most exciting thing about it. It's the most wonderful opportunity and greatest challenge.

Thom Schuyler's "16th Avenue."

That's right. And that can happen. That's what keeps you going back to the well. Just knowing that when you wake up in the morning that, "Hey, this may be the day." It could be.

And think of how many people don't have that. It's the same thing. They get up every day, go to the same job, and do the same thing they did yesterday, which is the same thing they're going to do tomorrow. I think the luckiest people in the world are people who can do what they want to—for free if they could afford to—and make a living at it.

It's been a pleasure. I appreciate you.

Well, ask me what time it is and I will tell you how to build a watch.

Photo courtesy of Lisa Sutton

Glenn Sutton — Side A

You're from north Louisiana.

I was born in Hodge, Louisiana, between Jonesboro and Monroe. It's a paper mill town.

Like Springhill, Louisiana. We could smell the Springhill paper mill thirty miles away In Bossier City on a good day, or a bad day, however you look at it.

My grandparents lived in Jonesboro and Beach Springs, which is where Jimmie Davis is from. My mother and him taught school together. They lived about two houses from each other.

I moved to Texas at a very young age. I went to the Louisiana Hayride about once a month when I was a kid. We lived in Henderson, Texas, which is just right across the line. I saw Red Sovine tons of times. Him and the Wilbur Brothers, the Louvin Brothers, Johnny and Jack, Slim Whitman, Faron Young. I saw Johnny Horton twice. I never saw Elvis.

I remember seeing Hank Williams there. I was there the night they did "Bucket's Got A Hole In It." They brought a bucket out and poured all the fan mail through the bucket and let it fall out on the stage.

When did you know you wanted a career in music?

Oh, I knew from the time I was ten years old. I started writing and singing when I was in Texas. I used to have my mother grade my songs. She'd look at the lyrics. She'd put "fair," "good." She'd put an "A" or a "B." I've still got all those things. They don't even make sense compared to what I write now, but they were just like giving me my horse, saddle and a wide open range.

When I got into Marty Robbins and enjoyed his music, everything that I would write would sound like Marty Robbins for a while.

Which was probably a good exercise for writing for artists.

It was. I would write tons of stuff. One month I'd write like Carl Smith. Everything he sang, I'd write something around that.

Old Tom Perryman and Jim Reeves used to own KGRI in Henderson, Texas. Jim Reeves was a radio announcer when I was there. He had just cut a couple records on Macy's out of Houston. "A Wagon Load of Love," "Penny Candy" and "My Heart's Like A Welcome Mat." Then he went on Abbott.

I had a little fifteen-minute radio show on Saturday when I was sixteen years old. Guests would come through and sing a song on my show, then go to Longview and play the Rio Palm Isle, which was a big country nightclub there. Hank Locklin and Slim Willett came through.

In the eleventh grade, we moved to Brandon, Mississippi. I joined the service after I got out of high school. I stayed in the air force four years. When I came back home, I went back to working in bands. I sold insurance, worked on electric razors. Did everything just to get by.

Before coming up to Nashville, Murray Kellerman and I went to Memphis to Pepper Sound Studio and cut a master. We cut two sides on him and two sides on me. That's all we had the money for.

We left about midnight and drove up there and cut the next morning on no sleep or anything. We pressed five hundred of them on Joe Cuggy's label, K&M. It got so much airplay in Jackson, Mississippi, where I was living, that Cuggy wanted to lease the master. He leased it just like it was—me on the back side with a song called "I Gotta Leave This Town" and Murray Kellerman on the other side with "Long Tall Texan." It became a hit, but when John F. Kennedy got assassinated the record stopped that day. It was fifty with a bullet in the pop charts and nobody wanted to hear anything about a Texan.

Billy Joe Royal had just reached the Top Ten with "Burned Like A Rocket" when the space shuttle Challenger exploded. It was immediately off the playlists, as well. What next?

I kept going to Shreveport trying to get on a Louisiana Hayride. I finally got to see Tilman Franks in his little office he had in a bank building. Tilman told me that the Louisiana Hayride had just quit a couple of weeks before I was over there. But he listened to a couple of my songs and said, "Let me cut a master on you." So we went to Tyler, Texas, to Robin Hood Bryan's studio. Tommy Tomlinson, Johnny Horton's guitar player that got hurt in the wreck with him, was the guitar player. We cut four sides. Tilman brought them to Nashville and he played them around. Tilman tried to get them leased. He never did, so I went back to playing in the clubs, just kind of hanging out.

I was writing songs, but I really wanted to be an artist.

In the '60s, you could bring finished masters to record labels and they would release them as is.

Right. They wouldn't sign you and re-cut you with somebody else. They would release your master.

Now, they got to get other people out of the way. They cut everybody out. They got to get the money in the right pocket. If you come in with a hit master, they didn't produce it. You did. They got to cut it so they're the producer.

"They" being the record label.

No, "they" is the producers that work for the record label. You know how it works. It's common knowledge. I'm not saying anything that's not happening.

Where were you playing in Mississippi?

I was working at a club called the Wagon Wheel in Jackson, Mississippi. We had a pretty good band, so we backed a lot of acts that came to town that played the VFW and the American Legion and places like that in the old phone shows—firefighters and all that. So Bob Luman and Justin Tubb came there to do one of those phone shows. They asked us if we'd back them. I said, "We know everything they do. It won't be no problem, if we rehearse with them a little bit." Justin brought one picker. Red Lane was playing guitar with him. Bob didn't bring anybody. So I went out to the Holiday Inn where they were staying to meet Luman and tell him we'd be cool for the show.

The first thing Luman wanted to know was if we had a bootlegger. He wanted to get a pint of whiskey. So I took him to the bootlegger. When we went back to the hotel, I got to talking to Justin, and I told him, I said, "I'm a songwriter. I'd like to get some songs to somebody in Nashville, if I could. I've been trying for a while." I sang him a couple of songs and he said the old standard thing, "Get in touch with me when you come to Nashville."

So we played with them that night. Never heard no more from them. About a month later, I drove up to Nashville during the middle of the week and called the number that Justin Tubb had given me. When the guy answered the phone he said, "Ernest Tubb Record Shop." I said, "Is Justin Tubb there?" He said, "This is Justin." I said, "Justin, I'm Glenn Sutton. Do you remember me? We played with you about a month ago. I'm in town and I brought some songs with me. If you've got time, I'd like you to listen." And he said, "I don't really have anything I could do with them. Let me send you out to Star Day. I'm going to call Tommy Hill and see if he'll listen to some songs."

So Justin set me up to go out to Tommy Hill's place on Dickerson Road. Tommy took me in that little old studio and turned on a mike and a tape. He said, "Sing everything you got." Then he left. I had a little old book of songs. I sang about fifteen things and sat there until the tape went off. He came back in and said, "You put them all on there?" I said, "Yes, sir." He said, "Well, I'll listen to them and get back to you."

Back in the car. Back to Mississippi. Back to the club.

What year was this?

That was in '62, '63, somewhere along there. I was selling insurance at that time.

I didn't hear anything for about a month and then one day I come home and Mother said, "You got a letter in there." I looked at it and in the corner it said Star Day Music. So I opened it up and it was a Star Day publishing contract for two songs and a letter from Tommy saying, "I like two songs. I plan on cutting them on the Willis Brothers and we'd like to publish you."

I'm sure you took the contract to a lawyer for review.

I took it to nobody. I signed it and got it in the mail immediately. I didn't care.

Same day?

Hell, yeah! I took it straight to the post office. I said, "All right!"

In fact, two days later the insurance guy was giving me a little static about not having a lot of life insurance sales. I said, "Look, do me a favor. Shove this company. I'm through. I just got a contract from Nashville. I'll be moving up there shortly."

Tommy Hill cut two songs on the Willis Brothers. One of them was called "Credit Card" and the other one was called "Gonna Buy Me A Juke-box." The jukebox thing wound up on the back side of "Give Me Forty Acres To Turn This Rig Around." And I kept seeing these ads: "over 300,000 sold," "half a million." I called Star Day and I said, "Look, I'd like to get an advance. This Willis Brothers thing looks hot. Could I get a little taste on the front?" The guy said, "Don't believe everything you read in *Billboard*. That damn thing ain't sold 30,000." So I got my first lesson on believing what *Billboard* said. I didn't understand the hype system.

The next break was Merle Kilgore getting Al Gallico to sign me for fifty bucks a week.

This would be where you learned the hype system. Fifty bucks a week. You were rolling in the dough.

I didn't have enough money to buy a meal or anything. Mel Tillis came by and said, "Let's go eat." We were all hungry. Somebody said, "Anybody got any money?" Everybody together didn't even have five dollars. And somebody's pet rabbit was out there. So Tillis threw a rock at it and killed it. We skinned that rabbit and with what money we had bought some potatoes and carrots and cooked that rabbit. We had a big time with the rabbit.

Every time I see Tillis, he says, "What about that rabbit?" But those were fun days.

Give me a Gallico story.

One day Al Gallico came in town. He said, "I'm going over to Chet Atkins's, kid, you wanna go?" I had never met Chet, so I said, "God, yeah!" He took me over to Victor and I was shaking. I couldn't even hardly talk, being in Chet's presence. And Chet said, "We're doing an album on Eddy Arnold. We're calling it *The Easy Way with Eddy Arnold*. You think your boy there could write a song called 'The Easy Way'?" I said, "I'll have it here in the morning."

So I went home and wrote "The Easy Way" and "Tell Them Where You Got Your Blues." I carried them two songs back and they cut them both. "The Easy Way" wound up the "B" side of "Make The World Go Away." I was tickled to death. I was about ten grand in on draws. That cleared me out and I've never owed a dime to a publishing company since.

How did you pitch those two songs to Chet?

Me and a guitar. I just put it down with me and a guitar on a tape.

Reel-to-reel?

Yeah. I just went in there and handed it to him. He played it and said, "I like it. Let me play it for Eddy." And they cut it a couple days later.

When did this instant gratification of cuts for a songwriter go by the wayside?

When everybody started making really good demos. Multi-track killed it. You could do so much more. The producers today, if you took them a guitar/vocal, they couldn't cut a record. They got to have a finished demo. There's not too many people out there right now that could just take a demo with me and a guitar and cut a record.

When I worked at Columbia for nine years, we got some demos from some publishing companies. But most of them were people just bringing them in and singing them to you with a guitar. And you'd say, "Put that one down. I like that one." Sometimes we'd put them down in the office. I don't remember ever cutting too many songs before the early '70s that were demos.

When Billy Sherrill and I were producing for Columbia, we just sang them to the musicians at the session. We let them write a chord sheet and then said, "All right, here's what we're going to do." Just went from scratch.

It seems like a lot of writers today are more concerned with the demo process than the writing process.

Oh, exactly. They try to make a better demo than they do a song.

But what's ruined the creative process, to me, is these writers' rooms and putting everybody together. Is there anybody left that can write a song by theirself? I think publishing companies hurt our business when they put these writers' rooms in and had everybody co-write. You don't really know who the real writers are anymore.

When there's three and four co-writers, one or two of them had absolutely nothing to do with the song but be there while it was written. I've seen that happen too many times. In fact, I've written an entire song while a guy put it in a computer. He had a laptop. He kept saying, "Yeah, I like that line." And I was saying to myself, "I got to finish this up and get the hell out of here so I don't have to come back. I don't want to have to work on this again with this guy and watch him with a laptop. He was too busy putting it in the laptop to even think to try to put a line in it."

When I see three writers on there, I don't know. I know I've never been in a process with three people who sat down and could get any good out of a song. I don't mind co-writing, if it's somebody I like or an artist, because nowadays you have to.

Why do you say "nowadays you have to"?

Well, who's going to cut it if you don't write it with the artist, the producer or somebody involved with the act? I could write the greatest song in the world, and I'd have a hell of a time getting it cut unless I wrote it with the artist. That's what it's come to. They're all spoiled. The publishers made the writers spoil the artists.

Come again.

By making so many deals, the publishers have spoiled the artists to getting a piece of everything. The artists all want everything now. They still want everything even though the writer gets the smallest share of anybody. They still want a piece of that.

The artist could probably do a great album, if ten great songs were brought to him. But instead he'll do ten songs that he co-wrote with ten different people that the publishers set him up with.

Some artists are great writers though.

You got a few. I'm not saying that everybody's like that. But I'm saying in general.

I signed a deal with Famous Music for a couple years in 1990. And they were into the "have you got your book?" They wanted you to co-write.

Your appointment book.

Yeah, your appointment book.

Everybody would say, "You got your book with you?" I said, "I ain't got no fucking book. I can remember what the hell I'm going to do. I ain't going to write every day with three or four different people. I can remember what few appointments I have. I don't have to have a book."

They all had a book. They cared more about their book than they did writing. If their book was full, they thought they were doing something, whether they wrote anything or not. So the book thing drove me nuts.

I got off track there of what I was talking about. Where the hell was I? How did I start that?

You were talking about publishers spoiling the artists.

Right. Writing with the artists.

I run into an artist one day and he said, "Let's get together and write." We had written before he had even had a record deal. And so, he said, "Have you got your book?" I said, "I got no book." He said, "Well, call my girl and get a date." This was in May when I run into him. She gives me a date July the 9th or some shit, you know. Well, I might want to do something else on July the 9th. Have I got to delay an idea until July the 9th to write with this guy? Let's do it today. You're standing here now.

Then if he's on the road somewhere, he cancels July the 9th and moves it to September. So I just quit fooling with that. Unless a guy wants to write within a couple of days, I ain't setting nothing up. That's just ridiculous. Hell, I may be dead. Or I may be in Africa, or in jail.

So you would rather write when the spirit moves you.

Exactly. Say I had five appointments in a row. Nobody can come up with five good ideas in one week that are going to be great songs. And everybody that I wrote with, I always took something—a verse or a chorus or a great title.

We'd sit down and I'd say, "Well, you got any kind of idea that's just burning a hole in your mind?" He'd say, "No, I was kind of hoping you did. I haven't really got anything." And these are people that hadn't even got a record deal. They're just writing for a company. They don't have a clue. So you wind up writing a song for them to get the hell out of there. Otherwise you could spend a month. If you waited on them, you would be writing two or three lines and then you got to go back. You got to meet them again. If you didn't like to write with them to start with, why would you want to go back and meet them again two weeks from now? It ruins you life.

If somebody really was serious about it, I could write five in a day and just get it over with. Demo them and be done with it and take off two months. But instead, the process they do now, you go and you work on a song for three or four hours and then you both say, "Let's go to lunch." When you come back you say, "Let's work on it next week. You got Thursday open?" Seven or eight years later they have a song. By then, the business is over.

Why all the co-writing?

You're trying to increase your odds, but you're actually diminishing them, as far as I'm concerned. The perception is my co-writer's publishing company is working it and my publishing company is working it. There still may not be nobody but you working it.

If I write a song for you that doesn't mean you're going to go out and work it. You might not even like it. In fact, most of the songs I co-wrote with people, I didn't like them myself. So I didn't work them, because I didn't feel like they were quality. You can have a great idea ruined by a co-writer.

There's another thing that killed a lot of songwriters: a quota. A guy guarantees to write you twenty songs a year. Well, he'll write you twenty songs, but will they be twenty songs that are worth a damn? Just let a guy alone and pay him within reason.

Are six-figure advances within reason?

Hell, I'm in the Hall of Fame. I bet I couldn't get two hundred a week from any publishing company in town. And can out-write most of the guys they got working for them. Talent has nothing to do with it. Deals and deal makers. I know guys that have been on draw for years and never even had a cut, and they're still on draw.

I guess their talent is getting a draw.

And that's the way they talk, too. They say, "Man, I got to keep my draw coming." So they turn in sixteen or twenty songs. But if you listen to them, you say, "My God, we paid for this?" All you're doing is filing stuff and paying demo bills. You're just wasting money. Of course, it ain't never going to change.

You don't see the pendulum swinging?

It's too far out of hand.

Personal credit seems out of hand. Credit cards were relatively new when you wrote "The Credit Card"?

It was a brand new thing. I didn't even have one then. Never even seen one. Just heard about them and saw all these ads on TV about them. American Express, Diners Club and Carte Blanche used to be the three big cards. There wasn't no Master Card or Visa. Now every man on earth's got one.

You can get an Alan Jackson Visa. I was over at the bank and I asked them, I said, "Hey, if I get one of these Alan Jackson Visa's, does he get anything?" They said, "The artist get a small percentage." I said, "God Almighty! How about me starting one with you? I can get a few people to use my card."

You wrote a number of award-winning songs with Billy Sherrill.

Probably more with him than anybody. He and I wrote a lot of great songs together.

Was he producing at a label at that time?

He had just taken over Epic when I met him. He had been there about six months. Before that Jerry Kennedy ran it and he went to Mercury with Shelby Singleton.

Gallico's office was in the same building, so Billy and I just got to running into each other at the old clubhouse next door playing the pinball machine. I'd play him an idea every now and then. We started writing some, because he was cutting the acts and I saw that this was the way to go. I said, "Hey, this guy here can cut me a lot of records and save me a lot of time fooling around hunting these guys."

And sure enough, we started writing just for the people he cut. Me and Billy Sherrill never did a demo of our songs. Billy was a good piano man and I played guitar, so he'd either sing it to them on the piano, or I'd sing it. We might just put it down me and him, but most of it, we just did at the session.

We didn't just stop with country. I wrote a lot of bluegrass. Cuts on Jim and Jesse. Then he hired me as an assistant producer. I stayed at Epic nine years.

A lot of albums now are piecemealed over time. Going in to cut a few things, going in to cut a few more things. But back then, I did the whole ball of wax. I'd do it in one day. I would book three sessions and cut the album. I could get five sides in three hours.

Now an artist puts out one album every year or two. Then we did four albums a year on every artist. That's why you see so many Stu Phillips albums in the bins, because they did four on him, too. The title usually was the single. And in three months it had sold what it was going to sell. I remember we had a big party when Tammy Wynette broke 30,000 on one of her albums. You had to be constantly cutting.

Describe working with Billy Sherrill?

Billy Sherrill was the most nervous man I ever met. Still is. Couldn't sit still long. Just a moving. You could go in and sit down and start talking to him, and he would get up and leave while you're talking to him. He might come back in an hour. Nervous energy. He's always nervous.

But he and I got along good because my office was on the first floor and his was on the second floor. Whoever had the idea would say, "Here's a couple lines I got, see what you can do with that." We'd work on it during the day. I'd come up with a couple of lines and he'd come up with a couple of lines, and he was great with melodies. He could get at the piano and really put some neat changes in them, where I'd just be three chords on a lot of stuff. The closer it got to the session, the harder we worked on them. We'd play around for a month, but if somebody was cutting in two days, then we'd get on it and really work.

So you co-wrote separately.

Right. We never sat down and wrote a whole song together that I can remember. Tammy Wynette is a co-writer on two or three songs with Billy and I. To be honest with you, I don't ever remember sitting down and writing anything with Tammy, so she might have wrote her part with Billy.

Billy and Tammy were working on "Stand By Your Man." And Billy gave it to me and told me to write another verse to it. So I went and spent a day writing a whole verse. Pretty damn good, too. I brought it back in and he said, "Yeah, I like that." Well, when they cut it, they left my verse off. The song was long enough like it was.

I ran into Billy when George and Tammy played the Ryman. Billy came up to me and he said, "You know, your life would've been a whole lot different if I had put that other verse on 'Stand By Your Man.'" I said, "I know it, you son-of-a-bitch!"

Billy Sherrill was very adamant about his opinion. I'll give you an example. One day he had cut Freddy Weller. Freddy wrote all of the songs except one Curly Putman wrote. And out of the session, Curly's was what Billy really liked. Freddy was writing for Bill Lowry. Bill Lowry calls Billy and says, "Billy, I'll tell you one thing. That is a really great ballad on Freddy. I think that's the single and I think that'll be a hit." I was sitting in there listening and Billy said, "That's your problem, Lowry. You think and I know." And then he popped that other record out on a three-day special. He didn't mince words. When he liked something, he liked it. That was what he went with. And he was usually right. He had a very good ear. His ear was great for knowing a good song. He knew what to do with it and what to change about it. He just knew. I saw writers that wouldn't change anything—the gender or whatever—and they didn't get a cut.

Billy Sherrill changed Thom Schuyler's "16th Avenue" significantly before he recorded it with Lacy J. Dalton.

Because he didn't feel like it would be good like it was. But a lot of guys were adamant about their opinion. They'd say, "Well, I like it just like it is. I think it's great."

What were your responsibilities for Epic?

I was looking for songs and I had several acts. I was cutting Jim and Jesse, Bob Luman. I did a couple things on Jody Miller. I did tons of artists, but a lot of them were like Mack Curtis—artists that sold five records. But we wasn't putting any money into them. Now an album costs $150,000.

Not counting promotion.

Jimmy Bowen did that. That's the one thing he did for Nashville. He changed a $25,000 album into a $150,000 album. As far as I'm concerned, that's all Bowen did when he was here.

When I was over at Columbia I said, "I will cut *Stayin' Alive* that the Bee Gees have got out. And I don't care what they spent on it, I can do it for ten grand."

I'll cut it in a regular damn day and I won't spend a year mixing it. I'll mix the damn thing in three hours, because if it ain't right in three hours, you can listen to the son-of-a-bitch till you go crazy and it ain't gonna change. Whatever is on that tape is on there.

If the song ain't no good, you can mix on the son-of-a-bitch for eight years and it won't be no better. They waste a lot of money like that. I used to mix an album in six hours, because once you get the basic bass, piano, drums and all that stuff set, all you got to fool with is the vocals, bring them in and out, and maybe tweak a steel here and there. A little echo and that's it.

I mean, these guys make a career out of a record. A guy sits in there and mixes on the bass for a week. A bass is a bass. That's it. But they make a hell of a lot more money than I make, so maybe they're right.

That's just my personal opinion.

Some people write with the artist, but you one upped that. You were sleeping with the artist.

Well, that's right. You got to sacrifice your body every now and then to get cuts.

How did you and Lynn Anderson meet?

Lynn was a secretary at Chart Records. She was working for Slim Williamson, plus she was on the label. Her mother, Liz Anderson, had come here and was writing. She was a good writer. I was working up at Epic and I used to see Lynn all the time. Then she went off to California to do the "Lawrence Welk Show." She came back for one week and I ran into her at a golf tournament. I asked her if she wanted to go to the BMI Awards with me. She said, "Sure, I'm not going." She had to go back to California, but we started talking on the phone a little bit, and then push came to shove. One day, I picked her up at the airport and when we got back to the hotel, I gave her a ring.

When was this?

That was in '67. We married in '68.

How long were you married?

Nine years.

After you were married, you started writing and producing for her.

I wasn't producing her when we got married. She was still on Chart. But her contract was coming up and I knew I could get her on Columbia. That was just our plan. I eventually bought all the Chart masters and sold them to Columbia. Al Gallico did some kind of deal.

He's always doing deals.

Well, him and Buddy Killen. I put them in the same context. They're deal makers. You could have done it yourself, but somehow they're in the deal.

It's like cue card guys at TV stations. I had a record out on Mercury, "The Football Card." It was one of them talking things—a week long. I had already blew it once. I'm standing there in Detroit. I forgot the damn song. I couldn't think of it. And I said, "Well, if you want to hear how it's really sang, you'll have to buy the record, because I don't know how it goes." So we went to a TV station and I took my cue cards the next time. Well, I get to this station and I'm already mad and the guy says, "Sorry, you can't use those. We don't have any of the guys with the cue card union here to hold them." I said, "You got to be kidding. Let me lay them on the floor. I'll never get through it." And sure enough, I didn't. If you get lost on a recitation, you're gone.

Kind of like "Blue Cyclone."

I never could do "Blue Cyclone" live. I couldn't remember it. I'd get down in there and get lost. Did you ever hear the dirty version?

No.

I'll have to get you a copy. I took my old demo tracks and did a dirty version of it. It's really raunchy.

Were you into wrestling?

Yeah, I really liked it. Buddy Lee was an old wrestler and he started a wrestling thing in here. Got a lot of investors. I was good friends with Buddy and I met the Kangaroos. They were from Australia. So Buddy got me to referee a couple of matches for them. I became good friends with the wrestlers. I would go to Knoxville with them. I'd drive to Chattanooga with them. I'd go every weekend just to watch them raise hell in their dressing room.

I've never seen a referee see a wrestler pulling hair.

Never sees anything.

One night Jerry Kennedy filmed when I was a guest referee. I was just trying to stay out of the way, because they're flying by you. They're going a hundred miles an hour. I've never seen the film, but it's a little old eight millimeter. A bunch of people in the music business went. Hank, Jr., was a referee that night. Hank, Jr., refereed one and I refereed one. It was two out of three falls.

So we're in the dressing room and the wrestlers are in there wiping their face off and drinking a beer. And Al Costello of the Kangeroos told me, he said, "Look. Here's what we're going to do. During the match, I'm going to grab you. I'll pick you up and spin you like I'm going to slam you, but I'll lay you down real soft." I said, "All right, but be damn sure you do."

We get back out there and they're in the heat of the match. Lorenzo Pereni of Lorenzo's restaurant is one of the wrestlers. I used to eat there a lot before they closed. Me and Lorenzo were good friends. Him and Don Green were wrestling the Kangaroos. Don's dad owned Green Appliances here in town.

Sure enough, Al picked me up and the crowd goes, "Kill him!" And by God, he slammed me, just nearly broke everything in me. And when we got back in the dressing room, I said, "You dirty bastard! What happened? I thought you was going to lay me down like a baby!" He said, "Well, I'm sorry, man. I was in the heat of the match and I thought you was Don Green." I said, "Your thinking I'm Don Green nearly got me killed!" I couldn't hardly get out of bed the next day from being slammed. I was sore for a month.

Now they explain wrestling is show business. Before they always wanted to act like it was really real. And they could never be interviewed. Wrestlers told me, they said, "Hell, we never get any TV, because the first question is 'Is it fake?'" What are you going to say? I mean, slamming somebody on the hard concrete ain't fake. They really get hurt now with all that jumping off them ropes. A lot of them really get hurt bad.

Or killed, like Owen Hart.

I wrote a song called "Hulkamania." I did it on an album for Mercury. It's a pretty good little old song. I sent one to Hulk Hogan, but I never heard a word from him. He's probably above the music business.

Photo courtesy of Lisa Sutton

Glenn Sutton — Side B

Lynn Anderson was doing pretty well on Chart, but it was Joe South's "Rose Garden" that changed her career.

"Rose Garden" really busted her loose. That song was cut several times before we did it. There were four or five really good versions of it. Joe South did an album on Capitol called *Introspect*. It was a ten or eleven side album, and it had "Walk A Mile In My Shoes," "Games People Play, "Birds Of A Feather," "Rose Garden." Just about everything in there had been a hit by somebody. And the "Rose Garden" had never really been a giant record. Lynn's the one that brought it to my attention. She loved that album. She kept playing it and I kept passing. I said it was a man's song. And if you listen to it, it is a man's song. I just didn't hear it for her.

Finally, one night we had fifteen minutes left in Studio B at Columbia. I'll never forget it. And Lynn had that album with her. She had carried it to sessions two or three different times. I said, "All right. We got fifteen minutes left. No use wasting the time. Let's do the 'Rose Garden' real quick. We'll do a track anyway."

We got the "Rose Garden" out and played Joe South's version. We got to playing with it and it was just bogging down within a couple minutes. We were doing it kind of like the record. Ray Eddington was playing guitar on the session. And Ray said, "Hey, let's do it like straight eights. That'll make it." So we started doing it like that and it felt great. So in fifteen minutes, we had a track.

How many tracks on the tape?

I think it was sixteen, because we put strings on it. I was just going to leave it like it was, because it was pretty full without the strings. But Billy Sherrill had a couple things on Tammy Wynette he wanted to put strings on. He said, "You got anything of Lynn's you can put strings on?" I said, "Yeah, I got two things." So I put strings on "Snow Bird" and "Rose Garden." But I still didn't think that much about it being a single.

I was in Studio B mixing it during deejay week, and Lou Bradley was doing a playback. Lou was the engineer. I was sitting out there listening to it on the big speakers. And they had picked Clive Davis, who was the president of CBS at that time, up at the airport and were bringing him down to Billy's office for a meeting. They led him in the back door and he came through Studio B. He stopped in the middle of the studio and said, "What the hell is that?" I said, "That's something we cut on Lynn. It's going to be on her next album. It's called 'Rose Garden.'" He said, "Run it back to the top. I want to hear it all the way though." So Lou ran it back. Played it again. He said, "That's a smash. That's her next single."

I had already planned on something else, but what can you say to the president of the company? He went back to New York and he called me and said, "Hey, I'm getting the ball rolling on this thing. Let's get it mixed and schedule it."

They played it at a sales meeting and Clive said, "I want this record. This is a monster. This is a number one record and it better be."

Five weeks at number one. They delivered.

It won a Grammy. It was a platinum album. It was gold in a couple of foreign countries, too.

You're working for CBS. You're writing songs that are on the radio. Who was your publisher?

Al Gallico was for five years. And then he and I started a company called Flagship.

So you had some publishing on your songs.

Right. I had half publishing.

You're producing Lynn Anderson. You're married to Lynn Anderson. Lynn becomes hugely popular. I'm sure your life is changing dramatically.

Oh, yeah. There were so many demands on her. She was gone all the time. She worked an awful lot.

"Rose Garden" becomes a prophetic song for your relationship.

Well, the relationship changed after she got to working so much. We were doing great when we were making the records, before "Rose Garden," before she started working constantly and doing all this TV. She was busy all the time and she was trying to be a mother, too, when our daughter, Lisa, was born.

It got to where I didn't see her that much, so we just didn't get along that well anymore. It drug on for a long time. And plus, for a female artist, it's bad because there's a thousand wolves hitting on them twenty-four hours a day when they're not around you. And they're around a lot of big people. They run into a lot of millionaires that's got a hell of lot more to offer than you have as a little old songwriter. So sooner or later, they're going to run into one that might change their mind about you.

We just got to where we really didn't see eye to eye. It got to where the music was a problem, too. That was really laid on it on the last album or two. I can remember overdubbing some horns on "Joy To The World," the Hoyt Axton song. When I brought it home and played it to her, she said, "That's disgusting!" I said, "What do you mean, disgusting? It's great!" And it wasn't that overdone. It was just a pretty little old thing with a trombone and a couple of trumpets.

There was one particular part she didn't like, and it made me mad, so I went back to the studio and just pulled it all off. Scratched all of it and put it back like it was. Then when the album came out, she listened to it again and she said, "Well, you took it all off." And I said, "You said take it off." She said, "I meant the one lick." I said, "Fuck the one lick! I took it all off. You don't want horns, you don't want horns."

We got to arguing. And there were other people saying, "You need to do this. He's giving you the wrong songs." Every artist goes through that. But basically, I was always just happy-go-lucky. I don't tend to let anything bother me for over thirty minutes, because if you do, you can waste a hell of a lot of time worrying about nothing.

So finally, we sat down and I said, "Look. I think it's just best if we talk about a divorce." And plus, she had run into Spook Stream, who she later married, and became great friends with him. That kind of strained our relationship, too. It wasn't really a big, bitter drawn out thing. I flew to New York, had the accountant figure up what percentage of money I made and what percentage she made, and that's the way we split it. No argument or anything. We sat down at dinner and I said, "Here's the way it figures out. What cars you want?" I had seventeen cars at that time. They were all antiques. She said, "I don't want the cars. I can't drive." So I said, "Well, I'll take them then."

If we'd have stayed together, we'd have probably been up there with Donald Trump, but it don't always work out that way.

Did you remain close with your daughter?

Oh, yeah. Me and Lisa have a great relationship.

You were involved at the beginning of Tammy Wynette's career, too. Her first Top Ten was "Your Good Girl's Gonna Go Bad." Followed by "I Don't Want To Play House" and then five number ones. You've had great success writing for females. You must be in touch with your feminine side.

I actually wrote for a man and just changed the gender. I didn't know shit from a woman's viewpoint.

I've had several people interested in doing "I Don't Want To Play House" as a male version, which could be done as a little boy instead of a little girl. Jerry Kilgore's told me several times he wanted to do it. And David Ball mentioned he was thinking about it the other night. I said, "Well, then quit thinking about it and do it." Writers starve to death while people are thinking about doing their songs.

Gary Allen.

Gary Allen revived "Living In A House Full Of Love." Oh, man, he did a great version.

I always say, "I'm a writer, not a politician." So if somebody's going to cut one of my songs, they got to cut it because they like it. I'm not going to beg. People say, "How come you're not out there. Boy, you ought to be out there working them songs." I say, "Look. I'm sixty-two years old. I don't want to spend the rest of my life begging some son-of-a-bitch to cut a song. I got five hundred of them out there. Let them cut one of them." And that's the way I feel about it.

I had such a great career. I can't complain about anything. I loved every minute of it. But I realize, I ain't going to do it all again. I mean, fuck, why would I want to? I got other interests. I'd rather put in a hardwood floor as to go meet some guy in a room somewhere and try to write something with him.

Your life changes, you know. Of course, there's a lot of people that are still just trying and bitching and moaning and groaning. I get so tired of people complaining. George Jones and these guys complain about airplay. Hey. Lonzo and Oscar don't get any air play. How many times do you hear Zeke Clements or The Bales Brothers on the radio now? You don't. So Jones and them, they had their window. That window shuts after a while. And if you want to just keep clawing to get back in, you can. But it's stupid, especially if you've got enough to relax. Why? Ego, I guess. Got to be in the limelight or something, I don't know.

I had a fantastic, twenty-year run. It started in '65 and ended around '84, when Complete Records sold and I got out of that operation. That's really when I moved on and said, "I ain't fighting this shit no more." I can't expect to do all that again. I'm just going to do it on my terms and on a limited basis. I still work catalog every now and then. But I just make compilation CDs and mail them to different people. If I run into them and they want a song or two, I give them a CD with thirty on there. If they're going to throw the one away anyway, let them throw thirty away.

One of your biggest songs is "Almost Persuaded." How did that song come about?

Charlie Walker tells this story to me every time I see him. He said, "You wrote 'Almost Persuaded' for me then you gave it to David Houston." We were working on something for Charlie Walker and the Honky Tonk Band. Meanwhile Charlie Walker was working somewhere and David Houston was coming in to do a session before him. We said, "Hey, man, we'll cut it on him. See how it comes out." We wrote on that thing three or four different times. Billy Sherrill would write on it a while and I'd fool with it. We didn't even have a title. And we're sitting at the piano at Billy's house at three o'clock in the morning. I'm about half drunk and I said, "What are we going to call the damn thing?"

We had the melody and we had a bunch of lines. I said, "It's got to be a thing where he goes back to his wife." We had the whole thing mapped out good. And on the piano was a Broadman hymnal. Billy picked it up and he was flipping pages. A song in there was "Almost Persuaded." I said, "What the hell's wrong with that? Let's call it 'Almost Persuaded.'"

I guess you could say you had some divine inspiration.

Yeah. So then after that we stole another title—"Where Could I Go But

To The Lord." We called it "Where Could I Go But To Her." That was a David Houston record, too.

That brings to mind the title "Stealing In The Name Of The Lord."

The Lord helped write a lot of them. But that's how "Almost Persuaded" happened. The record was another lucky thing. It came out as the "B" side of the record. The "A" side was called "We Got Love." They used to put out two sides. Now they wouldn't dare do that, because somebody might be a hero and play the other side. So we had the big red "A" stamped on the "A" side. Then we had the "B" side, too. If a jock wanted to play that, he could.

They shipped out "We Got Love" and the publisher was all excited about it. We were just on the "B" side. We didn't think it was a monster. Just another record, because we was cutting them every week.

Mack Curtis was the head disk jockey at WPLO in Atlanta and later he was on Epic. I did an album or two on him. He called Billy one morning and he said, "Hey, you're on the wrong side of the 'We Got Love' record. You better get that turned over." Billy said, "What's that? You mean 'Almost Persuaded'?" And Mack said, "Yeah, I flipped it over this morning and played it during drive time. We got 130 something calls in an hour to hear it again."

So Billy said, "All right." He called and had the sides switched. The publisher of "We Got Love" had already bought a full-page ad. So they went wild. They said, "You can't do that!" He said, "Hey. Would you rather be on the "B" side of a monster or off the record altogether?" So they were the "B" side then. At first, they raised hell, but they wanted to stay on the record.

I've always scratched my head that people actually get on the phone and call a radio station to play a record.

Me, too. Why would you call? I've never called a radio station, have you?

Maybe if they had a ten-thousand dollar cash prize going, but not to say, "Play David Houston again."

Or if I returned somebody's call. But not, "Please play that again."

But people do it. Now radio stations don't announce the artist or song title, so it would be kind of hard to call up and ask for it again.

You mentioned being half-lit at Billy Sherrill's piano. That segues into "What Made Milwaukee Famous Made A Fool Out of Me." Autobiographical?

Oh, yeah. It was kind of me at the time. I liked to drink. That one I wrote by myself. That has a great story to it, too.

Al Gallico called me while I was mixing something in Studio B. He called my office and they rang up there and finally found me. The receptionist said, "Al Gallico's on the phone." I said, "Jesus Christ, I'm trying to mix!" Gallico was in California and he said, "Jerry Lee Lewis is cutting in two days. He needs a song tomorrow. You got anything?" I said, "Yeah, I got some stuff. I'll get it over there to him." He said, "Now, be damn sure you do. I told him you're bringing something over." I said, "Okay, I'll get him something." I'm just trying to get rid of him.

Gallico had asked me two or three days before if I was working on something and I said, "Yeah, I'm getting it. It's almost finished. Don't worry. I've got it under control." He said, "I got to talk to Jerry Kennedy tonight. What's the title of it so I can tell him?"

I hadn't even started anything. I looked down on the floor and Charlie Bradley or somebody in the studio had read the paper and just dropped it on the floor. And right before my eyes was a full-page ad with a big beer can on it and it said, "Milwaukee's Best. The beer that made Milwaukee famous." I said, "It's called 'What Made Milwaukee Famous.'" And he said, "That's a great title, kid. I'll tell Jerry." Then Jerry Kennedy called me and said, "Al says you got a song about Milwaukee. Bring it over in the morning at nine." It was three in the afternoon then. I said, "God Almighty! I'll have to really get drunk tonight."

Did it take about a six-pack?

Probably a bottle of wine. I worked all night on that thing. So I went over to Jerry Kennedy's the next morning—just me and the guitar—and sang it to him. And he said, "I like it. Put it down."

I went to the session. They ran it down and Jerry Lee did it in one take. Jerry said, "Maybe we ought to fix that ending there." And Jerry Lee said, "What's wrong with that, Killer? Do it like it is." He wouldn't overdub nothing. Everything he sang was great to him. His country stuff to me is just phenomenal.

What were your thoughts when you heard that Rod Stewart had cut "What Made Milwaukee Famous"?

Money. I said, "God Almighty, a pop record!" When I heard the record, I almost vomited. It was awful. But I said, "Any cut's a good cut." That's always been a good motto.

He cut that in '69. Lewis's record came out in '68. I didn't even know Rod Stewart cut it. Al Gallico found out about it. And they wasn't even going to put it in a package or anything. I don't know if they even liked it or not. And all of a sudden they're putting together a "Best Of," and Gallico talked somebody at the label into putting it on the cassette version. It finally came out as a single, but it didn't do much. It made a little money off the album.

When the box set, *The Storyteller*, came out, it really made some good money. Then it was in two other Rod Stewart packages. So I probably made an extra thirty or forty grand out of three or four different packages on Mercury fifteen years later.

Has the life of a song amazed you?

When I get a statement of mechanicals I'll say, "Jesus, that is old!" I mean, my mechanicals amaze me. The secret of it is volume. I just had so many cuts by so many different people. And with the way they're doing stuff today, everything is repackaged thirty fucking times. It's the same song, but it's in this package, that package. "The best of." "The best, best of."

If I can just outlive a few more artists, mechanicals will hold up. I know one day they'll drop and I'll go on relief.

Even when record companies are only paying 75 percent of statutory on packages, it still adds up.

Right. There's five hundred different cuts on "Almost Persuaded" alone. And it's in hundreds of packages. I wish I had the publishing.

The back catalog carries a publishing company.

Oh, exactly.

The catalog carries the labels. And the ones that don't work the catalog don't do as good.

What's so sad to me is some of the people that record labels got running the special products. Some of them are good and some of them have just devalued the catalogs, because the people that are putting the packages together don't really know the music or the people. They don't know which songs to put in there or what would sell best or anything.

It makes me so mad sometimes when I see a package and I say, "Jesus Christ! These songs?" And the guy was a big artist. But whoever did it just went through a computer list and said, "Okay, let's get eight of these for that."

Whereas some labels will go and lease some sides from other labels to put with the package and make it a great package.

Has your career exceeded your expectations?

Oh, beyond my wildest dream. I figured I'd get a few songs cut. And like I say, when I came here I wanted to be an artist. I just wanted to have a record big enough that I could work the honky-tonks for ten, twelve years. I dreamed of working through Texas and Louisiana, because there was a lot of nice places to work. Old-line hillbillies like Hank Locklin and all them guys worked the Rio Palm Isle and the clubs. Those guys never played to a crowd of forty or fifty thousand. They didn't have a light show that came out of the ceiling and exploding rockets. They didn't come out of a piano. Their guys came out there and had on nice suits. They didn't get up with what they slept in and play in that, which is what they do today. It amazes me that as much money as Alan Jackson makes, he can't buy a decent pair of blue jeans. In my opinion, it makes him look like an idiot. I'd wear the nicest clothes I could wear on stage. I'd have one of Porter Wagoner's jackets on.

Why did the artist career not happen?

I had a record on MGM and got a chance to work a few shows. Once I saw how that was, I didn't like that at all. You go somewhere and you don't have a band and you got to play with a house band for a bunch of drunks. I said, "Hell, I ain't going to do this. I did that in Mississippi."

But in Mississippi it was different. We were hunting women. We played the club for nothing just to get at the women. We didn't care. But now it was serious. I was trying to make a living out of it. And I just got to where I said, "Heck, I don't need to be an artist."

Of course, I wasn't that good anyway. Most of my stuff was comedy anyway. If comedy had been as big back then as it is now, my records would have probably done more, because I had some good comedy records. But the labels didn't get into it like they do now.

What is Glenn Sutton doing now?

I'm just enjoying life. That's all. I get up every day with a good attitude and I say, "Hey, man, what am I going to do today?" My biggest problem is figuring out what I'm going to do all day every day. I usually find something pretty interesting to do. Any time you got a house there's always something wrong. Like two days ago, I put a ten by ten piece of rubber on my rubber

roof. I had a leak during this last rain. So I did that. I do all my own maintenance work, which is good for me. I'm what you know as a piddler, I guess. I
just piddle around with this and that. But I have a really good time.

Have you scaled back on the automobiles?

Oh, I don't have any of those now. I sold all that stuff. I still have a lot
of memorabilia. To really understand it, you'll have to drop by my house
sometime.

I'll take that as an invitation.

You just have to look in there and say, "God Almighty! What in the hell
is all that?" I'm a collector by nature. Have always been. Always. I have collected everything there is to collect, except maybe glass cows.

Beanie Babies?

No, I wouldn't get into that. Now I don't as much as I used to, but at
one time I collected everything. I would collect something until I got just
about all of it. I got into Hopalong Cassidy a few years ago. I finally had one
whole section of a room in glass cases. I had 385 different Hopalong Cassidy
items. I mean, just an unbelievable collection. I got tired of that and I said,
"Hell, there's about a thousand pieces, I don't want to have to spend everything I got on Hopalong Cassidy." So I started selling a few pieces, then I just
sold it all.

Why do you collect it in the first place?

Something to do that I enjoy. I enjoy getting it together and then I enjoy
getting rid of it. And I always figure out a way to make money, because I try to
buy it as cheap as possible. And I got an antique store with my buddy, Phil
Tomlinson, in Old Villa, Tennessee.

Where's that?

It's down off of Natchez Trace. It's about seventy-five miles from my
house. We got it leased out right now. We had our stuff in there at one time.
I take stuff down there and put it in there on consignment. We ran it for
two or three years ourselves. We just opened up on Saturday and Sunday,
but I got tired of driving down there every Saturday and Sunday. I ruined
my weekend. But I piddle with antiques. I buy and sell. I'm always buying
and selling.

I have too many guitars at all times. I'm a sucker for a guitar. I'll buy a guitar this afternoon, if I see one that I like. Then I'll sell it a month from now.

I enjoy being with my daughter, Lisa. We spend a lot of time together.

But as far as business, I just basically work catalog and stay in touch with the special products people to try to get in those packages. I don't really know what to pitch an artist today. That's why I make compilations of fifteen songs and press a hundred of them and pass them out to the guys. If they hear something on there they like, fine. I do a few demos every now and then, but the chances of getting something out of those is few and far between. And I understand that because there's too many songs. There's not enough artists for the songs.

There are some unbelievable songs that will never be heard, because you just can't do everything. People don't understand that. They get mad and bitter and they say, "They're not working my stuff." But they can't. And I understand that.

I had a couple little old writers with me and they nearly drove me crazy to work their song. I said, "Get out there and work your own song. You think Gallico Music's working my songs now?"

But really, I understand it. It's 90 percent luck. I've got so much stuff out there that I'm going to get something in the package. You're going to have to buy gasoline. If you do a package on one of them artists that was on CBS, you use one of my songs whether you want to or not. There was probably one in there that was a hit.

And you benefited from your position at the label.

Exactly. I mean, hey, a lot of artists hated the songs they cut. But they were my songs. I explained to them how it would help them. I set them down like a son. Said, "Hey, this thing's just going in an album anyway. What do you care? Hell, cut it. I need a good demo on it."

But most of them were good songs. If you're cutting an album with twelve songs, why would you want twelve outside songs? It's the same way today. I understand an artist wanting to cut his own stuff if it's good. But if it's bad, he's never going to be a star. He's got to go.

People can say they can do it with an open mind, but you don't. Every one of them is looking out for theirselves.

A record producer is overrated. *Record producer* is just a term that somebody came up with for a guy that just kind of coordinated everything. But now they act like these guys are gods. They have very little to do with the record. The musicians are the main ingredient. If you got an engineer and you got some good songs, anybody can do it.

And get points on the record.

Exactly.

If an artist on a label hits with another producer, well they got to get rid of the producer and move the artist over to them. It's points. I mean, I think that's great if them guys can get away with it. But the guys that built this business, like Don Law and Frank Jones and Ken Nelson, are totally forgotten. They got no points. They were salaried employees. I was a salaried employee at CBS.

"Rose Garden" sold ten million records. Did I get any points? I got my little check every week. I didn't get a damn dime, not a quarter.

When people get into a position to load up, do they do so because it's a short-term window of opportunity?

Well, most of the people don't realize that. They think that they're still supposed to be hot. They're my age, but they're still griping because nobody cuts their songs. I say, "How many did you take downtown last week? They're not going to come out to your house and ask for them."

If I get a cut, it's luck. I'm just not into working it that much.

What advice would you give a writer today?

It's a co-writer world and you got to have a good affiliation with a publisher. You can't just start out by yourself. The best thing to do is try to get a co-pub deal and work with a major.

I would tell them to try to write some stuff by theirselves, and not depend on someone else to help them with everything they do. If you can't do something by yourself, where are you? You look back at the old writers that really wrote a lot of great songs, there's not a lot of co-writers. Floyd Tillman didn't have a lot of people on his songs. Marty Robbins didn't have a lot of co-writers. Hank Thompson had only like one: Billy Gray. Those guys really worked at it and they wrote some great songs.

It's an altogether different world. People keep saying, "There ain't no country music." What we're hearing today is what country music is today. This is the country music. In the '30s, it was Roy Acuff. You don't hear a lot of Acuff now. It's evolved like a car has evolved from a Model A to a Cadillac.

When you put a Model A and a Cadillac side by side, there are huge differences. But if you look at the Motor City assembly line or the Music City assembly line year by year, the changes are subtle.

Right. It's a process of evolution. And what we wound up with now is actually what country music is. It's more modern. Used to be people thirty-five to fifty-five were the only ones that liked country music. Now fifteen-year-olds love it.

Do you think you could write for this market?

Well, yeah. You could take the same songs and just cut them like these artists today do them. The song doesn't change; the production changes. The people and the acts and the way they present themselves change.

You take a good song from the '30s and cut it today, it's just as good as it was then. Or even better. The song doesn't change. You can change the arrangement of it and make it new. Every now and then somebody takes an old song and does it.

Alan Jackson.

He popped a top.

A whole album of classics.

The reason they don't do a lot more of it is because they have publishing companies or they're a writer or a co-writer. It's a money thing. If I was an artist, I'd cut all of my own stuff. When I did my album on Mercury, I didn't go look for a lot of outside stuff. I already had the stuff. I could write it myself.

I mean, Reba ain't somewhere now trying to call me to write for her. She's got her own stuff working.

She may call you to come do her kitchen floor.

Hey, I'm getting good at that shit.

Then you could leave a CD on the counter when you leave.

Well, I'll tell you who I met like that. Became a giant artist. I met him laying carpet in my house. He had been with the Pozo-Seco Singers and they'd had a few hits. And he was working for a carpet company. He laid carpet in mine and Lynn's first house. We got to talking and he told me about the Pozo-Seco Singers. I didn't even know who the hell they were. He said, "We had a couple hits. I still sing a little bit, but I got to make a living for my

family." So he played me some tapes and sang me a couple songs. I went to Billy Sherrill and he said, "Nothing there." It was Don Williams.

Later Jack Clement cut a record on him and the rest is history. You never know.

It's a fickle business.

I firmly believe that anybody can write one hit song. But write forty or fifty of them, then you're a songwriter. If a guy writes one hit, to me, he's just a lucky man—some talent and some ingenuity. But there's a very small percentage that can make a living strictly from songwriting. It's always been that way. I worked two jobs even when I had the first records out. After I'd get off from fooling around over at Merle Kilgore's all day, I'd go over to Music City Recorders and work a night shift cutting dubs. It's a hard business.

But a lot of fun.

Oh, it's great fun!

Dallas Frazier

John D. Loudermilk refers to songwriting as the muse, so I'm curious when your song-writing muse started and when you realized it was going to be the path for your life.

I started writing songs when I was about ten years old. I still have a song that I wrote when I was about eleven. I turned sixty years old last October, so my songwriting goes back a ways.

I got my first job in the music business when I was twelve years old working with Ferlin Husky in Bakersfield, California. I met Tommy Collins at that time and we wound up being roommates. We were both living with and working for Ferlin. I recorded for Capitol Records when I was fourteen years old and I recorded some of the material I wrote.

So you were a teenage sensation before Tanya Tucker and LeAnn Rimes.

I didn't have that kind of fame and fortune. I was not really a child star, but I was in the music business as a child. I wrote and sang and did some pretty good things as a kid.

I had the pleasure of sitting down with Tommy Collins, and we conversed a little bit about Ferlin. I went over to Branson, Missouri, five or six years ago and saw Ferlin at the Christy Lane Theater. That was the first time I had ever seen him perform. It was a wonderful evening. He really worked the crowd. That seems to be a lost art.

Yeah. And also doing it moment by moment, because so many things are so rigid and rehearsed. But his is a spontaneous show. Of course, he's rehearsed

Photo courtesy of BMI Archives

the tunes, but it's a spontaneous thing, too. Somebody could say something from the audience and he would be right back with them.

Great singer and a comedian.

Yeah, Ferlin is one of the all-time, old-time greats.

Why did Ferlin take you under his wing?

Ferlin was holding a talent contest in Bakersfield, California, at an old

dance hall called the Rainbow Gardens. I entered the contest and won. That night he asked me, he said, "Would you like to come to work for me?" And I said, "Of course, I'd love to." He asked if I would like to live with him, because he was traveling some and it was just a short ways from where my folks lived. I talked my folks into it and then I started traveling with him. That was the beginning of it.

So at twelve, you talked your parents into letting you leave home.

My folks were separated. And I wasn't going a long ways off. It was just next door, about ten miles away. It wasn't something they really were cheerful about, but I was convincing. So they let me go.

So you grew up in the shadow of Bakersfield.

I sure did. My family, you might say, were some of the "grapes of wrath" from Oklahoma like the Steinbeck novel. We came out in '41 or '42 to California. My dad and mom worked in the fields picking fruit and cotton. So we were part of the Dust Bowl movement. We settled in little towns in the outlying areas of Bakersfield, like Arvin, Greenfield, Oildale, and Lamont. They were full of Okies, Arkies, and Texans.

Music was a big part of that culture.

It really was, because the people brought their music with them. There was a lot of country music. People with country music backgrounds moved to the Bakersfield area. I think that's the primary reason that Bakersfield became a West Coast music town.

And you stayed there through high school.

I sure did. I graduated from McFarland High School, which is north of Bakersfield about twenty-five miles.

Was there a rivalry between Bakersfield and Nashville at that time?

There was no real rivalry in the '50s. Of course, Nashville had the Grand Ole Opry. And, really, that's about all Nashville was doing at that time. Nashville was not a big recording town. Bakersfield just had a lot of local honky-tonks and dance halls. But there's never been any real rivalry, because Nashville overshadows the little Bakersfield thing. But for the size of the city, Bakersfield has had a lot of music product, a lot of talent.

I grew up in Bossier City across the river from Shreveport, which was famous for the Louisiana Hayride.

I visited the Hayride in '55. I've heard a lot of stories about Bossier City. I love that country. Louisiana is just mysterious to me.

So when did you make the move to Nashville?

I was living in Portland, Oregon, and I ran into Ferlin in '63. We hadn't seen each other in a long time. Prior to that, I had lived around the Bakersfield area and L.A. area. Ferlin offered me a job here, so my wife and I moved to Nashville in late '63 with our two little girls. Well, it kind of piddled out with Ferlin, because from what I could see, Ferlin was gone all the time and it just wasn't working out. There was no problem with being friends, it was just that I wanted a real active publisher.

I met Ray Baker, who was working for Jim Reeves Enterprise. Ray said, "Would you consider making a move?" I said, "Well, let me think about it." Ferlin said, "Fine, Dallas, no problem." So I made the move.

Did you have a relationship with Jim Reeves?

No, I didn't really know Jim. I met him maybe once or twice.

What was going on in Portland?

Nothing. I was working a day job in a music store and I was just miserable.

How old were you?

Twenty-three.

You were out there playing and performing as a teenager and then you found yourself at twenty-three working in a record store. What happened?

In 1961, I was living in Los Angeles. I had written "Alley Oop" when I was eighteen or nineteen years old. In the summer of 1960, "Alley Oop" was a monster hit, one of the biggest novelties ever. I wrote the song at a cotton gin. My stepdad was a ginner. And I thought, "I'll go back down to the cotton gin again and work another season, maybe there's another 'Alley Oop' down at that cotton gin." It paid good money besides, so I went down when I was about twenty-one, and I went to a revival meeting. And I really came under conviction. I became aware of God for the first time in my life. I knew there was something between me and God that had to be settled. So, long story short, I joined this church. In fundamental Christian terms, I repented and I was born again.

Then I left the music business. I did not feel it was compatible with my newfound spiritual life. And I still feel that way about some of it. It's what you make of it, too. You could be almost in any field you want to be in as long as you're in control and the thing's not in control of you. I think what happened was association problems. I was a wild man in the music business.

No one had ever been wild in the music business before. You were a pioneer.

Not hardly. I had a lot of predecessors, so to speak. I had a bunch of them to follow after and to learn from. But people have association problems. I was really wild. The music business is what you make of it. It can be wild if you're wild.

And sometimes it presents an opportunity for temptations that may not be as prevalent in other walks of life.

Let's face it—the music business has a few extra perks when it comes to temptation and glorifying the flesh and the glitter and the glamour. It has more snares and traps in it than farming, to say the least.

But I got out of it, to answer your question, Phil. I left the music business, and my wife and I wound up moving to Portland, Oregon. That's where she was from. I met her in Los Angeles, and we got married when we were eighteen years old. And we're still married. I thank God for that, because He gave me a real gift when He gave me my wife, Sharon.

That's beautiful to hear, because she stood by you through some difficult times.

Sharon is a sweetheart of a girl. She came from a real close family. Her dad was an Italian; her mama was an Austrian. They're both gone now.

She's a homebody, but not homely. I really was fortunate to have a wife like her, because I could have had a wife that was like me. And that would have been a disaster. But she put up with a lot over the years. The cold, hard facts of it are I really abused her and our marriage. Not physical abuse, but just all kinds of living wild. Just suffice it to say that she had every right to dump me. Every right. But she didn't. She stuck with me. She's a spiritual woman, too, and I wouldn't take anything for that.

I'm sure her loyalty magnifies your gratitude.

Oh, yeah. Looking back, I don't deserve any of this. This good life I'm living now with my wife and with my bride of forty-two years, I don't deserve this. But I have it and I thank God for it.

Your tribute to her is "If My Heart Had Windows."

A song like that, Phil, it's not dated. It has nothing in it that dates it. And you're fortunate when you write a song like that. For example, "Put Another Nickel In The Nickelodeon." Well, what in the world is a nickelodeon and what can you get for a nickel today? I have a lot of songs that have a figure of speech in them that does date them.

A song of yours that isn't dated is "There Goes My Everything." I remember my parents playing that when I was a kid. They were playing Engelbert Humperdink, who is a wonderful singer, but Jack Greene, in my opinion, is equally as good.

Jack did such a great job. I want to give honor to whom honor is due here. That's the kind of cut every songwriter just dreams of. You've just had time to put down this little rough demo with a couple instruments, and then you hear your song done like that. They captured your heart. They went beyond what you were hoping. You don't get very many cuts like that.

I remember another cut, "Johnny One Time," a song that Doodle Owens and I wrote. And, oh my goodness, Brenda Lee hooked it. And so did Willie Nelson. He really hooked it, too.

What was the inspiration for "There Goes My Everything"?

That song came from a divorce of a good friend of mine. His life was out of sorts at that time.

Inspiration from others is a wonderful thing. Sometimes you don't have to experience the pain yourself to share it with others.

That's right. A lot of songwriters can only write what happens to them. But to be a good songwriter, you have to have a great imagination. You have to be able—like an actor—to put on a role and get into that role just like it's happening to you. And write it.

For an example, "Beneath Still Waters." I lived on the Cumberland River at that time. And I remember seeing the water looking real still, especially early in the morning. I had been told about the undercurrents that were beneath that. It looked pleasant on the top, but underneath you could get in trouble, especially trying to swim across it. I was thinking about that one day. Had I not had those thoughts, I would not have written "Beneath Still Waters."

I know a writer who had a really big hit. It stayed four weeks at number one. And he was almost apologetic, because his body of work had so much more depth than this particular ditty that was dominating the charts. You're a person who has written some songs of wonderful depth, but one of your biggest songs is "Elvira."

Now, that's interesting because I'll tell you something: You cannot put all these songs on one scale and weigh them. You cannot. "Elvira" is one of the best songs I've ever written. Now, is it real deep or poetic? No, it's not. But it has a streak of simplicity and commercialism in it that you just don't come by every day. If I did, I'd write them every day.

It's infectious. You released that as an artist.

I had it out in early '66.

How did it do?

I had a southern and southwestern hit down in Texas, Alabama, Oklahoma, Georgia, Mississippi and all through there.

I recently learned Kenny Rogers and the First Edition recorded it.

Yeah. He cut a real different version of it.

But nothing did as much for "Elvira" as "um papa mow mow."

If you took Richard Sterbon's bass lick out of it, it wouldn't be the same. But the song is soulish and it cooks. If I were comparing songs, it wouldn't be fair to take that song and have it in the same category as "If My Heart Had Windows," because it's two completely different categories.

How did the Oak Ridge Boys cut of "Elvira" come about?

Ronnie Gant plugged it to them. Ronnie was working for Acuff-Rose at that time, and he's the one that got it to them.

One thing I admire about you is that you embody the idea of "it's never too late to learn." You celebrated your twenty-five year high school reunion before you went to college.

Going to Emmanuel Bible College in east Nashville. Being interested in the ministry and being interested in spiritual matters prompted that.

How was college life?

I loved it. I really did. Being older, you're real conscientious about your learning and getting good grades. I was just like a little third grader trying to please my teachers. I worked hard. I got good grades.

But this went beyond college. It was a calling for you, as well.

Yes, it was. And it prepared me for what I wanted to do, which is to be a preacher.

Did you waver on answering the call?

Oh, yes. I waited a long time. I would think about it and decide, "Naw, it's too late. I don't want to start that now." It was just one excuse after the other. But when God wants you to do something, He won't leave you alone until He gets His way.

Where are you pastoring?

I'm pastoring a small church in White House. We're renting the civic center now. We're hoping that we can get some property and build.

How long have you been pastoring?

About six months.

So this is a new venture.

Yeah, it's new. The pastoring thing is new. I've been a minister for a while. I've traveled and spoke here and there. I had a couple trips to Africa.

Were you a missionary?

Not missionary work in the real sense of the word, just a guest speaker.

Pastoring is a lot different, because for one thing, you have to come up with a new sermon every week. That's kind of like having a new demo session every week.

Has you songwriting career had much gospel writing in it?

No. I'm really not through writing yet. I know that I'm going to write some gospel things.

Are you ever the featured vocalist in your church?

Yeah. I participate every once in a while. We have a good music program in our little church. We have some good musicians and singers. It's fun.

I'm seeing some new Dallas Frazier songs and some old-time favorites on your gospel album.

I don't know how much I'll be involved in the secular music business. But I am going to write some gospel songs. When I'm writing, I'll just write. I don't mind writing whatever comes to me if it's good, if it's the truth.

You can write anything if it's the truth. And it should be accepted. Ronnie Schaffer and I wrote a song called "The Devil Ain't A Lonely Woman's Friend." And it had a line in it about cocaine. I got a lot of flak about that. It doesn't glorify cocaine. It puts cocaine in its place. But it was taboo to even mention the word, and that's not right. Of course, that's been a while back, but it shouldn't be that way.

Looking out at your garden, I'm reminded of picking green beans and tomatoes, cutting okra and cucumber, and hoeing weeds. I've noticed that gardening puts me in a rhythm to receive creativity.

I think you're putting it in a creative manner there. I have times when it just comes to me. The channels are clear. It's hard to say exactly how it happens. Sometimes stuff just comes out of the blue. I mean just falls down on you out of the blue. You don't know where it comes from. Sometimes you can trace it to something that triggers it.

Sometimes it can be like chasing after a butterfly with a net. You can't quite catch it, because you're chasing it too hard.

I know about the net and the butterfly. You know there's a butterfly out there. You can feel it. But you start trying to write it before you comprehend it. That doesn't work, because you're pushing. It's not coming to you. The flow is not natural.

How did you balance letting it come to you, yet having to generate a lot of product?

Sorry to say, I didn't use my head. A lot of times I pushed. I generated when I didn't feel like generating. And, consequently, a lot of times, you wind up writing mediocre stuff. I used to book demo sessions and I wouldn't have a song. This is the kind of stuff I will not do again. I would book a demo session, because I knew that if I was dry, I was going to get wet. If I booked that demo session, I had to come up with something. I would panic. I would be up the last three days and nights, straining and struggling. And compromising. It's really not tight yet but, hey, I'm out of time.

Close enough for the radio.

It's close enough, yeah.

And did you find some of the songs you would call mediocre getting cut?

Yeah.

Did you find them becoming singles?

I wrote a song, "Until My Dreams Come True." Jack Greene had a number one hit on it. I was in Florida on a vacation and my publisher, Ray Baker, called me and said Jack's going to cut and he really wants a song. I said, "Ray, I'm down here on a vacation." He said, "Well, I just thought I'd tell you."

Ray knew how to nudge me, and it worked out good for both of us. But, anyway, long story short, first I had to go rent a tape recorder. That was a hassle. I walked down the beach and I wrote that song. I come back and put it on tape and sent it to Ray on a Greyhound. But Jack cut it. And it was a number one.

What was the value of your relationship with Ray Baker?

We were both hungry. Not poverty stricken, but close to it. It was do or die. And that's what really got it going. Plus he was good at what he did; I was good at what I did. It was teamwork. Needing a break, you work harder. You really do.

Do you and Ray still have a relationship?

After I moved up here in '75, I lost track of Ray. Now he lives down the road from me. I see him every once in a while. He got into producing Moe Bandy, George Strait, and Connie Smith. He published for a long time. He did very well.

Did you consider him a good song man?

Ray Baker's a good producer, but he's got an ear. Sometimes he'd have a good suggestion like let's slow this thing down or let's start with the chorus. You can always stand some good constructive criticism or changes.

Where did the idea for "Mohair Sam" come from?

Out of the blue. Ferlin gave me an old pair of mohair pants. I was intrigued with mohair. It was supposed to be top-notch material. But "Mohair Sam" actually come about under pressure. Ray come by my house one evening and he said, "I saw Charlie Rich today downtown and I told him you had a smash for him." And I said, "Well, what did you have in mind?" He said, "I figured you could come up with something." So I went to work that evening and I struggled and strained. I couldn't come up with anything. Then I got up real early, about four-thirty or five o'clock that next morning, because he was cutting at ten o'clock.

I started working. Just beating the bushes. And it come to me. It was just a little old quick thing, but clever. It had a real good beat and feel to it. Ray took it down there just in time, and Charlie listened to it and loved it.

Charlie Rich is one of my favorite all-time guys. He took out of here young. Great talent. I loved his piano playing.

The Silver Fox.

Good-looking dude.

What instrument did you write "Mohair Sam" on?

Piano.

Did you mainly write on keyboard?

I wrote some things with a guitar, but most of my things I wrote with a piano.

I love "Fourteen Carat Mind." Driving out here I was amazed at some of the mansions sitting on the hill. But you live very modestly. Certainly well within your means. Why are you choosing simplicity when you see so many people chasing the acquisition of things?

I don't like debt. I've been conservative. I come up real poor when I was a little kid. I started making some money as a teenager. I just don't believe in owing any money. There are things that I like to do, and I like to have cash to do it when I want to do it.

I blew a lot of money on cars. I had a weakness for cars. I finally got over that after I sobered up. I used to get drunk and trade for color. I bought a brand new two-ton truck one night when I was drunk. It was a five-speed with a two-speed axle. It didn't have power steering. I couldn't wait to get one with power steering; I had to have it that night. So anyway, long story short, I lost my shirt on that, because after I sobered up three or four months later, I said, "What am I doing with this?"

I went through some things like that that was just absolutely ridiculous.

But I have some acreage, old barns, a shop, and a little study outside where I have a getaway with a piano. It's enough.

It's beautiful. And you don't seem to be defined by your things.

No. And I'm just like everybody else. Sometimes I can get a wild hair for something. I'll think, "I ought to move into something bigger. I ought to do this; I ought to do that." And why? For other people's eyes. It certainly wouldn't be for mine. We find ourselves straining and working and spending our money for one purpose—for the other people's eyes. It's ridiculous.

Now I'm not saying I'm not going to get another sports car. I might have to get me one more hot rod. But I wouldn't have it if it wasn't within my means.

If you wind up with a woman that's got a fourteen carat mind, it'll bleed you dry. I'm glad my wife was a real simple homemaker. Sharon is not extravagant at all. If she were, there'd be more stuff around here. But she's a very conservative woman. Cadillacs are foolishness as far as she's concerned. I had the car bug.

When I moved out here to Gallatin, I actually retired from the music business.

Really?

I laid the pencil down on purpose. When I moved up here to Gallatin in the summer of '75, I had a real problem with drinking. I had serious problems with alcohol. I got sober around the first of '76. And I knew that God helped me get sober. I knew that I wanted to stay that way and I wanted to get back involved in church. I had been involved in church at a younger age.

I severed my old contacts and hibernated out here, you might say. I thought I would rest up a year or so because I was doing well, financially speaking. And still am, by the way. I'm thankful to God for that. I thought, "I don't have to work, I'll take it easy for a year or two. Take a good sabbatical, and then I'll ease back into songwriting on my own terms, at my own pace." And it never really happened. I lost the desire for it, to tell you the truth.

You're still pacing yourself.

Yeah. I'll tell you one thing. When I wrote, I worked hard. I really did. My decade, my earning era was the '60s. I poured the coal on in the '60s. But sometimes I found myself in a marathon trying to keep up with all the demand. "Hey, Dallas, you got a fast one, you got a slow one, you got a waltz, you got this, you got that?" And I thought, "I'll have to come up with something for these guys." So I burned the candle at both ends for a long time. And I thought, "If I ever really get on a commercial kick again, I'm going to take my time and do my songs just like an artist paints pictures. I'm going to take a good, long look before I let them go." And I still feel that way.

For a songwriter, getting called for songs sounds like an enviable position to be in.

It is. And I'm grateful for that. But the demand gets kind of heavy. If you're hot, you have to work hard. You have to produce. It's an assembly line. You can't just wait around for the bright ideas to hit you. You have to go out and start beating the bushes to keep up with it.

"What's Your Mama's Name, Child."

I was with Earl Montgomery down in Alabama on the river. I had the idea, and Peanut helped me write it. Peanut Montgomery, that's Earl Montgomery. But when it got started, it was just there.

I'm glad you mentioned the song, because that's one of the most interesting story songs that I've ever had anything to do with.

Was that purely a work of fiction?

Similar to a thousand stories. But it was just imagination.

When I first arrived in Nashville, one person who was so generous and kind to me was Doodle Owens. You spoke of Doodle the night he was inducted into the Songwriter's Hall of Fame. Doodle missed his evening in the spotlight, as he lay in a coma at an area hospital.

That's right. And died a couple of weeks later. He was informed that he would receive the honor, so he died knowing that.

This book will not be complete without a discussion of Doodle.

That's right.

Doodle Owens was the most prolific writer I've ever known. Doodle always had a pocket full of pencils and colored pens. He was ready to go. I mean, this guy could turn the songs out. He was just full of them. Doodle and I had a real good rapport. I met him in '65, and we started writing right away. We were good friends and we wrote a lot of songs, including "All I Have To Offer You Is Me," "I'm So Afraid Of Losing You Again," "Johnny

One Time," and "Just For What I Am." Jerry Lee Lewis had a number one on "Touching Home."

Doodle pulled his weight when we was working. And he was a very artistic man. He had polish and style and imagination. He was great when it come to bouncing things off. I could say something and he could finish it. He knew where I was going with it.

Doodle was a polished old pro and a lovable guy. A funny guy. Sometimes we'd just travel the roads. We'd ride these old country roads drinking and what have you. I had a farm in the country with a cabin up on the hill. And after about two days of just running around, we'd finally land up there on top of that hill and put on a pot of beans and drag a couple cases of beer out of the trunk of the car. We'd hole up there for two or three days and just crank 'em out. We'd stay up there until we'd come home with something.

There's not room for ego when you're co-writing. If you've got a dog line, sooner or later during the songwriting process, you're going to realize it's a dog line. Most of time when we wrote together Doodle would say something, and I'd say, "Let's think about that." And vice versa. But we knew it wasn't there yet. I could handle that from him, and he could handle that from me. Just like with me and Whitey Shafer, same way. Because they know it's not there yet, they just need some confirmation.

But sometimes you at least have to put something on the table and volley it back and forth.

That's right. I used to hate to write alone. I wrote a lot of stuff by myself, but it's a lonesome job. Sometimes I would take my wife with me and I'd say, "Sharon, what do you think about this?" I'd bang it out for her. She'd say, "Well, honey, I don't know." And I'd say, "What do you know about songwriting anyway?"

A songwriter asking his spouse, "What do you think about this?," is the equivalent of a wife asking her husband, "How do I look?" You don't want an honest opinion; you want them to say, "Great!" You're looking to them for support. You know you're going to take one on the chin when you actually pitch it.

Yeah. Yeah. Yeah.

Did you have a lot of co-writers?

No, there was just a few. I don't really know why. It wasn't planned that way, it just happened that way.

I love the title, "Son Of Hickory Hollow's Tramp." It's been cut by Merle Haggard, Kenny Rogers and Gary Puckett.

A very, very powerful story. But it's not a true story. It's wild imagination, you might say. But it's one of the most powerful stories I've ever wrote.

It's about a woman whose husband leaves her. It's a country setting. He leaves her with a bunch of kids to fend for herself. And she sells her body to raise this family. One of the boys in the family is telling the story in retrospect. His mother became labeled as the Tramp of Hickory Hollow. But he's the son of Hickory Hollow's tramp, and he brags on her. It's a real touching story.

What is your advice to songwriters?

A songwriter is in the word business. Choose your words just like you would choose fruit at a market. Don't be too hasty with grabbing the first thing you see. Take your time and have respect for words and the different meanings and connotations that even the same word can have.

If you're an aspiring songwriter, there's two things that can happen to you, as far as publishing goes, that can be real negative. First of all, you can be with a publisher that had no contacts. Somebody is just working out of their back pocket. You're not going to get anywhere like that. Then again, you can wind up with an Exxon and if you do, it can be just as bad, because they don't really need you. They don't need your few little dollars. You can wind up being some executive's whim. If you're signed with an Exxon, you need somebody really rooting for you. It's hard to get started unless they're really behind you. A songwriter has a certain amount of stuff in him. And when you're fresh, they might get all your fresh stuff and those songs might just be shelved. They paid you two-hundred-and-fifty dollars a week, but they've taken the firstfruits of your brains and it's just on a shelf. They don't need it. You can just get lost in the shuffle. I think the middle ground is best for the beginner.

I noticed you have "Psalm 37" on your license plate? What is the significance of Psalm 37?

I'm glad you asked. That's an interesting story. In about '62, after I quit the music business, I was living in McFarland, California. And Sharon and I really got down, really broke one day. It didn't happen in one day, but it come to a head one day. And I remember praying. I was desperate. I got down on my hands and knees and I said, "Lord, you say here in Psalm 37 in verse 25 that David said he had lived to be an old man, but he had never seen the righteous forsaken nor his seed begging bread."

And being righteous does not mean righteous in my own acts. Righteous according to His blood being shed for me. I said, "Lord, I'm your child, and it looks like if something doesn't come through for me pretty quick, I might have to be begging bread. But You say right here that I won't."

And you know what? God did come through for me. He come through miraculously. As a matter of fact, He sent a man to knock on my door the next day and offer me a job. I didn't even have a car that would run. He had a grocery store that was within walking distance of the house. He said, "Dallas, what are you doing?" I said, "Nothing." He said, "Won't you come and work at the store for me?" I said, "Oh, Mr. Watson,"—his name was Albert Watson—"thank you so much. I need a job. I've been praying for one."

God come through for me, and I'll never forget it. About twelve years ago, I got to thinking about that verse I had claimed. I applied for the tag and I got it. Psalm 37.

You were worried about begging for bread and God supplied a job in a grocery store.

Yeah. That is ironic, isn't it? Led me to a grocery store. It was just a minimum wage job, but it was just what I needed. Mr. Watson gave me 10 percent off my groceries.

Christianity is the most important thing in my life. Jesus Christ being my Lord and Savior—that is the most important thing in my life. All the other parts of my life have to work around that and fit in with that. And that's solid as granite.

Curly Putman

I remember this room of your house, because it was real popular the night you put up the tent and had a guitar pull.

We had to come in out of the rain, if I remember correctly.

I was leaving, and Jamie O'Hara started singing "The Cold Hard Truth." It stopped me in my tracks.

That was a George Jones single.

About four years after I heard it here.

It is hard to get out there.

The Mavericks were out here that night. Tricia Yearwood came out here. They hadn't made it at the time. And all of a sudden, they're big hit acts.

Fifteen-year overnight successes.

This area right here is where Paul McCartney and his band practiced. It wasn't finished out and done, it was like a double car garage, and we did keep it just a place to lounge around out here.

Buddy Killen produced some sessions with them. They recorded "Junior's Farm" and "Sally G." They just kind of laid around for six weeks. They were going over their act, getting ready for a tour.

Photo courtesy of Sony/ATV Music Publishing

What year was this?

I believe that was 1974. I'm not sure.

Got a picture over there on the wall that Linda McCartney made up for us of she and Paul and the whole group. They took it around the farm here.

After Linda died, the world gained insight into how special her and Paul's relationship really was.

Well, it had to be. They stayed married for so long. It had to be a special thing. I was around for just a little while with them together. I do know that she was down to earth, both down-to-earth people.

You've logged quite a few years as a husband. Coming up on forty-five years, I believe.

That's a long while, isn't it? With the wrong woman. I mean with the right woman.

Be careful, Curly, I got the tape recorder running. I have a friend who's been married for ten years and he says it feels like ten minutes. Underwater.
You wrote a song called "The Older The Violin, The Sweeter The Music."

I'm trying to think where I first heard that saying. A lot of those things I heard from my mother. She used to say things that just popped out of her mind. And that kind of stuck with me. Hank Thompson, of course, was an older star at the time and he had a big record on that. It's amazing that I still get a lot of BMI earnings off of that. Every time I get a royalty statement, that particular song gets played a lot.

So does your mother's saying hold true?

Well, I'd say so. In a lot of ways.

Like a Stradivarius?

I always loved that little saying. And it can mean a lot of things, depending on how you wrote it, of course.

I guess Jamie O'Hara was taking notes from you when he wrote "Older Women."

I tell you what, all of us guys worked pretty close together. Jamie and Kevin Welch and Rafe Van Hoy and Don Cook were all around at the same time. We took from each other in our thoughts. I was always too serious minded to write anything real funny. I could really kill people off in a song.

Like "Blood Red And Going Down."

When I wrote that song, I didn't really think all that much about it. I liked the Delta-ish, down-home flavor of it. I wrote it for a guy. I played it for Billy Sherrill. And then he called me up and said he wanted to cut it on Tanya Tucker. Tanya had just come off of the big hit "Delta Dawn." She was about fourteen years old. Man, she could sing.

Did you ever think you would see a plethora of young artists singing country music as we have today? Billy Gilman is pre-pubescent.

I thought not about the age, but the type music. To me, a lot of it's just not what I call country. I love the Dixie Chicks. But the younger stuff, I can't get any feeling. I guess that shows you that I am getting a little older. A lot of the young people can sing a little bit, but a lot of them don't have that control that shows up in people like Tanya Tucker and LeAnn Rimes. But anyhow, it's a different business altogether right now.

Than when you wrote "Green Green Grass Of Home."

When I wrote "Green Green Grass Of Home," I hadn't been in Nashville all that long. Less than a year, I guess. It was a down-home type song, and those kinds of songs just wasn't necessarily happening at that time. I played it for a lot of different folks. A lot of them turned it down, as usual. You know how that goes.

Then I played it for Bobby Bare, who at that time was doing "Detroit City" and "Five Hundred Miles Away From Home," all that stuff. Chet Atkins took the song, and I won't get into the long story here about it, but he took the song to play for Bobby, so Bobby was holding it. In the meantime, Johnny Darrell, who was running the Holiday Inn down on West End, loved Bobby Bare-type stuff. His singing kind of leaned towards that. So he asked Bobby could he take that song. So Bobby said, "Yeah. Go ahead."

Bobby Bare undoubtedly hadn't necessarily wanted to cut it real fast, so he gave it to Johnny Darrell. The first week or so it was out, man, everybody started calling me. It just lit a spark with an unknown. And then Johnny got covered by just about everybody in the book.

Jerry Lee Lewis cut it. By the way, that's where Tom Jones heard "Green Green Grass of Home." He was a big fan of Jerry Lee's, so he decided he wanted-ed to cut that song and everybody tried to talk him out of it. Porter Wagoner then covered Johnny Darrell's record and, of course, he was established and he went to number four or somewhere in there.

I remember watching the Tom Jones Show as a kid, because my mom wouldn't miss it. It was a little risqué for the time period. He would kiss the buxom girl dancer from behind a silhouette screen at the start of the show. "Green Green Grass of Home" was somewhat uncharacteristic of his persona. He must have really loved the song.

He did. He fell in love with the song. Gordon Mills was his manager and he loved for him to do this kind of middle-of-the-road country stuff. He managed Engelbert Humperdink, too.

There's a new biography out on Tom Jones. All of the chapters of this book are named after songs. The first chapter is "Green Green Grass of Home," which was a pretty rough start for him back in the coal mining country there in Wales.

You came from humble beginnings, as well.

I was born in North Alabama, up in the mountains there in Putman. Was named after our family. My grandfather talked about his dad working in the coal mines. My father worked in the sawmill business.

I started at Tree in the royalty department, so I had an intimate knowledge of what different songs would earn. "Green Green Grass Of Home" is a handsome annuity for the Putmans.

It is. It came out in 1965. Last time we counted at Tree, it had been recorded over seven hundred times. Every major language in the world, you might say. And it still—after that length of time—counts for a big, big part of my foreign BMI and foreign sales.

It still buys my kids and grandkids a new pair of shoes.

Speaking of grandkids. You now have a granddaughter working at the publishing company where you wrote.

I'm still with them as far as a contract. I've been there ever since I moved to Nashville in 1964. I stayed even longer than Buddy Killen, who owned the company. Gina wanted to be in that part of the business, and she went after it.

She works with Greg Matthews, son of the late Neil Matthews, who was a member of the Jordonaires and created the Nashville Number System that is used by musicians in recording sessions.

There's a lot of tradition that goes on, I guess. Of course, the music has changed so much. Looking back, it seemed rough at the time, but now I think it would be a lot harder for me with the type things that I write. I can't feel a lot of the stuff I hear now. They're good tunes and they're commercial. But it's hard to say if any of these songs here today will stand up. There might be a few. A lot of them are safe records. They're safe with the younger people buying them. But if "Green Green Grass Of Home" was out right now, it would probably sell. No telling how much money it would make compared to what it did.

How was your wife, Bernice, instrumental to your songwriting career?

The basic thing was providing a good home environment for our kids while I was really working pretty hard at it. She loves music. And she did follow me around. I wrote the song "My Elusive Dreams." It was kind of like our life, really. We wasn't making it all that great, so I moved from Nashville to Memphis. I was selling Thom McCann shoes. Then I still wanted into music and we moved back to Huntsville, Alabama, where I started from. We kind of made a circle around through Nashville and Memphis and back to Huntsville. Then, finally, I got to come back up here. It wasn't an easy thing. Didn't know if I could write or not, either. I felt like I could, but I wasn't like a Roger Miller that could just spit them out. I had to work at what I did. More, I'd say, than a lot of writers have to work.

What's your favorite cut of "My Elusive Dreams"?

Mine. No, I was joking about that. That was my first record on ABC Records. I had so many. Tammy Wynette and David Houston covered my record. And then Johnny Darrell fell in the picture again and he recorded it during that time. Lee Hazelwood and Nancy Sinatra had it out.

If you had a hit, every country artist in the business would put it on their album because they wanted that draw in buying power. They don't do that anymore.That shows you how important the songs were then, because the cover would help sell their album.

That still seems like a good idea.

Actually, it boils down to that bottom line. That dollar, don't it?

You sold Thom McCann shoes. You sold storm doors. And, in a sense, you were selling songs as a song plugger. I've had several people tell me you were a good salesman.

I never considered myself a salesman. I always tried to be open and honest. The old saying is: "You sell yourself before you sell anything that you've got." I didn't try to hype anybody into anything when I was selling. I think that came off for me as much as anything. A lot of song pluggers and salesmen hype everything to try to sell it. I didn't do that.

You were writing songs and plugging songs for yourself and others. Most songwriters tend to bellyache when a song plugger gets one of their own songs cut. But a number of writers speak highly of the job you did at pitching their songs. How did you balance this perceived conflict of interest?

Well, it's not easy. And I've talked to people that have that problem. And just about everybody sooner or later does. I always tried to pitch other people's songs first before I'd even think about pitching a song of mine. But after I had a hit, of course, they'd say, "What have you got, Curly?" I got to pitch mine, but I tried to get everybody else's up front. And it might have even helped me to do that, I don't know. I didn't think about it that way. I just tried to pitch songs that I thought would fit the artist.

Were there some grumblings you had to deal with?

A little bit. Not much. Now and then I'd have people look at me and you knew that they might be thinking that. But I tried my best not to be just strictly for me. It's just a fact that if you had a hit or two, songwriters get to saying you're holding back on them. Some more than others. That's typical. That goes along with it if you're in that position. Even though their song wouldn't even fit the people you're pitching to, they still wonder why you didn't pitch their song.

You signed with Tree a little bit before Bobby Braddock did.

It wasn't very long after I went there that Bobby came.

You and Bobby took different roads in terms of your finances. I'm wondering if you were more successful financially from your songwriting or from your investments, such as Cracker Barrel.

Well, I'm the world's worst business-minded man.

So finances are Bernice's department?

That's Bernice's niche.

I have made a few little investments like the Cracker Barrel thing, which was just laid in my lap. And it's like "Green Green Grass Of Home" money-wise, if you stop and think about it.

The founder, Danny Evans, is a neighbor of yours.

The headquarters are right here in Lebanon.

We had just moved up here in this area and had met Danny at little get-togethers and stuff. I know he wouldn't mind me telling this. He had been to Las Vegas, and I guess he probably might have lost. A banker told me that Danny had some Cracker Barrel stock for sale and would I be interested. I said, "Well, I don't have the money." He said, "I'll take care of that for you." So I went out to see him and I bought forty-five hundred shares. It was four dollars a share, I think. That was probably 1972 or '73. So that's how I got that.

Over the years it became, well you know what it's done. You know how many stores we've got now. But, anyhow, I sold some stock last year when it was up about forty something dollars a share. It has split a couple times over the years, so I'd say whether I ever make another penny off of it, it's been a good investment.

Has it been your best stock purchase?

Oh, yeah. And like I said, it wasn't something I was smart about.

At least you picked the right horse to ride. Some music business people began to resemble their investment in Po' Folks.

I didn't get into that, luckily. I did try some other things that didn't make it during that time: Roger Miller King of the Road Hotel and then Hank Williams, Jr., Bar-B-Q.

They went the way of Terry Bradshaw Peanut Butter.

But you try things. It was no big money back then, because I didn't have any big money.

Not long after I started at Tree, you had major knee surgery.

I believe it was in 1990. I had to go to Boston and have a bone graft, because I had a type of ligament cancer. It wasn't the kind that you could treat with chemo. So it had to be removed and I had a bone graft put in there. But, that's right, I was on crutches when you first saw me.

So you're a cancer survivor.

Ten years now. It was a kind that when you got rid of it, the chances of it ever coming back were just almost zero. And we got rid of it. Later on I did have a knee replacement. So that knee's doing good. I can walk good. I can't do as much as I used to.

Can't kick much butt with it anymore?

No, not much. Or football either.

I'll race you once around the house for some Cracker Barrel stock.
You've seen several changing of the guards at Tree from Jack Stapp to Buddy Killen to CBS Records to Sony Music.

Well, I'd have to say that it wasn't good for me. But I'm still a writer with Sony.

Which part wasn't good?

When we first started out with people like Roger Miller and Don Wayne and Justin Tubb and Red Lane and Bobby Braddock, we was a little bit closer knit. And we knew the boss and the bosses. After it was sold, you just feel like you're just on the edge of the music business with the people in New York. They're thinking a lot bigger than a Curly Putman writing "Green Green Grass Of Home." I don't know, you just feel left out or unwanted. I don't think you're important to them at that point.

It changes your whole attitude about writing. Because, like I say, you feel kind of like nobody's interested. I think writers need that. The way we built Tree was with everybody helping everybody else. Saying, "Hey, that's a great song." It was more fun that way.

Was it difficult losing an office in the building during the corporate transition?

I was ready myself personally to get out of an office, because you always feel obligated when you have an office that you've got to get with people. I was kind of burned out with that end of it.

In fact, I was offered an office over in the fire hall. So I said, "All right, I'll move over there." Well, I packed all my things and I went in there one day and stuff's still in boxes. I sat down at the desk and I thought, "Man, I'll just go crazy if I have to sit here." And it was my decision then that I get out.

You do get burned out. I think I did. A lot of us worked so hard doing it. And every day it's just a continuous pressure on you. Even though you're enjoying it, it's a lot of pressure. Also, I've had ulcer problems. I'm not an out-going person like a lot of people, so it kind of eats you up inside. If you can't get something done, you wonder why. Why didn't I? Why couldn't I?

Are you effectively retired from songwriting?

I don't know if you ever completely retire. I still sit around and think of things and write down little things. But until I feel that I'm in tune enough to write a hit song or a good country song, then I'm not going to work at it. I can't write what's happening now. I'm just not geared to write that kind of stuff. I'm older than all of these people. Even though there's a few older writers that still hang in there, it is a young man's game, actually.

Are you enjoying this season of your life?

I think I'm enjoying it. I missed it for a long time. I felt like I ought to be at Tree doing something. It took me a long time. Every day I'd think about it for a little while. And, finally, I got to where I said, "Well, I'm just not going to worry about it."

Is Dan Wilson still your neighbor?

Yeah. Dan lives down the road about a couple miles. I saw him yesterday.

How's he doing?

Doing good.

What's he doing?

Well, he started a magazine called *The Scoop* over in Murfreesboro. He was doing pretty good with it.

He's a good writer.

A good songwriter. He's had some hits.

"War Is Hell On The Home Front, Too."

He and I and Bucky Jones wrote that. And he wrote "Good Ol' Girls." That was a number one hit.

I always thought if he had gotten away from the plugging, he would have had a lot more hits as a writer.

That's something that he never did concentrate on much, other than sitting down with me or Bucky or somebody that was a friend of his. And he was good at plugging, because people loved him.

Great storyteller and jokester.

But he knew a good song, too.

The last time I saw him he was in a print ad for a casino.

He told me about that. That's somebody I think he knew up there and they liked him.

You said earlier that you can't write for this market, but the Urban Cowboy '80s era is not too much unlike what is going on today. You co-wrote "Baby, I'll Be Coming Back For More" with Sterling Whipple.

Well, I kind of think maybe that I could. I guess I always want to write something that's really fantastic and will leave a mark somewhere.

I think Sterling's probably one of the better writers that was at Tree. I thought he would be good for this type music that's going on now. He and Rafe Van Hoy, they could write country or they could write something a little bit more than country. And we all got into a groove of writing at that time. He would come in my office and sit down and if we had an idea, we'd write it in one sitting. We'd try to do it quick.

That's the way we did that T.G. Sheppard cut. It was a number one country record.

You've left a mark with "Green Green Grass of Home," "He Stopped Loving Her Today," "My Elusive Dreams" and others songs. Is there something about a writer not being hungry that is part of his demise?

It's possible. And like I said before, burnout. You just get tired of being in a rat race. As I get older, that doesn't appeal to me at all. As I get older there's more important things. I still love music. I don't love it like I used to. I lived and breathed it during the time that I wrote it. And now, sometimes I don't even listen to music.

I'll hear a great song that I love and love the record, but country music needs to come back around with a little bit more tradition to it than what we got right now. And that's not sour grapes. I admire anybody that can get out there and sell millions of records. But some of it's a little weak, I think.

If a man can have three or four songs like "Green Green Grass Of Home" or "D-I-V-O-R-C-E" or "He Stopped Loving Her Today" in his whole career, I think he's done a good job. You can mention the title of others that you've had number one records and BMI awards on and most people wouldn't remember them. The main thing is you never know which one's going to do it.

There's nothing more interesting to people than love and dying and losing somebody that you love more than anything. Those, to me, are the things that would make chill bumps come up on your arm if you say it right.

You won CMA Song of the Year two years in a row for "He Stopped Loving Her Today," a song you co-wrote with Bobby Braddock. Describe that moment of walking up on stage.

Well, it was a great experience. I was surprised. But to get to do that a second year in a row was exciting. And you don't soak it in as much as you should have. You try to get out there and say the right thing without being overly thankful.

Because if you do, they're going to start playing the "exit stage left" music.

I don't mean this derogatorily against a song I co-wrote with Bobby, but I wouldn't trade "Green Green Grass Of Home" for two or three of "He Stopped Loving Her Today." I'm talking royalties and money, because there's no comparison. The Jones boys—Tom and George—are both great singers. But worldwide, Tom Jones is another Elvis.

You briefly ventured into music publishing with Green Grass Music.

I signed some good writers like Jim McBride, but it slowed me down in my writing. Nothing that I wrote during that time was big. Green Grass Music could have made it if I had stuck with it. I could have done like a lot of these people did that started publishing companies and later on sold it and made a lot. But I just felt like I needed somebody else to handle all that business part of it, so I went back with Tree.

Are you still playing pedal steel?

Never did play it well, so I just sat around and fooled with it. My wife bought me one. I couldn't even tune one good. But one of my great loves is steel guitar music. I wanted to be a good steel guitar player. I'm glad I skipped from it to songwriting, because I feel like steel guitar playing wouldn't have made me quite as much money to live on.

Steel guitar itself is not easy. If you play like Jerry Bird and Roy Williams and all of those people that didn't play pedal steel, it's still a hard thing to learn. Pedal steel makes it much more complicated, but it's prettier, I think.

I read you were an avid reader. Your bookcase can attest to that fact.

You can see I've got more books than the law will allow. I could start a bookstore. I read everything from Stephen King to Elmer Kelton, who is a guy that writes Westerns. He's from San Angelo, Texas. Larry McMurtry. I got all of his stuff. I try to read a few classics now and then.

Have you read any of the Harry Potter books?

No, I hadn't. I told my son, Troy, I said, "I've got to get me one to read even though it's for young children." You ever read *Watership Down*?

Oh, I love that book. In fact, I once had a rabbit named Hazel. Never go into a pet store around Easter or you'll come home with a rabbit.

I see an autographed picture of Jack Palance on your wall of fame.

Buddy Killen produced an album with him. He did a couple of my songs. He was around town for a week or so. We got to know each other pretty good. Went out to dinner with him and everything. He was a nice man. He didn't claim to be a real singer, but he could sing pretty good. He's a good actor, though. On his picture there, he wrote, "I wish I could act as good as you write."

This is a picture of the whole Putman clan made in Hot Springs, Arkansas. That's my mother, my daddy and my grandfather, a one-armed Methodist preacher. I must have been about five or six.

My dad's grandfather was a two-armed Methodist preacher.

Is that right?

Here's you and Roger Miller.

I used to go to Vegas with him. He wrote the liner notes on my first album. That was made in Las Vegas at the Landmark.

Billy Sherill writes "40 percent of a great team."

In his mind. I told him that the 40 percent was his.

There's Tammy Wynette.

We were very good friends. We used to see her all the time. She was a great gal. One of the most down-to-earth persons that I was ever around.

She wrote "To Curly & Bernice, For twenty-five years you have both been wonderful friends. I hope we have twenty-five more." That didn't work out, did it?

No. She was some little talented old gal, though. I loved her.

Photo courtesy of BMI Archives

John D. Loudermilk — Side A

Gatemouth Brown is a dear friend of mine. He's an interesting old fart. He's a deputy sheriff down in St. Tammany Parish, Louisiana. Gate wears his pistol and everything. He's just a great old guy. Son-of-a-bitch, he's so sweet.

I roasted Norro Wilson for Spina Bifida and I talked about the muse of Nashville. She's a girl in a cave under Broad Street combing her hair and humming. I told Gate about that recently. I said, "There's a muse in Nashville who's a goddess of a particular art form." Well, Gate is almost illiterate. He's just plain raw talent. He says, "Where is she at? I'd like to bite her on the ass and she if she hollers like a steel guitar." He's just so wonderful.

In this society we equate illiteracy with ignorance.

Oh, no, man. Illiteracy is with wisdom. Illiteracy means you haven't been book fucked. My daddy was illiterate. He couldn't read or write his name. I learned to appreciate real wisdom from that.

Gatemouth Brown is so unaffected by pop culture and he is in the middle of it. He has such clear vision of how things really are. Gatemouth says, "There are two types of people. There are those on the box and those on the floor. I've worked all my life trying to get off the floor onto the box. And then for me to stand up on the box and for them to tell me that everybody's standing on the floor, that's disgusting to me. Now when I go to the doctor, I'm on the floor and he's on the box."

He's a very interesting man to associate with. I've been associating with him since '72, '73. He comes and hangs out here. As a matter of fact, this is the Gatemouth House. He stays out here and writes, and we hang around together.

He's seventy-five; I'm sixty-five. I think everybody needs an older person. Whenever life gets fuzzy, you say, "How does this look?" And they tell you. They don't have to worry about it. They don't have to think about it.

How have you seen the music business change?

Old record producers used to make the decisions upon hearing the song with a guitar. They would make the decision and go in and cut the record. And many of the songs I had cut years ago, you'd go in and the artist would listen to it as part of the three-hour session. They would listen to songs and decide on one and cut it without rehearsing it.

But nowadays you have to go through a bunch of lawyers and bunch of accountants and a committee. There's two types of people: those who create and those who make money off of those who create.

You have to really fight today to keep art alive. And in spite of all of these different ways of doing it, I guess we have more art today than we've ever had. Certainly the songs are better today than they've ever been. The artists, minus the electronics, are better demonstrators of songs today. The vocalists are much better today than they used to be. The musicians are much better.

My son plays with Crystal Gayle on the road. He is so good. At times, I say, "Just play something for me, man." And he'll just play and just fool around. It's so warm to listen to him play. I'm very fortunate to have three boys all in the entertainment business. One is a printmaker. He's an etcher out in Austin. One is a musician on the road. Then I have another son who has a little CD company. My wife is an artist and we understand art. Art is what happens. How would you live without art?

I used to be a commercial artist. I started out as a sign painter and window dresser. Folk art. And then songwriting. That's all I've done since '56. Made a good living at it. Enjoyed every minute of it.

I've had to turn down a lot of possibilities and chances. George Hamilton IV and I started the first tour in Nashville of country music stars' homes. National Life said, "We want the tour. We're not going to buy it from you. We're going to take it from you, unless you come with it and run it and own half of it." I had to make a choice of being a songwriter or a tour director, so I turned that down.

Songwriting is the greatest art form. You can cover so much time. It's much better than a poem, because you tickle them while you're telling the poem. I took a course at a university in Louisiana in poetry. I was doing fine until the bastard found out who I was, and then it ruined his authority. Then he wanted to be a buddy, see. Solomon was a songwriter. David was a songwriter. Solomon was also a magician, did you know that?

Did not.

Songwriting to me is the most valid art form there's ever been and ever will be that I know of within our scientific knowledge. And I'm so glad to be a songwriter. I'm still writing songs, but they're not recordable songs. A sixty-five-year-old guy writing a song—how the hell can he write for a twenty-year-old mind to appreciate? It's hard.

I am writing a song now that I've been writing for twenty years. I've got enough money to where I can live fairly comfortably the rest of my life and my family, too. I can take time with songs now, so I overwrite. That's what wealth will do for you. Wealth will ruin you creatively. You have to stay poor as long as you're creating.

I'm directing my son's career over in Austin. I could leave him money right now and he'd never have to work anymore. And he wouldn't. He'd never make another print. You've got to be poor to produce. It just is that way. And once you get enough money to where you don't have to write, you will not.

I'm forcing myself to write this one piece that I'm writing now. And it's built on the Evangeline theme of Longfellow. It's about a French girl and a boy getting separated during their exodus from Nova Scotia on their way to Louisiana and looking for each other after death. So you can see where that's not recordable. But I'm into stuff much deeper than the country jockeys are playing. It's my duty as a writer to do that, and I said, "I don't have any choice."

I can stay stupid and write that shit back then. A lot of guys try to do that and it'll drive you crazy. But I don't want to stay stupid. I'm stupid enough as it is. I enjoy reading and I've known what my later part of my life is going to be like all my life and that's why I'm happy with the direction it's going.

Have you pursued other written art forms other than songs?

Yes, I have a book of poems in my shoebox. Right now they're asking me to do a movie. I have an Indian friend who has just retired from being a doctor. He's written an Indian movie and he just came back from a year in India producing. He said it was a life of hell. And I said, "Do I want to do that with the rest of my life? I don't think so." What the hell do I do? So I write a successful movie, then what? Then you got them desperately asking you to write a second successful movie. So I write a bomb movie. Well, that gives me an ego crush. Do I need that? I don't know if I need that or not.

See, I have to turn down careers. I turned down a career as an artist. I turned down a career as the Minister of Tourism for South Africa. I was over there in the '60s. I had a number one record for sixteen months over there. "Blue Train." I opened for Duane Eddy for a while, then he opened for me.

I had written "Blue Train" in the bathroom at Studio B. I needed another song to make up my album. We got over there and they took me from the airport to the damn railroad station. Said, "There it is." Here sat a yellow train, a red train, a green train, and a blue train for their illiterate black population that they sent out to the reservations at night to get them out of their damn hair and out of their cities. Just like we did the Indians. Their situation is very much like our Indians, not like our blacks. And they thought I had written about their blue train. So I drove the blue train and spent a wonderful six weeks over there.

They came to me and said, "You need to be Minister of Tourism." The kid who inherited all the diamond mines was a young kid then. He came in his red car and said, "We're so thrilled about South Africa."

I got back home and I had a stack of eight by tens that big with copy written on the homes that I'd be given if I were the Minister of Tourism. I was a dumb, uninformed American redneck who had come over there and loved what I saw, but they were not showing me the whole damn country. They only showed me the white part. They didn't show me the black.

So my first wife was very wise and said, "I don't want any part of that." She could see it objectively. See, I was over there and they fed me little movie starlets. Beautiful little girls. I hear from them now and they know Susan. And they kept me very happy. With unlimited wealth, you can absolutely buy a mind. There's no question about it. So they had me hoodwinked into thinking that their country was the most wonderful thing in the world.

But, God, were they racial. Oh, Jesus, you talk about racism. God Almighty, they had one waiter per person in restaurants. Four waiters would be standing around a table of four people. You'd dump your cigarette and it was taken. I mean, it was incredible. I've never seen anything like it. I wouldn't want to live around it, because you'd have to carry a pistol all the time.

So I've had a lot of chances in the business to expand out of songwriting.

But songwriting has been so good to me. It's given me so much time for reflection and reading. I'm so happy with the choices I've made.

This last year I've had two of the most important things— professionally and personally—happen to me. I wrote "The Lament of the Cherokee Reservation Indian (Indian Reservation)." That came out years ago by Paul Revere and the Raiders. You may remember the song.

I was eleven in '71. I remember it well.

The Chief of the Cherokee Nation, wrote me and said, "You're being given the Cherokee Medal of Honor." I went out to Tahlequah, Oklahoma, and met some of the most warm, real people. In this business, you have a lot of phony bastards. They're so phony that their skin is made out of plastic.

But these people out there don't look like Indians now. They're so watered down. They look like us. But they have something to prove. Trying to find your quest you've got to be screwed. If you're not screwed, then you have no drive. You have to be screwed to drive fast to beat your peers. It really is important. These people have been the Trail of Tears, have been sincerely taken advantage of. So I met these people. And it was the most meaningful award I've ever been given.

The second thing, I wrote a song as a result of a dear friend of ours out in Texas. We've been family friends for a long time. She called up and she said, "Look, I'm going to die. I want you to write me a song to die by." She had come off of dialysis. Her life had gotten so bad after her kidneys failed. It lowered the quality of her life to the place where she said, "To hell with it, I'm just going to stay off of it."

So I wrote her a song called "Over Yonder On The Other Side." I made a tape of it and I sent it to her and her son played it for her. She loved it.

She invited us down for her dying. Susan, my wife, held her hand and I held her other hand. Her kids were all around. And her son started playing this song. I didn't have it on a tape loop. You had to rewind it. It took her four-and-a-half hours to die and he played that song the whole time she died.

About two hours into her death, she had gotten to the place where she was so still and so glazed and so long between her breaths, that I said, "Surely she's passed." As far as her attention is concerned. So I said, "There's no use in playing the song anymore." I got sick of my own song. But she wanted it to continue. Four-and-a-half hours.

She died looking up through the window at some lights. She was seventy-five years old. It was the most incredible thing I've ever experienced.

Do you feel a certain kinship to the Native American?

I got into reading seriously about the Indians and found out that I had an ancestor on the Trail of Tears. A Stonewall Loudermilk. His wife was named Ruby. Both of them were in their nineties when they walked from Cherokee County, North Carolina, to eastern Oklahoma in the winter, and they came right down this road out here.

My first hit in Nashville was by Stonewall Jackson. Synchronicity. So I'm reading a lot about synchronicity now. I'm reading esoterically. I have been now for the last ten years. Heavily into it. We went to see the crop circles in Wilshire, England, a couple of years ago and ran into some old friends over there. They were following the same news we were.

Now I'm finding out from going through and putting my family's history together, they were all Cherokee. They were all intermarried with Indians up there in Cherokee County. And that was a real "social no" back then.

My grandmother is eighty-three. I was visiting with her in Atlanta and she began to tell me about my Cherokee ancestry.

Oh, good.

I read Trail of Tears years ago and really felt a connection. Now I'm just finding out some of the pieces of this puzzle.

Well, you know, I'm sixty-five and just finding out who I am. That's natural for you to find out more and more about yourself as you get older. Young and dumb rhyme. In a strange way, that is true. Thank God I didn't know what I know now when I was young. I'd have been in prison now for not obeying the law, I tell you.

"Youth is wasted on the young."

I want to live again. I really do. I'm not through this passage.

Do you think you'll come back to this place?

Oh, yeah, man. I've got to come back because I love to feel. The senses are so sharpened by reading what I'm reading that I've just got to keep on smelling and hearing and seeing and tasting and touching. I can't stop that. My soul's not there yet.

The gift of reading, to me, is one of the most precious gifts—book fucked or not.

The freedom of speech is our dearest heritage. Our whole business is built around it. If we didn't have freedom of speech, we couldn't have commercial songs. We couldn't have transmission of thought through the airwaves.

You're geographically close to Middle Tennessee State University. Are you involved in their recording industry program?

No, I'm not. I could be, but I'm not. We've been out here for eleven years. There's two types of horses. There's the long running racehorse who will run till he dies. Then there's the quarterhorse who will run like hell as fast as he can possibly run for a quarter of a mile, then he's exhausted. I am a quarterhorse.

Bill Denny and I started internships, where college kids come in and work in the business. And I am about ready to say that was a bad mistake, because they've watered down the form. In other words, the form should be kept alive by guys coming off the road from playing country music in front of mass numbers of people. Those guys coming off the road should come into the leadership of the record companies, instead of somebody academically protected and isolated coming in with their old Beatle records. I think that's a mistake and should be changed. And will be if I can talk to the right people.

You had your first cut while living in North Carolina.

I had my first two hits from North Carolina. I was working at the television station as a commercial artist doing scenery and slides and stuff. As part of my duties, I was performing on the television every day, on the local *today* show type thing.

I had written this song about a rose and a Baby Ruth. I don't know where the idea came from. I was going steady with a bunch of girls at the same time. My age group was strongly sexually driven and I don't know where the hell that came from. I haven't had to deal with it so much, but it's really been a problem for my generation.

You didn't need to be neutered.

No. That will come naturally.

I did "A Rose And A Baby Ruth" on television and Orville Campbell heard it. He had the newspaper in Chapel Hill in the '50s. Big college U.N.C. guy. Printed the yearbooks for the school. Knew the president and all. And he called about that song. He had a little artist, George Hamilton IV. So I wrote the song and it became a hit. I got into the music business in Nashville. But I started, really, in North Carolina. I came here with money in the pipe.

Nobody is found in the hinterlands now.

Orville later told me, he says, "George has charisma; you don't. You should stick to writing." I was insulted, but now, I see the wisdom of that. I am so glad he did that. It took a lot of courage for him to risk friendships by telling me the truth.

Boy, I had such good advice from Orville. He's dead now. I wish he was still alive. I'm going back and seeing a lot of my old friends. We're vacationing together and hot-tubbing together and going to mineral spas. Doing all the stuff that old guys do. We're hanging out. I've missed thirty years of them. I'm going back and finding out what they've done. And they all have lived terribly boring lives, have not raised their intelligence very much over the years.

I have just read myself silly. And everybody says, "Hell, you're reading yourself stupid." I said, "Well, maybe so. If that's the way you see it, then it's all right with me. If you say I'm reading myself stupid and I think you're stupid, then I'm getting something out of it."

In addition to Nashville and North Carolina, you lived for some time in south Louisiana.

Because of the quarterhorse thing. I came up here in '56 and I stayed until about '70. I had a divorce and a child custody case that was so exhausting.

I had run fourteen years. I had run hard. And, I mean, back then, man, as soon as that artist got off the plane, you kept that artist with you and kept him either drunk, whored up, doped up, whatever it took to keep them isolated from the other songwriters. There were only about a dozen songwriters in Nashville when I got here. So we all were competitors like we are now.

You weren't co-writing amongst yourselves.

Hell, no! Co-writing is for sissies. I don't know where the hell that came from. Co-writing waters down a concept so much you wind up with a bastard thought.

The best co-writes seem to be where someone brings the music to the table and someone brings the lyric to the table.

Yeah, but these bastards around here won't allow that. They all come in and sit around and try to bullshit each other and try to win intellectually. Nobody brings just music in. Nobody brings just words in. And the reason for that is pride.

I come in with a melody and a guy comes in with the lyrics. He wants to change my melody and I want to change his lyrics. Well, hell, that ain't the way you do it. You come in with the melody or the lyrics and you say, "Here it is." And it's in stone. It's finished. They take that and they work with art. They work with a piece of art and decorate your art. But the writers won't do that. They want to sit down and change each other.

In Nashville, the lyric is king. A great melody writer might feel inferior because he didn't contribute to the lyric.

Well, the British have a saying: "And this is the thing, isn't it?" It works on just about every statement that's said.

We need more nice melodies. We need melodies like fallen leaves. Things that are picturesque. And we should be more visual. We should be more theatrical in our presentations of ideas. It's wide open for real theater art—for magic and for playettes and little operettas. I've written a three-piece country operetta that takes ten-and-a-half minutes to do.

You were a recording artist for a season.

I turned down a performance career, because it's too damn hard. I don't have the energy for it. I made five or six albums for Victor.

With Chet Atkins?

And Bob Ferguson. I had a couple of hits. "Language Of Love" was a hit. But it was an "ooby, dooby, dooby" thing and I said, "Well, down the road, I'm going to be sixty-five some day. I don't want to be going out with my shirt unbuttoned down to my navel with gold chains singing this shit."

So I knew what I was going to be. I think your life is predestined whenever you're born and you have a few little choices in there just to keep you interested in choices. You're back here to live your karma that you earned in the last lifetime. I swear I believe that with all my heart.

I know that my second wife, to who I'm dearly devoted and attached to and engrafted onto, I know that she was sent to me as part of my karma payoff. We've been married twenty-eight years now. She was the positive payoff. My first wife was the negative payoff. Somehow I got involved with that. It could have been my kids needed to come through her. But this wife, when she walked in, damn, I knew it. And I said, "Oh, God!" I just saw what I was going to have to go through to live with her, but it has been absolutely wonderful.

Were you married when you met her?

I had just gotten divorced.

But I knew when I met this girl. I had prayed for her. That's the way you get them. You pray for them. And I prayed and meditated desperately for this woman. When she walked into my life, it was a tremendous jolt. I knew. I knew that the rest of my life was going to be spent with that woman.

Of course, men are so romantic. They're more romantic than women. But she knew it, too. I would advise marriage over any other alternate lifestyle. I really would. That definite commitment to another individual is a very holy and noble thing. I enjoy every minute with her. She's such a wonderful person.

What made this marriage different from the first?

The first one was under an old system of beliefs that were given to me by my family that were horseshit. And I changed. Susan, too. She had come through with a heavy Church of Christ attitude. I had come through with the Salvation Army fundamentalist sense of values.

We sat down and we said, "Look. That shit didn't get it. We know we don't have to keep that going." So we said, "What does work?" We started reading. We read a little book called *The Lessons of History* by Will and Ariel Durant. They wrote ten wonderful volumes of the history of the world. And we absorbed that book word for word while we were together. We would look up dates, wars, movements that we didn't know about and read extensively of those. From that little, tiny book and the complete works of Carl Sandberg, we made our new laws to go by.

Mutual agreements?

Mutual agreements. Exactly right. And it's just worked beautifully for us.

But the Indians, I am so thrilled with their culture. I'm going to show you something after while that's going to blow you away.

What we're talking about now? I had a senior moment.

We were discussing the horseshit of the old marriage and the new agreements that you and Susan made.

After this divorce and child custody case, I laid back.

I'm assuming you did not get custody.

Oh, yeah.

You got custody?

Yeah.

Quite unusual for a father from your era.

Exactly. And it was so exhausting. You can imagine what it would have been like. But after that, I was so tired that we said, "To hell with it." Susan and I stored our furniture and moved out and went to England for a year. Put our boys in school over there. Man, we had the best time. Then we came back and I touched base in Nashville and I did not want to stay.

So how did you land in Lafayette, Louisiana?

Honest to God we did this. We took a road map and put it on the wall of the door of the men's room in the airport in Latvia. We threw a damn dart at the thing and it landed just north of Lafayette, Louisiana, in a little place called Sunset. Well, we went to Sunset and I couldn't live there. It was only a village. So we went to Lafayette just three or four miles south of there. We rented an old history professor's house built in '44. It was the first Hayes Town house in Louisiana. He became the architect for Louisiana. All the bigger office buildings and all the big governmental buildings and big homes was built by Hayes Town, a remarkable French architect. So this was his first house.

Lafayette was just wonderful. We raised our children there. When they got into college, we came on back up here and started the Songwriters' Guild chapter in Nashville. I had been screwed so heavily by publishers. All of my peers had. It had killed many of them being imprisoned by long-term contracts that were unfair. It was indentured servitude is what it was. Professionally enslaved.

Why?

Well, the nature of the contract was if you sign this contract, and you made x amount of money, then you had to pick up the next contract. It was one on top of the other as you continued growing in your income. You were working yourself into slavery; and therefore, your copyrights and your children's copyrights into slavery.

Well, I said, "I am not going to die as a result of this. I'm going to start a songwriters' organization that will tell writers about their contracts." So we started checking around and we founded a songwriters' guild. It was called the American Guild of Composers. Irving Berlin and the Gershwin Brothers started it. It had worked in New York and in California, but it could never get into here because of the Jews. I used to laugh and tell them that's what the publishers said down here. "We don't want the Jews coming down and taking over."

Don George used to say, "And sure enough, the Jews took over." A wonderful old man. Brass headed cane. He had a version of "The Yellow Rose of Texas." He was kind of a gopher for Duke Ellington. Had his pants split right here up to there. They draped over his shoes. He was an old beatnik and he carried a gold-headed cane and wore a pan sideways and said, "Daddy O." And shit like that. It was just wonderful. He was real.

And we got in with these people up there in New York and found out that Nashville needed the guild. So we started it in our apartment. Our phone was the first guild's telephone number in Nashville. Now there's a thousand members, or several hundred members anyway.

How did you get out of your exclusive songwriting contract?

It just finally ran out. See, a writer has a run of time when his dialogue, his jargon is contemporary with the age group of the people who are buying the product that he's producing for. You follow me, know what I'm saying?

Yes, sir.

After that musical jargon and literary jargon runs its course, and then the words start changing and the musical impressions start changing, then his run is over. Most writers have a run of ten years. The stuff that they listened to as kids, they use from that to make their run. After they use that up, then their run is over and kids are coming along with new impressions. So there is a run that all writers have.

I had about a fifteen, twenty year run. I've been very fortunate. I think studying classical music, classical guitar and having the old Victorian hymns at the turn of the century helped me tremendously. Plus, the early black rhythm and blues really helped me. Eddy Arnold was my big flame as a fan. Roy Acuff I liked and Bill Monroe I adored. I came over here and signed with Roy Acuff and that's part of the thing.

I got screwed and so did the rest of the guys. Yeah, we got screwed. We got screwed out of half of our life's earnings. But everybody else got screwed. I mean, I wasn't the only one that got screwed and there were guys in California getting screwed. But I have resolved that.

See, copyright is a brand new thing as far as creativity is concerned. Henry VIII—as soon as the printing press was invented—he got five of them for his friends, man. And they started gathering these old folk tunes up. Cecil

Sharpe and the Lomax Brothers, they came through. What did they do? They stole the publishing on all of these folk tunes. That's all the hell they did. They weren't after preserving any kind of literary stuff. I've talked to folk collectors before. They're into the publishing of it. And that's what Ralph Peer is in the Hall of Fame. He's gone all over South America stealing the publishing from those poor bastards down there, those old guys up on mountains and stuff. That's the duty of a folk collector.

And as part of the splash-off from that, people hear the music and that gives it another generation of acceptance. And that's not bitter. That's the truth. That the inside. I know. I know publishers and I know how they think.

It's not to save the folk music of the working class. They couldn't care less. They want the copyright earning power for the publishing end of the copyright.

We started the guild and we got threats on our life. We put our energy that was killing my peers into starting the guild here. Susan was the first director and I was the first vice-president from here. We went to New York every six weeks and were in on all the change in the copyright law. It was wonderful, but then I got tired. I'm a quarterhorse.

What year did you come back to Nashville?

I came back in '80.

So Loudermilk's been gone a decade and comes back as a troublemaker.

Hell, yes. I hope so. And I had a couple hits, too, as a writer then. I got some things recorded that were published with Acuff-Rose. Forever. But my basic run was over. Now I have my own publishing company and I had just had a Jimmy Buffett cut the other day on his new album.

As a publisher, what would you like to see change?

We need to build standards. The publishers are so eat up with new writers coming in that the song is over—Boom!—it's gone. And this is what Wesley Rose was so wise at. Yeah, he was a thief. I don't think he had any morals. I think he was amoral. I think he hated his father. His father, Fred Rose, was a delightful, wonderful man. He was a writer. Boudleaux Bryant knew him real well and so did Fred Foster. They said he was a marvelous man, a real good man. His son came along and I think he just wanted to be opposite from his daddy or something.

But Wesley Rose knew how to publish. By God, he was the last great publisher that Nashville's ever had. They don't make them now like that. And the reason I went with Acuff-Rose is because he promised me things orally and didn't write it down, but he promised it orally. His answers were not relative to the questions. He would tell you one thing, and when you got your contract, it said something else. But he said that's the way legalese is and that it has to be that way. A young kid coming through from the ghetto would sign anything to get a break. So you sign away your entire life's efforts. It's happened. It's happening now. It hasn't changed. The same story. The same song. Just a different arrangement.

Anyhow, I had a real good run with Acuff-Rose because I knew Wesley as a publisher. Not as a friend, as a publisher. When he was on your side, you were all right. But when you were in contractual opposites, you were screwed. Pretty much so because he was a sharp guy. He was sharp. He was wrong, but he was sharp.

He was a good publisher, and he believed in getting songs cut over and over and over. Hank Williams's catalog was not all that great as songs were concerned. But what the publisher did with those songs. Every artist that Wesley produced, he cut Hank Williams songs. He cut Boudleaux Bryant songs. He cut John D. Loudermilk songs. He cut Mickey Newberry songs. He cut Roy Orbison songs. Everly Brothers songs. He continued building those copyrights. And today we're enjoying the good life because of his efforts.

Did he own Hickory Records?

Yes. He did. And we had a lot of the Hickory hits. We wrote and produced them. But we didn't get anything for producing them. Producers weren't getting points back then. They were just getting salaries.

Wesley Rose was caught in a paradigm shift of business morals. And it was the old way from Henry VIII to Queen Anne. I was working under those copyright understandings in 1909 when all my songs were signed. All of us were. Imagine what 1909 automobiles looked like. So the new copyright law was necessary and we were instrumental in getting it passed. We put all of our efforts toward that. After we got that done, I got tired of going to New York. I hate the goddamn town, and I just said, "I am not going to lower the quality of my life by coming up here anymore. I just can't do it anymore." So I turned it over to the younger kids and let them run it. Susie and I came out here eleven years ago and have just lived in heaven.

Have you ever lived in the country before?

I have not, but I intend to. Growing up, I used to go to the country every Sunday for lunch at my grandparents. I spent many, many hours next door to a cow pasture. Bovine make good neighbors.

When we moved to Louisiana, the schools were falling apart, the cities were burning, the blacks were raising hell, and it was just going down the tubes as far as the white guy my age could see. So we pulled our kids out of school. We built a school in Louisiana. We got within a local family of teachers who had five children and we went out into their rice field and built a big old wooden house and started a school and we all taught. We had twenty-one students and thirty teachers. Everybody taught what they knew. It didn't matter what they knew; they taught what they knew.

So you had a village home school.

Yes, we did. We put our children in that and they were raised in that. They did French folk dances, instead of running into each other and brutalizing their future bodies. Mike learned all of his French music down there. It was just wonderful. We just enjoyed it so much.

I would seriously consider, if I were a young parent now, some way to get that child home schooled in some area. The teachers now are so hampered to be politically correct about everything.

"God winks at the survivor." Durant says that. Hell, he doesn't give a damn if it's politically correct or not. God winks at the survivor. Isn't that wonderful?

And a lot of that surviving is not politically motivated. In other words, it's very brutally motivated. We have two Great Pyrenees dogs out here, a German Malamute combination and three cats. We have extended our understanding and our education past the human sphere with these animals. It's incredible what you can learn from an animal. We've got a dead possum under our deck up at the house. Stinking to high heaven. The dogs can't get under there because they get into wires and pipes and stuff. I've got to get it out. But it doesn't really matter. It used to offend me to smell carnage. But out in the country, you're lenient. You become different out in the country.

I would highly advise you to consider that as you get old. And you will. With your knowledge of yoga, you're understanding geometry, you're understanding physics, you're understanding medical things. You're understanding a lot when you understand yoga. Yoga is not taught enough at schools. It's not taught enough in our current society. So you don't get the truth about yoga until you happen upon it or you search for it.

You have to search for the truth. They give you truth pills as a kid. You eat that truth pill and you don't know if it's a lie of not. And most of it is a lie.

Once you understand the truth of a certain thing, then you'll suspect the truth of other things. And that's enlightenment. You'll wind up in the country.

Yoga changed my life, and in some ways, it's brought me home.

Define home.

Home in terms of the values you're talking about, like country and simplicity. Living close to nature. Not only did I experience that growing up, but I think it is compatible with our spirit. Yoga created change.

Define change.

Less materialistic. Developing a meditation practice opened up a lot of creativity. It put me in touch with synchronicity in my life, which I believe is going on in everyone's life. They might not be aware of it, but it's there nevertheless.

I began to have experiences that are intricately interconnected and synchronistic, like your Stonewall Loudermilk/Stonewall Jackson story. I had experiences like that with Columbine High School.

You went to the high school where they had the shooting?

I visited it.

After the shooting?

Yes. I was in Littleton, Colorado, six weeks after the massacre and I visited the school. I went to stand as a silent witness against the violence. People with good intentions were visiting from all over the world. It definitely created sacred space. I eventually wrote a song about it called "Columbine Blue."

Songwriting is the greatest dodge of psychiatric care that you can imagine. You'll never have to go to a psychiatrist if you're a songwriter. If you tell the truth, you'll just stay empty all the time. Therefore, you can get more in. Your vessel will be available if you empty it. That's right. That's the truth. Songwriting has just saved my life. I wouldn't change a thing in my life if I could do it over.

Grandkids at this point?

No, not yet. I told them, I said, "Don't you bring any kids home for me to raise. Put all your time in your career right now. Have your kids after you get older. Get you some money ahead of time, so that you don't have to make a choice between your kid and the money."

You came late in life.

Yeah, I came late in life. But I had children early in my career and I had to pay so much attention to my career. That and my sex drive. I avoided the children a lot when I shouldn't have. I caused 50 percent of the breakup with my first wife.

In Louisiana, when you were teaching school you were getting quarterly royalty checks in the mail.

Oh, yeah.

I'm from Louisiana.

Where abouts?

North Louisiana.

You're not from the Louisiana that I know then.

Correct. Go south of Alexander and the state changes.

Hot Wells, Louisiana. The best mineral water in the world. But that's another thing.

They know how to eat in Louisiana. No question about it.

When we were living down there, we found a family-owned restaurant in Lafayette with big oil paintings in gold frames of the family members. We ate lunch there every day for five years. Until the two sons went to the Culinary Institute of America up in Hyde Park. They took one chicken and sixteen months later, what they were cooking had a part of that chicken. However minuscule, it was a part of that chicken. That's their whole deal: to keep what you have left over from a meal and make another meal from it.

They came back and one was the cook and one was the maitre d'. They started wearing tails down there for lunch. And one boy said, "I'm going to introduce you to a wine a day." I was kind of somebody down there. I mean, he had heard about us and everything.

You had written popular songs for goodness sake. You had number one hits.

Right. So he said, "I'd like for you to give me some feedback on the wine." It was the most wonderful wine, Hügel. H-u-g-e-l with the two dots over the "u." So I brought up a case of that to Nashville, and I gave it around. A day later I went and looked in the refrigerators and I found bottles with no corks in them. Nobody understood the wine. And I realized how terribly authentic Nashville is. See, we're the crudest fuckers in America, right here in the middle of this state. And I'll tell you why. The sharp ones were left over on the coast. It took crude bastards to get over the mountains. Man, you had to be crude and hard to get over those mountains. That's why the hillbillies have such coarseness about them.

That's why it's wonderful when musicians and writers come in from California and from London and from Connecticut and from Oregon and bring in their music. It just invigorates and makes our music more civilized. But when it started out it was really coarse. And it's held on to a lot of the coarseness.

But if you're into yoga, and you're into other things that have opened your mind, and then you settle down in Tennessee, it takes a stretch. It takes a negative stretch. And that's what's so hard about living here—the narrow view that you're forced into doing. That's why we live out here in the country where we can be natural.

Phil, when we go through that gate down there, it's like you enter another world, another country with different laws and different languages. It's like going off in a fast plane and landing in another country. So this is our little place that we have identified as being our free world out here.

You have substantial acreage.

Yeah, we got a lot of acreage. And we got a lot of woods. We've got the biggest chinkapin oak in Tennessee. It's eighteen feet around.

Your ancestors might have walked by it on the Trail of Tears.

Could have. We've had tree huggers come out. We have a lot of friend who are Yuppies. We have a lot of tree hugger friends. People who are ecologically driven. And there's nothing wrong with that. But they come out and they hug this tree. They get poison oak off the tree, but they hug it and I understand it. It's a wonderful living thing. It's been dying ever since we've owned it, or since we've been around it. But anyhow, I don't know. I'm probably wandering. If you're interviewing songwriters though, I'm giving you some good shit.

Yes, you are!

Yes, I am. There is a songwriting thing down at Florabama Club down in Florida. You know about that?

Sure.

They've tried to get me down there for several years and it's nice to be wanted. But I wouldn't go down there with these bastards. Every one of them are competitors. I look at a songwriter just like a real estate guy would look at another real estate guy. This idea of "Let's get all the songwriters together. They'll know each other. We'll buy them a whore and some drugs and booze and an apartment, and they'll come down and they'll make records for me that I can sell after they're dead." That's bullshit to me. I said, "No, man. I see through that. I don't want to do that."

I gave up that business of singing in front of people, because I'm gifted as a writer, not as a singer. I don't have the charisma and the stamina to ride those big buses, man. I ain't going to do it. My son's riding those big buses, and it's horrible. It's not a quality life. When we were young, that was the only way to get out of Durham. Either play ball or play music, but play something.

I don't know what I'd have done if I'd had to stay in that place, man. We went back for my fortieth high school anniversary reunion and I saw my dear friends that were so cool when I left. They were cool. They've been cool in the same place, man. For forty years. They are forty years cool, man, I'm telling you. That is so sad.

What's cool to you?

I'm into Chopin real big. The only music I listen to now is classical music. I don't want to hear folk music, because you can't define who is real and who's not. But classical music, you can define who's real and who's not. I like new age music and I love folk music. I love blues and I love bluegrass. But there's a lot of people in it who have never worked a day in their lives, and they don't know what the pathos of the working class is all about.

But classical music, you don't have to worry about that. Yo Yo Ma is a great musician. He studied to be that way. And he's damn good. Did you see he left his cello in the damn cab? Did you see that? He left a million-and-a-half-dollar cello in a cab in New York. Walked off, just bopped off, man. And had to call the police to get it. The guy didn't know what he had or he'd been in Mexico by now.

We missed Pavaratti in New Orleans when we were living down there. This new guy came to America. A tenor. We didn't know anything about him at the time, so we gave our tickets away. His first tour. But classical music just elevates my spirit. It's like going to the mountains when the leaves are beautiful. We just came back from Asheville. I think this is a thing for older people.

As you get older and you see something beautiful, it just takes your breath and you get light on your feet. What do they call it in the psychic field?

Levitation.

Levitation. It's akin to levitation.

We found a place called Hot Springs, North Carolina. Just over the border, just east of Knoxville. Out by the French Broad River. Deep tubs out there. The water runs in. The water runs out. There's no chlorine. There's no chemicals. It's just all mineral water. And you feel so wonderful when you get out. It must have lithium in it. There's springs down in Mexico that are just lithium. You go down there, you drink it, you bathe in it, you eat it.

Just north of Alexandria, Louisiana, the state owns a thing called Hot Wells. And it's closed down now. It had a big commercial three-story hotel, a big Olympic-size swimming pool. Twenty years ago they would wrap you in sheets and give a massage for seven dollars. I went up there one time with my father-in-law, mother-in-law and Susan. We checked in, the woman said, "Do you have any scratches or cuts on you?" I said, "I have a scratch right here on my hand." She says, "Now it's okay. I'm not saying that that's bad. I'm just saying 'Look at it when you come out.'" We went in there and took a thirty-minute bath. The water was iron red. Awful, nasty looking with items floating around in it. I came out and the scratch was gone. I'm not kidding you.

The Indians started it, but it is sitting down there waiting for some young person to take that over. You could buy that whole thing I bet you for a million dollars or less. The Longs used to go there to sober up. It's wonderful. They have a campground and everything. But it's just sitting there closed up waiting for somebody to come along.

The young people in this country are starting to understand the beauty of mineral water. The cleanliness of it. And it comes from deep in the earth. And, buddy, it's really good. It's really wholesome. It's a noble pursuit. I'd just love to live in a tub of it, man. I really would. I wish we could hit it out here. I'd drill as far as it took.

Speaking of water, when did your penchant for chasing hurricanes come about?

It came about from a trip when I was working at WTVD in Durham. I was a photographer and would cover news. They sent me to the Outer Banks to cover Hurricane Hazel in 1955. I was on a wooden bridge with this white station wagon and it started moving. The bridge blew out ahead of me and I called on the radio for the Coast Guard and they came out and got me. That was the first hurricane that I was ever in, and I felt the God Spirit. I felt the enormity of it. It was way bigger than me.

I don't have the words to describe it. Imagine seeing a hurricane for the first time and being thrilled by the bigness and the hugeness and the godliness of it. I started going to experience that. I've been to, I don't know, twenty or thirty hurricanes. Just within the last few years we found out that there are tornadoes in them and I haven't gone to anymore, because I don't go to a tornado.

I'd usually go to a courthouse or a church. Somewhere where they were prepared. And I would volunteer to help people evacuate their homes. Ride big old military trucks. It was a lot of fun, man. I helped deliver a baby girl in Jacksonville Beach, Florida, during a hurricane one time. It blew the antenna off my car.

I see God in these enormous things, and I just love what we call God.

John D. Loudermilk, right, with Eddy Arnold.   Photo courtesy of BMI Archives.

John D. Loudermilk — Side B

You ever heard of Art Bell?

No.

Art Bell has a talk radio show at night and I sit and listen from twelve o'clock midnight to five o'clock in the morning.

You're a night owl.

Well, I've arranged my sleeping around his radio show.

When do you sleep?

I sleep from nine o'clock to midnight and I sleep in the afternoons say from whenever I get sleepy to around six o'clock. But I sleep, because I'm a quarterhorse.

It's UFO's, it's aliens, it abductions, it's conspiracy theories, it's Roswell, it's all the new stuff that young people and researchers are delving into. Thank God for Jimmy Carter with the Freedom of Information Act. That's a wonderful thing. That and the Habitat for Humanity. He's going down as a good president.

I've always said, "As a president, he was a great home builder."

That's exactly right.

I met him at Emory University. He's a genuine guy.

Yes, he is. I want to go down for his Sunday school class.

That would be cool.

Yeah, it would be. I want to do that sometime when I know he's there. But I've been reading on this subject for a long time and it's just the most overwhelming thing. I just can't wait to get to my books. I read several at a time. But anyhow, we were talking about Art Bell and what he was talking about. What the hell were we talking about?

UFO's and four hundred thousand years ago.

Yeah. What the hell did all of this have to do with songwriting? Well, it has a lot to do with songwriting. A damn lot to do with songwriting. Because songwriting is, no question about it to me, the most valid art form. And I guess I would feel that way, being a songwriter. But it is the most valid art form.

Graphic arts can't touch songwriting. Because you go stand in front of a painting, so fucking what? You don't hear any beat. You don't hear any tune. You're not tickled into delightfully listening or watching. Now, if paintings had tunes, that would be different. But a song, you can say so much and tickle the person into liking it and believing it and concentrating for three minutes.

So do you believe there's still U.F.O. visitations and the crop circles are coming from that?

Well, I don't know what crop circles are coming from. I think they're military. I went over and I talked to a lot of people. I've noticed a lot of extreme jealousy and very base emotions among the people who follow that. Enough to where it turned me off. I've had a career of singing in England over the years and my biggest fan was the head of the BBC.

Phil Louis and his wife, Diane, would set up specials for me. I'd go over on vacation, and these eighteen wheelers would pull up at a little theater out in the country somewhere and I would do a special. He'd run it on BBC three or four times that year. Then next year the same thing. So I've had kind of a nice career over there with that.

Phil retired and it scared him to death. He's frightened to death he's going to die because he had twenty-six producers working for him. He's used to allocating great ideas. Go out and produce this and watch it on television. So he's become addicted to this creativity.

He called and said, "I'm retiring and I want to go to Ireland. Where would you like to go?" I said, "I've studied stone circles and I've started studying crop circles. I'm reading about circles. I'd like to go to Ireland because they've got a lot of them over there." They've got a thousand stone circles in the British Isles. A thousand stone circles. He and his wife set it up, so we went over. We went all over Ireland and we saw these wonderful stone circles. You'd sit in these circles and you'd look up on the hill and you'd see a stone up there. You'd walk back and you'd sight behind this stone and it was a in line with that stone. And then you'd see the sun come up behind that stone and up on to it.

I mean, it goes thousands of years back and you would live with that person. That person's alive that set that alignment. And you just were introduced to him. It was the most delightful study in the world.

What about the crop circles?

We wanted to go to Abrey where 90 percent of the big crop circles happened. Phil was frightened and scared about it. He thought it was a bunch of hippies that were trying to take him to the cleaners or something. So Susan and I had to go back the next year. He lives five or six miles from Abrey, so we went on to his house.

We went over the next year without him knowing it and hung out at Abrey. It rained for fourteen days. And all we saw out of the window was no crop circles, but a flower on a tree. It opened up for fourteen days. That's all we saw. I said, "I'll be damned. I came over here to see that flower bloom." I don't know what the meaning of it is, but I know it's meaningful.

The apparent purpose of the trip is never the real purpose of the trip.

The lesson.

I'm sure some people would be incredibly pissed that they didn't see a crop circle and it rained for fourteen days.

That's right.

But how can you be judgmental when you see nature work so subtlely? It's not waiting on your determination of what the facts are. It's there all dressed up.

I almost had my thread back. It was some pretty good thought, too. Oh, yes. I just read about Singing Wolf. He was on Art Bell. I made it back. That's wonderful when you can make it back.

Absolutely.

He was on Art Bell and died five days later. I heard his five-hour spiel on what he learned. He was the Hopi elder that has retained much of their culture, their prehistoric culture. Old culture as anybody has. And he quoted Faulkner. Very interesting—Hopi and Faulkner. Faulkner said, "The day they built the courthouse and the jail in our county was the day the little man quit thinking on his own." That was the day that he quit making judgments because he was enforced. The law was enforced. He had to obey the law. Well, you could say the church is the same way.

And Singing Wolf said that there is no such thing as right or wrong. He said, "There is nature and in the heart is where you go to decide what's right and wrong." So, sure, murder's wrong. But your heart will tell you if you murder somebody or get ready to murder somebody. It will sure tell you that that's wrong. It's wrong to steal. It's wrong to lie. It's wrong to do all those things.

But we're overburdened with laws in this country—all over the world— because there's too damn many people. We have to have laws to have bumpers or we'll crash into each other. But in nature, before there was too many people, the primitive man—those words don't match—but the old man would go to his heart when there was a decision or judgment to be made. And I try that now. I do that all the time in my meditations. And it's there. It's very simple to make a decision now. You just go inward.

You can't rationalize it and say, "Damn, but I'd like it to be this." If you do that, you're wasting your time. It's the same as me blowing a whistle for my dog and him coming running because he heard a whistle. He doesn't know how that works. And so something is starting to tell me things. I'm seeing lights appear. This is very much in the norm for people who are reading into what I'm reading. They hear voices or they see lights or they hear melodies or they hear sounds. It's very current. Over in the crop circles, they get into crop circles, they see the same thing. I've talked to people who study them over there, who are in them all the time, and they're nuts.

To be a songwriter and to hear stuff and put it down is nuts. But that's accepted insanity. And this is not insanity, but it would be thought of by people in the 1400s as insanity. Even if you were Christian, they would think of you as being insane if you were hearing something that they didn't say.

So Singing Wolf.

This is where Singing Wolf is so right. Because I don't believe there is evil or there is good. I think it's all good. And this is the way the animals feel.

They don't feel it's wrong to go out there and stomp something and just chew its head off. They don't see that as being wrong. That's just part of nature.

The Earth religions were into nature and they understood that—where we don't. We've been de-evolved down. Christianity, I think, has really done that to us. I really do believe that. The whole concept of Christ has been lost. We don't know what first-century Christianity was like.

The Church of Christ has tried to go back and get it. And I think this thing of not having music in their services—other than the human voice—is so noble and so perfect and so valid. I rather like the Quakers' way of doing it. Of just being quiet. I think Buddha found that. Just be quiet and just go into the center. The little voice is there. It'll tell you.

And it all goes in cycles. That's why death is not a dangerous thing to me. I don't fear that at all. As a matter of fact, I kind of look forward to it. Huxley said before he died, "And now, the great mystery."

See, we are so materially focused on this body as being what's alive. Hell, this is just what our soul is living in and our soul has been alive since the universe has been. I know that this is definitely not the end of life when this body dies. That's foolish to believe that. I don't think you can die. That's why criminals and murderers and people like that are doomed to live, see. They're doomed to die by us, but they're doomed to live by nature. You understand that?

I struggle with the death penalty. But if a person was truly guilty of murder supported with DNA testing, maybe society should take them out, so they can get a do-over. You're not really killing them, you're just saying, "Game over."

Yeah, exactly. Just go somewhere and stay over in death for a while.

In this reading that I'm doing, I have read both sides of "Who are these aliens?" and "What are they here for?"

You say the aliens are here?

Oh, yeah, they're among us as we speak. I don't know how many is in this room right now.

Invisible.

That's right. Non-entity. They're not into their five senses. But there's one sense that they are into, and that is the sixth sense. You can feel them at times and you know they're around. But the Christians, the Catholics, call it your guardian angels. The spiritualists call them your guides. My mother and daddy's picture is this far from me at night when I sleep. I pray to them and pray through them and pray for them.

So you're saying there are invisible alien beings here from other solar systems, as opposed to the spirit hanging around after the body dies.

Well, your spiritualists think that they're the ones that have not gone over, have not let go of this existence on this side. People who study this think there's seven civilizations represented in our visitors. They're not just from one place. And they can go and come out of this reality.

The boys down in Florida at the Eglin Air Force Base are going and coming with their triangular machines. We have reverse engineered the crashed ships that we found that have been hung up in this reality. Philip Corso just wrote a great book about this, *The Day After Roswell*. I don't know if you heard of him. He was Colonel Corso. He was the guy that was given the technology to give to the corporations of America and all over the world to reverse engineer these things. Night vision was one of them.

Susan and I interviewed Jesse Marsail for four hours. You know who he was?

No, sir.

He was the guy in charge of public relations for Roswell Air Force Base when the two spaceships crashed. He went out and picked up the garbage and brought it back in his old Buick convertible. He saw the three dead and the one still alive. That was July 5, 1947. And that was when this latest wave of this sort of activity started. We're in the middle of it now. It was in existence all the way back into prehistoric times. We've seen examples of this sort of mythology—it's been relegated to the myth—but it was actual reality. We know now that this has been going on for probably millions of years. Probably as long as we have.

Forbidden Archeology is a book that tells of pieces of coal that break open in people's fireplaces that has gold chains. It takes sixty-six million years to make coal. They're finding things now—like a series of brown balls in South Africa. They found thousands of them by now in the gold mines in South Africa. They're hollow metal balls about three inches around. The metal is so hard you can't scratch it with diamonds even. The ball has three bands around the middle part. And they don't know what they're from, but they're finding them inside the veins of the ore that the gold comes from. It's incredible.

But this reverse engineering from Roswell—the computer chip is part of it, the night vision is part of it.

So they're working backwards from this technology.
That's right.

To catch up to it.
That's right. And that's why our government is being quiet. They're desperately trying to get technology that will enable them to compete with whatever these things are.

The space program is part of that?
That's right. Exactly. That's part of the front. They're already shooting at each other. I mean, there's films. An astronaut took a video of a flying saucer coming across. He's looking down at the Earth *now*, flying saucer comes over and here comes the thing out toward the flying saucer. The flying saucer holds and goes that way. Outruns the damn shot. That's already been filmed.

Now, here's the good thing about it. I've read both ends of it. Should we shoot back? What are these bastards here for? Over here, you've got the tree huggers and the pro-peace people saying, "No, they're here to help us."

A guy named Jacobs is the head of the, I think, history department at Cornell University and has written a book on it. Now that's radical at this time in our history. He's taking a hell of chance and he's catching flack. The head of the psychology department at Harvard, John E. Mack, has come out with a book where he's interviewing twelve people who have been abducted. And he just peers in the box, you know? They're just jumping all over his ass. But that's the job of a hero.

So I've read this whole scope. I've read the extremes. The guy over here's saying, "They're going to take over our planet." And this guy over here, a Dr. Greer from North Carolina, is saying, "If they wanted our planet, they would have taken it over before we got the atomic bomb and while there were just a few people here." That's valid. That's very positive.

Maybe they haven't perfected the sauce to serve us with.
If you put it in the context of homo sapiens, we have been a people of conquest, especially the white man. See Manifest Destiny.
Well, yeah.

Our ships must have looked like a spaceship to the Indians.

It was a spaceship.

And if you take that model, we're screwed.

That's what Jacobs is saying. He's saying that he thinks it's about twenty years off.

Down in Del Fuego, South America, at the tip, when they saw Cook come around the corner with his big sailing ship, they just looked away. They thought it was a mirage. They couldn't believe their eyes. They just looked away.

They had no idea how fucked they were going to be.

Oh, God. Yeah, that's right. And we probably don't know. Ignorance is bliss. We probably don't know how fucked we're going to be. But if these abduction stories are true, which I believe they are. I really do. I believe they really are. We are being changed for a reason. And nobody knows exactly what that reason is. But we are being changed.

I can tell you right now, kids that come along and write songs are so far ahead of what my concepts were. That wasn't true between my age and the guys back in the '20s. There wasn't that much difference in our songs. But there's worlds of difference in the songs here now. They're much more spiritual. They're much more wisdom oriented. The visors have been broadened.

But that was present in the music of the '60s.

Yeah, I know. But I believe that there's genetic manipulation in the kids that are coming along now. They're all so much more literate now. They seem to have a wisdom now that they didn't have then. And I don't know what that's from. There's these people in this genre of literature that are saying that it's from the genetic manipulation. And you know if they've done sheep, they're doing humans.

What is happening to the people who are being abducted?

There are several scenarios. One, and a lady that we know right here in Murfreesboro, she's been taken four times right here in Murfreesboro. She worked in accounting over here at the university. She is a nervous wreck. She's scared to death of this. She said the last time she was taken that she saw stitches. They call them grays, and this gray was over her doing the physical examination. And she said she saw stitches in the eyes, in the big almond-shaped eyes, where the dark part was stitched on to the gray part. She's afraid of government danger. She's afraid. She's just afraid. She's scared to death.

She said she's seen military officers standing behind these grays. The patch where their names were you could see underneath there was light green. Now, if that be the case, our government is doing a lot of this examination, this manipulation of their time.

The first time that she was ever taken she was working at a dime store on the base in Tullahoma and a guy came up to her and said, "I can get you a better job than this." He said, "We're landing a shuttle here and I'd like for you to go to it." She was not married then. Strangers approached her and she's confused about how she got into this. There's missing time in her mind. There's missing reasons. There's missing direction.

And then, of course, this has led me into another field of mind control, which is just incredible.

Please proceed.

There's a girl who has been used in the mind control experiments in this MK Ultra Majestic Program that's going on. She mentions people that I know personally in her book, and she has not been sued by anybody. And she's bringing in personalities that we know like Barbara Mandrell and Charlie Pride. I sang at a CMA convention in Washington, D.C., at the White House. While we were singing, Senator Byrd came out to play his fiddle. And he had a little Mongoloid guy carrying a red velvet pillow with a fiddle on it. Now this was in '78. It was just not the right thing to do to be seen with a little Mongoloid guy with a red pillow with your fiddle on it. And she's saying that he is her controller. And she tells things about him such as that a person off the street couldn't know.

Who is the controller?

Senator Byrd from West Virginia. So I read deeply into this subject. And it's just the scariest damn thing in the world. Everybody I've given the book to—I bought a dozen of them and given the book to people in the music business—have just not spoken to me afterwards. It's such a deep and horror-type thing, that it's just frightening.

But I feel our government is in this. I feel that we are being prepared for a huge paradigm shift. The Christian churches call it the second coming of Christ. Buddhists call it other things. All the religions are realizing that we're getting ready. The Aztec calendar ended on the thirteenth of August,

1999. Their five-thousand year calendar ended. And there's not another one to replace it. So those people are worried about the big change that's coming along. I'm just reading and holding on. I don't know what the hell it is. But I know that there is a change coming, and Art Bell says, "Things are out of the box."

Charles O'Leary is an astronaut that has gotten out of the box. And he's being avoided now by his peers like a plague. But he's saying that science only taught him half the truth. He said he got out of the box and he saw the other half of the truth. He's real big on the UFO circuits. We've seen him speak several times. And he's a very courageous young man. His career's over as an astronaut. But he's taken the chance going out.

This is bigger than songwriting. Can you see the drift? Where I'm going with it? It's talking about the same thing where songs come from. But this is a bigger thing than that. Songs come from this. I didn't know where the hell "Indian Reservation" and "Tobacco Road" came from. But people have told me it's changed their lives. Those two songs.

I played for the governor in Georgia and for the whole Legislature. A young black man, a representative came up to me and he said, "You wrote 'Tobacco Road'?" I said, "Yeah." He said, "How could you know about that?" I said, "Because I've been poor, too. You're a politician and I'm a songwriter, but we both have lived this story."

Lou Rawls said the same thing: "I thought you were a brother." I said, "No, honey, I'm a cousin." But we're both from the same social economic background.

You must have witnessed your share of racism.

It's everywhere.

I graduated from high school in '54. We were the last segregated high school class. Back for our fortieth reunion, now Durham High School is nothing but blacks. There's two students that are white. They wouldn't even let us have the school flag for our reunion.

Martin Luther King said Chicago was worse than anything he was ever up against in the South.

Sure.

How did you overcome the institutionalized racism in America?

You know how I've done it. When I hated the niggers, I hated them. My daddy hated blacks. I was taught to hate blacks. I have hated people because of their skin color totally.

I'm an extremist. I hate the middle of the road where it's lukewarm. I'm just like Jesus.

"Then You Can Tell Me Goodbye."

That's exactly right. For a million years hang around and then you can tell me good-bye.

No, I am a white man living in the South. It's my duty to have hated blacks. But it's also my duty to feel sorry about that and feel repentant about it and erase the guilt that I have inherited by saying, "Hey, you son-of-a-bitch." And finding a black man that's worth loving. I don't love them all. They ain't all worth loving. Just like all the whites ain't worth loving. But my wife, Susie, is damn sure worth loving. And Gatemouth is worth loving.

No, there's nothing wrong with being racial. Experience it and go on past it, because we're all in this shit together.

Amen.

The music that we have in Nashville, Tennessee, is different. And the reason for that is the dead Indians under the ground. It's so pathos driven.

"He Stopped Loving Her Today."

It is the best country song that's been written in my lifetime in Nashville.

I had a log house in the '60s over on Noelton Lane and Granny White Pike. The Noel Hotel. The old Noel family built it for their daughter. Putting in a fallout shelter in the Cuban missile crisis, I uncovered in solid rock a clay vessel with a skeleton in it in a fetal position. In solid rock. It is now at the Parthenon in their collection of stone box Indians. I took it over there and gave it to them. Now, limestone takes six hundred million years to form. Somebody put that fucker in a jar, in mud, in clay, or in dirt that later turned to limestone. Yet, we're supposed to believe that we came here just recently. That's the biggest load of horseshit we're teaching our children I can imagine.

Forbidden Archeology goes deeper into that. There's a coal cave in Kentucky just north of here. The coal company closed it down because they came across a black marble wall in coal. Sixty-six billion years it takes to form coal and here is a damn black marble wall. And you can't go to the University of Kentucky and find anything in their museums about it. All of that shit has to be deleted to support our Christian thing and our Creationist thing that says we're only so many years old. It's horseshit.

But I hope I have told you something about songwriting.

Wesley Rose is not dead. See, there was no funeral for Wesley. There was no funeral. There was no funeral for his wife several months later. There's no place that they were buried. I know he's in South America. I know he is. I don't know exactly where he is, but I know that he's in South America or Great Britain or France.

Doing?

Living the comfortable life off the people he robbed.

I heard he died of Alzheimer's.

That was the story. But nobody saw him. Have you ever seen anybody that went to see him while he had Alzheimer's? Never have seen anybody. I told him, I said, "The day you die and the day you're buried, I will bomb your grave with dynamite. And then I will stand there and piss on your casket." They called me the day he died and said, "Would you like to make a comment for the newspaper?" And I said, "Yes. He was always on time."

And he was. He was always in a suit, and he always opened the door. He kept the publishing company open. He was a good administrator like that. But as far as dealing with the people on a contractual basis, he was amoral. I have gotten rid of my animosity toward him through deep prayer and meditation. I cannot afford to take that sort of hatred that he caused to my grave with me like others have. He killed Hank Williams. He killed Audrey Williams. He would have killed Hank, Jr., but Hank, Jr., stayed away from him.

His father died thinking he was Roy Acuff. Boudleaux and I both on the same night went to Roy Acuff backstage at the Opry and said, "You've got a thief running your company. He's not fair to people. He needs to be replaced and you're the only man that can do it." And Roy Acuff whined and carried on and we realized that he was being screwed, too. By Wesley.

I pray for Wesley Rose all the time. I know he's living a good life. I hope he is. And I do, I pray for him. I can't let that bother me. But that's why I never had a publishing company. I cannot do that to writers. I cannot do that. Did you ever know Don Gant?

I met him, but I didn't know him.

As far as publishing, he had learned from Wesley a lot. He said, "I don't like publishing because you have to sell your friends." That's the way a publisher makes money on his capital gain—selling his catalog. And over your years of building the catalog, you get to be friends with the writer.

He died awfully young, Don did. But he was a fine man and a fine publisher. He would have been a great publisher like Wesley. Wesley Rose was the greatest publisher in Nashville, Tennessee. Jack Stapp was a fool. He didn't know shit about publishing. Jim Denny, Bill Denny's daddy, didn't know shit.

One night in the Black Puddle, a rainy night, Jim held a sawed off shotgun with a bullet sticking that far out of the end. I had just sued him and he said, "I could blow your fucking head off, man." "Yes, sir, you sure could." And I jerked and ran out the door. I've had some things happen to me.

But Jim Denny was not a publisher. He was a street kid. God, he was as mean as they have to be. And I appreciated his drive. He helped to start the business here.

What was the lawsuit over?

Well, I had signed with Cedarwood Publishing Company. Jim was running the Opry at the time. And he had the power to tell the Opry stars, "You either cut that song, or you're off the Opry." So I used that leverage for my benefit as a writer.

It's never an even playing field.

Oh, no. Hell, no. If it is, then you're not dealing. But I was dealing with the kings, the guys that were starting all this stuff.

I said, "I need two thousand dollars to buy a house for my family." Jim said, "Okay. You'll sign an exclusive songwriting contract with me. I'll take out a life insurance policy on your life. I'll take a second mortgage on the house." And there was one other security that he demanded and I forgot now what the hell it was. But I had in my contract with him that the minute I paid that money back, I was free of my contract. Well the minute I paid him back, he would not get me a release. So I had to go to chancery court to keep him from telling the producers that I was signed to him.

They were having the disk jockey conventions at the James Robertson Hotel. I went up to the RCA Victor suite at two o'clock in the morning. An older man got on the elevator with me. And in the seven floors up to the RCA Victor suite—he and I were the only ones on—he said, "You're having trouble with a man here named Jim Denny. For three hundred dollars and first class, round-trip expenses from Chicago, I'll take care of it for you." I said, "I'm not interested in that." So I got off and Jim Denny was at the Victor suite.

Jim and I were on the first CMA board that founded the Country Music Association. Everybody in the business had to serve. The next day, we were on a committee. And Jim said, "You know, Loudermilk, last night I got on the elevator coming down from Victor. There was a man on there and he said, "You're in a lawsuit with a young writer here. For three hundred dollars and first class, round-trip from Chicago, I'll take care of it for you." I said, "What did you tell him?" He says, "Aww, naww." I said, "That's what I told him on the way up." We always laughed about that, Jim and I.

You were on opposite sides of the fence, but you needed each other. Similar to the player/owner relationship in professional sports.

Oh, yeah. And you can't keep everything you make. Shit, a man out here selling shoes don't keep everything he makes. So I don't think I'd have done it any differently, if I'd have done it all over again.

These guys were hard, but they did a lot for the music business. They did a lot for me. We all got along and we all have had a good career because of it.

God, back then you had to be a fool to get any attention. We all had to do our own press. And Roger Miller and I used to raise hell. God Almighty, I'd do things that you wouldn't believe to do today. I was just telling a retired captain about it. He said that he had heard stories about what we had done. I thought nobody even knew who we were, but people knew who we were.

Did you have a close relationship with Charlie and Ira Louvin?

We were first cousins. They're country boys from down in Georgia. Around Stone Mountain. But, no, we have not had a close relationship. They were of another mind-set. I'd be considered a sissy to their mind-set.

They're fine guys, but we have nothing in common at all, except our genes. My wife's doing research now on the Loudermilk genealogy. And she's run into the Louvins quite a bit. We don't know who the hell we are. We're Americans. We ain't supposed to know who the hell we were.

How important was Chet Atkins to your career?

Very important.

When I first came to town, I brought a classical guitar. A gut string guitar. Nobody had seen one around here except Chet. I had run into an old house painter, Ernest Moon, when I was delivering telegrams. I was fifteen years old and I heard him playing Bach and Fernando Sor with white paint under his fingernails. I had been listening to the Grand Ole Opry and never heard a guitar played like that. So I studied some with him and got into Burl Ives and Bellafonte and folk music, along with Eddy Arnold and Bill Monroe. I was playing fiddle for square dance.

Chet had heard "A Rose And A Baby Ruth" and he'd heard "Sitting In The Balcony." So I came announced. Not unannounced, but announced. I had given myself one year. I did George Morgan's television show in the morning. I worked at Cedarwood Publishing Company listening to songs that people had sent in.

The end of the year was close. So I got down by the chair and I prayed about it. I was doomed to go back home and work in the goddamn hardware store. My wife's daddy's hardware store. I said, "Shit. Is this it?" So I went out the last day for lunch at Ireland's, across from Vanderbilt, with Chet. And while we were holding our menus, he said, "Would you like to work for me?"

Tears came to my eyes. And I realized that this is out of my hands now. This was a prayer answered. Why would he have asked me at that particular time immediately after a prayer? He didn't know the year was over. He didn't know any of these things.

Chet tries to tell people he doesn't believe in God. He's the most religious, holy son-of-a-bitch I've ever met in my life. So I started working for him, helping him produce and rehearsing artists. And it grew from that. But very early in my career, he and I felt very much alike musically. I don't feel this way about anybody else in the music business, but I feel this way about him: That he's divinely guided and divinely joined with other people in this latest breath of the song. And I just feel very strongly that he's divinely oriented. All the earmarks of great art is in his life. I can't listen to his music without crying. The beauty is there. The softness. The tenderness. The pathos. The warmth. I've had several psychic things happen with him that's led me to believe that synchronicity is there. Something special that I don't understand.

He's got the biggest heart. He's helped more people than anybody I know get started.

Steve Shoals was Chet's boss. Big fat guy. He's dead now. But he let Chet choose the songs, choose the artists, choose the release dates, choose the album covers, choose the album liners, choose everything. Chet produced the piece.

I think drugs had a lot to do with the stopping of that. In the late '50 s, early '60s, guys couldn't finish projects. Jack Clement, who was the dean of marijuana smoking in Nashville, worked on an album of his own for ten years.

He sent me a copy of it. A test copy, a pre-copy. We were living in Louisiana. And I realized this was so rare. I put it on and I leaned back in the bed and I listened.

We had just been studying about the Navajo weaving in a mistake into their rugs to show that it was done by humans, and not God. It was not perfect. And so I was listening and suddenly I said, "That son-of-a-bitch." Jack's one of the most creative men I've ever met. I said, "He has done that. He put that scratch in there just like they did the rug." So years later I asked him about it and he said, "I don't know, man. I dropped one of them before I mailed it. That's probably that one." He didn't do it. That was just a scratch. But I admire him so much, I just knew that he had done that.

Jack's very realistic, but he's a dreamer. He's a card. He's the sweetest guy. He's helped a lot of people, too, man. He's like Bobby Braddock—not a mean bone in him. All creativity. All God focused and God strung. He's attached from a string.

Fred Foster is a great guy, too. A great creative person. I've been around some really top people. Of course, Owen Bradley was tops. Jesus! He was more of a realist. He was not a dreamer. He was a record man first. Chet was a musician first, then a record man. Chet never actually really got to be executive quality. He's always been above that. Your idiots can run record companies. But they shouldn't choose the material and choose the artist and choose the direction. That should be left up to the musicians and to the music oriented people.

See, you have your idealistic and you have your realistic. And you can look at any subject in both of those ways—idealistic or realistic. And Owen was more realistic. But he had a lot to do with changing country music. There were two people that were more important in the growth of country music in the '50s and '60s than anybody else. One of them was Floyd Cramer and one was Anita Kerr.

Anita Kerr was a background singer.

Yeah. She had the Kerr Singers. They were the female sounds. It was a quartet. Two girls and two boys. They were on everything. And a lot of changes went through with those kids.

I want to read a quote of yours from CSR *in 1968.*

CSR, what it that?

Hell, I don't know. Some magazine article you were in. You said something that struck me. I just wanted to read it back to you, because I found it very really interesting.

"I think that the songwriter/composer has a tremendous obligation. Because the composer today is the poet of our times. The poets are sitting around writing stuff that's far out and doesn't rhyme and all that, but the little cat that's writing songs that fit the man, he's the philosopher. He is the poet of our times. When you get in this position you have an obligation to not give the people out there the wrong thing to think. Don't mess up their minds, don't scream about peace and don't put political motives into your philosophy and into your entertaining song. That is cruel and I think there are several writers that are great writers and probably better writers than I'll ever be who have used their vehicle or they have been used by others as a vehicle for political messages."

Yeah, that's right.

But at the same time, I look at your songs like "Brown Girl," "Indian Reservation," "Ma Baker's Little Acre."

Political overtones.

Right.

But they were innocent political overtones. I had no idea I was saying that. I talked with Bob Dylan about this. See, if there's anybody that's responsible for the direction that record companies have gone as far as controlling everything about their output—the accountants and the lawyers controlling the musical content—it's Bob Dylan. He scared the shit out of people when he brought in innocent political messages in his songs. He didn't know what he was writing.

You don't know what you're writing when you're young and twenty. You don't know what the hell you're writing. It's coming through you so fast you don't know what you're saying. And then it's people who see messages in that material, who bend it and focus it and push it and offer it. I think Bob Dylan was that way. He did not know what he was saying. I've had a couple conversations with him. He was on the opposite political spectrum from me. He was a liberal and a socialist. I was a conservative and a socialist. I'm a very strange political animal. I believe in Republican socialism. I think you need to be free to make all the money you want to make without any kind of government, but you still owe a debt to the people that can't make it.

I think right now if you were to come up with political messages or social messages that Bob Dylan made in the '60s, you couldn't get them recorded, because the establishment is very comfortable. I was invited to a party one night where Bob Dylan was going to be. I told the guy, "If I come, I'm going to hit him in the nose with my fist as hard as I can. I'll be sorry the rest of my life and you will and he will. So just don't invite one of us." He didn't invite me.

I don't think it's the job of the entertaining creator to fuck up people's minds with deep thoughts. Hell, they're out wanting to hear light thoughts. They're paying you to think about sex and getting drunk. They don't want to hear about philosophy and politics and shit. It just so happened that Bob Dylan came along at the right time, he said the right things that were taken at the right time the right way, and he became a political observer, a social observer.

The reactions are slow to get started, but once they get started, it's like a battleship. You can't stop it hardly. And the record companies are very sensitive to messages.

They prefer the up-tempo dittie.

They like anything that will sell sex, you see. We are so controlled. We go out daily and consume our fix of packaged philosophy and packaged religion and packaged social. We've fed our culture.

Me-ism is the crux of democracy. Winston Churchill said, "It's a sorry damn system, but it's the best we got." And we've been led to believe that everybody's equal. That's why Gatemouth Brown is so wise, because he knows there's two classes of people. Those on the box and those on the floor. And there always will be two types of people. That's why we have a two-type political system. When you have a three-type political system, it gets cloudy. Four types, and then you have Italy.

I think what happened in the '60s ruined a lot of America. I had to give a lot in the '60s. There were people needing what I had in the '60s. I think America slipped backwards, started toward the Third World nationhood in the '60s. I know damn well it was better in the '50s than it was in the '60s. I know that's normal for a guy my age to say. But I talked to other guys that's felt the same way. Gate feels the same way and he's black. Hell, he's ten years older than I am. But he's stood up there and seen young people for fifty years and he knows it's going backwards.

The de-evolution of human species. Breakdown of health, breakdown of drive, breakdown of everything. It's going backwards. I just spent twenty-one thousand dollars on a damn bridge. The bridge you came over. I spent eighteen thousand dollars eleven years ago when I built the damn thing. So eighteen, plus twenty-one. The first house I bought when I was twenty-two years old for my mother and daddy was eight thousand nine hundred dollars. How many of those fucking houses is in that bridge? Now, I've seen the devaluation of our dollar over that period of time. The mayor, who was the richest guy in Durham, lived in a twenty-one thousand dollar house. Our money has gone down. Everything's gone down. Our cars are better, but there's more pollution. You damn sure don't see any electric cars. You can't tax electricity going through the air.

We don't have great men giving. We have great men taking. I'm praying and meditating now like I do this time every year for somebody to come along that I can give money to for Christmas. That's in our culture. Americans give more to the poor than any other country in the world. We are a giving country. That cannot last if we turn internally and be me, me, me. And that me, me, me shit is created by saying we're all equal and we're all individuals. Me, me, me, me, me. That is uncivilized. It's anti-human.

The whole concept of Christianity is to give.

When you give, you gather.

Exactly right. You have to believe in something bigger than yourself in order to get anything out of that concept. You got to believe in the hereafter.

I know that's true. Over the years, the more that Susie and I give, the higher our income gets. It just works that way, I don't know why.

Photo courtesy of BMI Archives

Ray Stevens

How have you observed songwriting change over the years?

Songwriting and songs today have shifted to the craft side of the endeavor. What I mean by that is, to me, there are two main ingredients in writing a song. One is the craft of writing a song and the other is the intangible, the spark. It separates the standards from the "here today, gone tomorrow" songs. And don't get me wrong, there are some "here today, gone tomorrow" songs that are amusing and clever and good. But the songs that really become standards and make a lot of money over the years and make catalogs worth millions of dollars are the songs that have that spark, that unknown, that intangible thing about them in addition to being well crafted. And some of them aren't even well crafted. So given a choice of whether you can have one or the other, I would pick the song with the spark rather than the craft. But it's been proven time and time again that a well-crafted song with that intangible spark is the one that you want.

A lot of the songs that I'm hearing on the radio today don't have the spark. They're well crafted. They're written by professionals. And that's about all they got going for them. They just don't have that something about them that will make them hang around very long.

It was like this back before rock and roll took over, before rhythm and blues kicked in the door in the early '50s. The songs were just hack. They were coming out of Tin Pan Alley. All the records sounded alike, all the singers sounded alike. Everybody was trying to imitate Frank Sinatra and Tony Bennett. They're worth imitating, don't get me wrong. They're great. But all the singers were of that ilk and all the songs were of that ilk and it was getting pretty boring. And that's the catalyst for something totally new. I think we're there again.

Obviously, if you could control that spark, you would do it every time, but no writer is able to do that.

No, and let me say this: a well-crafted song, as opposed to no song, is the desired thing. If you're going to be a songwriter, you got to get in there and do it. You got to set aside some time, if not every day, then every week. Sit down and try to come up with something. If the spark don't hit you, craft something. Then maybe down the road, you'll look at it and a spark will hit you and you can modify it and it'll really be something.

How did you get your start in the music business?

I was living in Atlanta, Georgia, and met Bill Lowry. He had a young music company, Lowry Music, and he needed material. At the time, he was a radio personality in the Atlanta area and doing really well at that, but he wanted to build a catalog.

He loved the record business. He loved the music business. So he encouraged all the young kids in the Atlanta area that showed any talent at all to write and bring him songs so he could get started. I was one of those lucky kids. I was still in high school and I had wanted to write songs and make records ever since I could remember. My first efforts were pretty bad, but I was trying and learning.

After I met Bill, I wrote a fairly good song, I thought. I took it to him and he agreed. I was seventeen and a senior in high school. He took the little demo I made to Ken Nelson, who was one of the hot producers at Capitol at the time. Ken lived in Los Angeles, and he would come to Nashville periodically and record people like Sonny James, Ferlin Husky and Faron Young. Bill played Ken this song, and he said, "We'll sign him." So on the strength of that song, I got a record deal. And they put me on Prep Records in 1957, which was a new subsidiary of Capitol.

And the name of the song?

It was called "Silver Bracelet." It was a hit in Atlanta, but it wasn't a hit anywhere else.

Was Lowry's place on Clairmont Road?

No, it wasn't on Clairmont at that time. It is now.

It was a couple different places. He started out in the basement at his house in Brookhaven. Then he moved up the street to an old converted schoolhouse that was near the railroad tracks just past Buckhead and Lenox Square. He then located on Clairmont Road where he is now.

You stayed in Atlanta went to Georgia State, then moved to Nashville.

I moved to Nashville on January 2, 1962, to go to work for Mercury Records with Shelby Singleton and Jerry Kennedy. I was chief bottle washer. I was assigned to screen songs, and God, there were a mountain of demos. Back in those days, people pitched songs on disk, as well as tape, but mostly disk. Cassettes weren't around yet. It's amazing how many disks you can get in a stack that's only a foot high. It takes you all day to listen. But I listened to songs, most of them really bad. I got an education as to what was going on out there.

I would find a song and take it to Shelby or Jerry and they'd say, "Yeah, this is good." "Naw, that's no good." "That's good, but it's not for this artist." We would talk about and plan the sessions that were coming up. Sometimes I would rehearse an artist. Teach them a new song that they needed to know.

In January of '62, I had a session and I cut "Ahab the Arab." It came out in the spring and was a big hit. And I sort of drifted away from my job listening to demos and rehearsing artists at Mercury. But I did play on a lot of Mercury sessions and a few other sessions during the ensuing years to supplement my income.

Your recording career is very unique. Most artists who cross over from country to pop, or vice versa, do it with the same song. But you had a pop career that shifted to country and then back to pop. A few songs crossed over during the transition periods, but most were represented in one genre.

I think the definitions of the different categories are like the desert sands. They are ever shifting. It's hard to classify anything anymore. This may be a curse, but I like all kinds of music. I love to hear classical. I love to hear jazz. And certainly, I like popular music. It's an umbrella category in my mind that includes country, rhythm and blues, pop and the things that most people who are not necessarily into music like.

I think radio stations that have such strict rules against crossing lines are very limiting and it's cheating the listener. I think it's time for a little more liberal playlist. Mix it up a little bit. If they need an excuse not to play something, they say, "It's not country." Then you say, "You played this." And they mumble something and go away. It's really strange.

Aren't record labels as much the culprit as the radio stations?

I'm sure they are.

What really mystifies me is how *Billboard* can put out two charts. One is the country chart according to God knows what yardstick, and the other down at the bottom is the sales chart, the records that have sold the most. And usually, the records that have sold the most are not the top records on the main chart.

The difference is enough, so that ought to be telling somebody out there something. When people put their money where their mouth is, that's really the bottom line. When you go out and plunk down sixteen dollars for something, that ought to scream the loudest. I don't care what a radio programmer has told a group of radio stations to play from his ivory tower. That's the tail wagging the dog.

You sold a lot of singles in your career. Do you see the Internet as a way of bringing back the sale of single tracks?

I don't know. I'm not that familiar with the Internet yet. From what little I do know about it, I hope it does. It seems like it could. It seems to me, though, that it's still an exclusive group of folks that are really using the Internet with any regularity. Most people don't type. The Internet is foreign to me. I've got computers here at the office and we're on the Internet, but I've got people that work them.

I have been too busy to learn. If I ever get some time, that's one of the first things I'm going to do—take some courses on how to work the computer and get on the Internet. But I think you're very limited with your marketplace at this point. It's growing, and I hope it continues to do so. I think one of the things that could help would be for the Internet and computers to become more user-friendly.

Not too many years ago you needed to know keystrokes and now you just need to know how to point and click.

Well, that's great, because we've got a store on the Internet. We'd love to sell product that way. The problem is proliferation. There's only so much shelf space in the stores. People are paying money just to get their product on the shelves. And then they're paying a lot more money to let the public know that it's there. To jump over these hurdles, you do direct marketing. When that proved to be successful, everybody jumped on the bandwagon. Now the time available to air your spots for direct marketing on cable is very limited, because everybody's doing it. Even the big corporations are doing info-mercials. Let's face it, there's only twenty-four hours in a day and there's a finite number of cable channels. It seems like they're endless, but really, there's only so many channels with enough viewers to make a difference. Marketing has gotten to be such a science with people aiming their darts at the right demographics. The sellers are targeting what they perceive to be their audience. And most of the time, they're right.

You certainly have a strong sense of who your market is.

I know who my market has been. I don't want to limit myself though. Don't get me wrong, I do want to target my market. But I don't think anybody wants to limit themselves. You have to experiment with other demographics to see if you can appeal to a broader range of people. Especially with comedy records, I think the demographics are very broad. I don't think you are confined to any age group or any ethnic group. By and large, you can get the kids and the old folks and all the people in between with a comedy song. And you can get a lot of different walks of life.

I remember being in the fourth grade when "Along Came Jones" was a hit. My parents were laughing as hard as I was. It was unifying music.

I was on MCA many, many years ago. I've been on MCA two or three times. We talked them into direct marketing twenty sides of comedy songs. And that was when direct market was not known to be that effective in selling records. We went in and shot a little cheap commercial with a couple of guys dressed up as clowns. I think it cost about $25,000. We did little bits and pieces of "Misty" and "Guitarzan" and all of these different strange songs. And the darn thing went gold.

Then we came out with the videos years later. We did it again as *Ray Stevens Live* and *More Live*, which was the up sale. Then the marketplace just got jammed. I didn't produce another product until a couple years later when I did a video movie called *Get Serious*. It was ten songs that were done in the context of a story. We acted out scenes between the songs to tie it all together. I guess you could call it a video musical. It was successful, but nothing like the first two products.

You're a father and a grandfather. With your success with novelty records and family appeal, you seem the perfect candidate to do a children's project.

A lot of people have said that and I've thought about it. I just haven't had time to really sit down and figure it out. But I plan to do a children's project as soon as I can.

What was your motivation for opening a theater in Branson, Missouri?

My show, with all the comedy songs, screamed for a production that was too much to carry on the road.

How was Branson in terms of performance and in terms of lifestyle?

Branson is a great place. It was a wonderful experience. The Ozark Mountains are a beautiful part of the world. The people are really great. They're down-home, friendly folks and I love them.

I couldn't do a big armada of trucks and buses. And although some of your bigger acts have trucks on the road today, back then I wasn't pulling that kind of money. So I was looking for a place where I could have the production that I wanted to surround these songs and not have to cart all this stuff around the country. I considered Branson and Pigeon Forge. I even considered Nashville, but at that time, Nashville was not really an option.

I got a call from a friend of mine and he said, "Why don't we build a theater in Branson?" So we went over and the people who were selling a vacant lot on the strip backed out of the deal. We talked to another gentleman who had a piece of property, and he went in with us and we built a theater. Back then, it was just kind of out of the way. Turns out it's the most desirable location in Branson.

When we built this theater, I crawled out on a limb. I borrowed a lot of money and signed my name to a big loan. I was shaking in my boots hoping that we would do well. And, of course, the results were phenomenal. The people really wanted to see the show. We sold out just about every show for three seasons in a row. We did three shows a day, six days a week for six months every year. Then you had to spend time gearing up and gearing down. That didn't leave much time to do other things, such as record. After three years, I was just really tired. I loved what I was doing, but I was just worn out. But I couldn't leave that big 50,000 square foot monster just sitting there, because it eats.

With a huge appetite.

Oh, man. The heat bill in that baby is really good. It gets cold there, so you have to heat it, otherwise the pipes will freeze and you're in big trouble. I didn't want to be a landlord, so we sold the theater at the end of the '93 season. I had always maintained my home here in Nashville. I just had a little condo over in Branson.

Who took over your theater?

We sold it to a corporation called Casino Resources and they put a review in there. It's called "Country Tonite." They have the same review in Vegas and Pigeon Forge. It's basically very talented newcomers who put on a show with all the new things that are hot. It's a great show.

I'm for Bossier City, Louisiana, and when I was growing up, Shoji Tabuchi lived there.

David Houston's from Bossier.

Absolutely. Shoji played fiddle for David Houston at that time. He lived right around the corner in a modest home. When I was in Branson, I visited the men's room in his theater. It had a pool table in it. I thought, "He's come a long way from when his bathroom was about the size of a pool table."

Well, you know, that's all showbiz, man.

I'm not a fan of the concert venue. Don't get me wrong, I've done a lot of them. But as a member of the audience, I had much rather go to a Vegas showroom. My favorite venue to work is a showroom like Vegas where people sit at tables, and not row after row in a theater-type environment.

You hooked up with Jerry Reed and Joe South in your early days. How did that come about?

We all met through Bill Lowry. I was a pretty good piano player and Jerry was the best guitar player I had ever heard. Joe South was no slouch either. Jerry and I were the main ones in the band. Sometimes Joe would play with us. We hired a drummer, a bass player, a sax player, and we'd go out and play dances. We played fraternity parties at Georgia Tech. You name it, we played it. If you had a hundred fifty bucks, we'd work. We were just doing it for money. We were mainly into writing and recording.

Are y'all still friends?

Sure. Had lunch with Jerry not long ago. Jerry Kennedy and Shelby Singleton went to lunch with us.

Oh, to be the proverbial fly on the wall. You did some recording for Fred Foster.

Yes. Fred had Monument Records, and he was as hot as a pistol. He had Roy Orbison. When I left Mercury, I went with Monument. Fred let me produce some records. I was really into that. Had a good time with Monument.

The hits I cut with Monument were "Unwind," "Mr. Businessman," "Guitarzan," and "Along Came Jones."

You also produced Dolly Parton.

I didn't cut any hits with Dolly. I cut a session with her where we did "Happy, Happy Birthday, Baby," the old R&B song. I really had high hopes for that, but it didn't make it. I think it could have been a little ahead of its time.

Speaking of ahead of its time—"Sunday Morning Coming Down."

Kristofferson.

Classic song.

Yeah.

You released "Sunday Morning Coming Down" at the end of '69. It was your first country chart record, which went to fifty-five. Then a year later, Johnny Cash releases it. Two weeks at one. CMA Song of the Year.

His record was totally different from mine. Mine might have been over-produced. His was a Johnny Cash record. And Johnny Cash was a hot country performer. Ray Stevens was a sometimes country performer. It could be a curse that I like all kinds of music, because I waded all those different pools.

What was it about that song that made you record it?

I liked it. The words were great for its time. I don't know if it would be that commercial today, but back then I thought it was very commercial.

Do you think the song may have been closer to Cash's persona than yours?

Sure. Back then I could not see myself in the mirror very clearly. I couldn't see myself as others saw me. So I think you hit the nail on the head. I think Cash's persona could sell that lyric more than my persona. He might have flopped with "The Streak."

Where as you sold five million copies.

"The Streak" came out of the blue. I had some help from the universal mind when I wrote that song.

Are the songs out of the blue your best songs?

Absolutely. That's the spark I'm talking about. It feels like you're getting a little help from somewhere.

Writing and recording "The Do Right Family" and recording "Would Jesus Wear A Rolex" and "Ten Percent's Good Enough For Jesus," you certainly understand the religious context of American people. What is your religious background?

Southern Baptist.

The production on "The Do Right Family" certainly captures that tradition. The production value of your novelty or comedy records elevates the lyric. If you put those songs into the wrong production hands, you've got a train wreck.

It's real slippery to come up with a great final product, because you've got so many facets that have to blend together.

You bring so many talents to the table—your writing, your performance, your arranging skills. When you're in the process of writing a song, are you envisioning some of the production values?

Sure.

It's very simple. You spend your whole life being involved in making records and writing songs. It's all one big ball of wax. When you're writing a song, you're also hearing the way it should be recorded. How do you walk and chew gum at the same time? You just do.

It's simple?

It is simple. Some of the hardest things to talk about and conceptualize verbally are very simple, like writing a song and making a record. I'm not saying that you hit the nail on the head every time, but you do know what you want. What you want may not be successful, but it's a very simple process.

I played golf with Peter Jacobson one time. I'm a terrible golfer. He looked at me and said, "Hey, it's just a stick and a ball."

That's like saying a guitar is just a piece of wood with strings.

To Chet Atkins, it is just a piece of wood with strings.

And to you, a piano is just some black and white keys.

That's right.

I worked hard at it and I cultivated my abilities. I enjoy it. We all have God-given talents in one area or another. Some of the talents are not as lucrative as others; but nonetheless, the talents are still important and make up who we are.

I could spend years playing scales or hitting golf balls on the practice range, and still not be a studio musician or play on the PGA tour. Did you recognize your talent at an early age?

I didn't know anything. I still don't. I suspected. I'm still suspecting that it might be. I'm still open for something that could come along that would be more—I'm being facetious now—that would be more meaningful to my life. No, I got lucky. I sort of figured that this is what I should do with my life.

Some people are songwriters, some people are producers, some people are perform-ers. End of story. You synthesized all three. Do you think you could have picked one and been satisfied or fulfilled?

Maybe I could have, but I didn't want to. I have always felt the freedom to do what I wanted to do. I have tried a lot of things. I have not been suc-cessful at everything, but I have enjoyed trying. I have gotten lucky and been successful at a few things.

It's all one big package, or small package, in my mind. It's all one thing. They're all parts of the whole. I understand that a lot of people like to sepa-rate them. They can move faster, but they're dealing with a lot of people. I'm just dealing with me, so I don't have to move as fast as somebody who's got a whole stable of artists.

I'm a producer. I'm a writer. I'm a musician. I'm an arranger. These people all work together in concert, and they turn out a lot of product for a lot of dif-ferent artists. But doing all these things just for me, I can keep up with the schedule just as good as they can. I've only got one guy to worry about.

Do you find that more satisfying.

Not only is it more satisfying, but it's quicker. You don't have to have all these meetings.

Are you an independent person?

I guess. I feel like I'm out here by myself.

But I sense it's important for you to be the captain of your own ship?

Yeah, it is. In some ways, it works very well. In other ways, it's not good.

If you're doing everything and you give somebody a product that they had nothing to do with to sell, they're not all that enthused to sell it. It's the old "What's in it for me?" axiom.

They are not emotionally invested.

Right. And it can work against you. You can't blame people. People are people. If you come in cold and say, "Here's a hit," it could be the hit of the world, but they're not going to be bowled over and work it all that hard if they didn't have anything to do with it.

That's very observant.

It don't take a rocket scientist to figure that out. That's the downside of doing everything yourself.

A one-man band.

Right. You better start learning how to sell stuff.

"Mr. Businessman" has a timeless quality. It is as relevant today as it was the day you wrote it.

I had gotten the raw end of a business deal. It really grated on me. So instead of tearing my hair out, I took out my frustration in writing that song. I woke up one morning and bam! The whole arrangement came to me as I was writing the song. I recorded "Mr. Businessman" at Owen Bradley's Barn in Mt. Juliet. It turned out really good.

Who influenced you most in Nashville?

Shelby Singleton, Jerry Kennedy, Fred Foster, Chet Atkins. I've always been a fan of Owen Bradley. I sort of watched what they did.

Let me read a quote from an interview in 1969: "Things are changing all the time," Ray said. "A songwriter may pass a point in his way of thinking where he can no longer communicate with the majority of his audience. When he can no longer put his finger on the emotions or mood of the public. This happens to 99 percent of creative people. I hope to have five million successes before it happens to me, but if not, I'll tap someone else and say, 'You write me a song, Daddy Rabbit, and I'll sing it.'"

That's pretty good. I don't think I've lost touch with what people want to hear. At times, I didn't have time to write. I would hear people's songs that I thought were great and I'd cut them. The most notable among that group would be Buddy Cabb, who wrote the "Mississippi Squirrel Revival" and several other songs that I recorded.

Daddy Rabbit. Why did I say that?

It was '69. You might have had your bellbottoms on. How important has Buddy Cabb been to the Ray Stevens?

Very important. Good friend. Knew him in Atlanta. One of the Lowry guys. He used to hang around with us and write songs back when he was in high school over in Decatur and I was in high school in Druid Hills. We were archrivals. You could throw a rock from one school and hit the other.

How does sixty feel?

I don't feel what most people perceive as being sixty. I don't feel those emotions. I don't feel any different than I always have. I feel the same. I feel thirty.

You still have the fire in the belly.

Yeah, I just hope that I can be accepted in the field that I've chosen to pursue for a little while longer even though I am sixty.

You had a recent bout with prostate cancer?

It scared me pretty bad, but I was very lucky. They caught it early through a PSA test. I can't stress enough for guys to get the PSA test. Do you get a physical every year?

I placed a call to my doctor just yesterday.

Ask your doctor to do a PSA test on you. It's a little blood test. He's going to take blood anyway. My doctor could not detect any abnormalities in my prostate through the normal DRE—digital rectal exam.

We've put a man on the moon and we're still doing DREs.

It's not a very pleasant thing, but it's not all that bad. I just hate it when they turn the lights down and play soft music.

The only reason they found it early was because of the PSA. They said, "Your PSA's a little high, we don't think there's anything wrong, but we need to do a biopsy." I said, "Okay." So they did a biopsy and said, "Surprise, surprise, surprise. You've got it." And I said, "Woah!"

It was contained in the prostate and there are all kinds of ways now of dealing with it. A lot of guys are doing the radioactive seed implantation where they don't remove the prostate. They shoot these radioactive seeds in there and they have a shelf life of three to six months. The radioactivity dies, but in the meanwhile they've killed all the cancer.

I chose to do the surgery where they just take it out for several reasons. And I hope I was right in my reasoning. But I found a doctor, Patrick Walsh, in Baltimore at Johns Hopkins. He's one of the best in the world. He has lived up to his reputation a hundred percent, because he was great as far as I'm concerned. I would recommend him to anybody. After the operation, he told me that it could not have gone any better. They biopsied all the tissue around it and it's all clean and I'm fine.

I dodged all the undesired aftereffects, such as incontinence and impotence. I came out smelling like a rose and I'm so thankful. I feel very lucky. They caught it early. If it metastasizes—spreads from the origin in the prostate—you've got big trouble. So get that PSA.

When cancer strikes, how does one find a way to sing "Everything Is Beautiful"?

Something's going to happen. One of these days, we're all going to leave here for one reason or another. And we know that since the time we're little kids.

Life is fatal.

You ain't going to get out of this world alive. Smell the roses.

Photo courtesy of Acuff-Rose Music

Whitey Shafer

What led you to songwriting and what led you to Nashville?

I didn't start writing until I was thirty years old. I was just doing it for my own amusement. I lived in Waco, Texas, and I always wanted to come to Nashville to be a singer. Not necessarily a songwriter. I didn't even know songwriters. I thought they just wrote for theirselves.

I had about three songs written. I finally raked up enough dough to come up here and hang out for a while. Doodle Owens introduced me to Ray Baker. I sang Ray them three songs and he said, "I guess we better demo them." And George Jones cut a couple of them. I had written them in the morning sitting on the commode waiting to go to work.

I signed with Ray Baker at Bluegrass Music. Ray got me on RCA Records and I never did chart a song. I was on there for about two and a half years. Usually, when it come time for me to record, I had already given my good songs away. But back then I really didn't have my singing style. I could sing, but I didn't have any oomph in my voice. I sing better today than I ever have in my life. Unfortunately, it doesn't make any difference.

You didn't have your rich baritone back then.

You said that, I didn't.

Did that have to be cultivated with Jack Daniels and cigarettes?

Yeah, Jack Daniels and cigarettes. And Lefty Frizzell kind of pulled me all through it.

Doodle Owens helped me out a lot with the ropes in this town. I met him in Texas. We both sang at the same old honky-tonk down there called the Circle R Club.

Doodle was one of the first people I met in the music business. He was such a kind soul.

He was a great guy. We wrote a lot of songs together. We had a lot of Moe Bandy cuts. We wrote Moe's first hit, "I Started Hating Cheating Songs Today."

Dallas Frazier was telling me how prolific Doodle was.

He wrote all the time. I figured that's where he got his nickname "Doodle," because he was always doodling on a piece of paper, you know? And some of his doodling was pretty good. But when he was a kid, he would crawl backwards like a doodlebug. That's where he got his nickname.

How did you get tagged Whitey?

I got that while I was in high school. We were building this dam right outside my home town of Whitney. For two summers in high school, I worked out there with iron workers as an iron worker's helper. Iron workers don't remember names, they just look at you and say, "Hey, you with the pink eyebrows." They started calling me "Whitey." I never did really like the name Sanger. I held on to Whitey pretty good.

For a country singer, Sanger's a pretty good name.

Yeah. My old buddy Pete Drake always loved that name Sanger. Sanger D. Shafer.

Where did Sanger come from?

This guy named Sanger Clark was my mom's basketball coach in high school. I think she had a secret crush on him.

Although he didn't sire you.

No. I don't think. There might have been a Whitey in the woodpile somewhere.

What was family life like?

My sister and I were raised in a musical family. She's two years younger than I am. Everybody sang. My mom and dad had a Satellite Stamps Quartet out of Dallas. My mother would play piano. She'd take us up to the singing every Thursday night at the courthouse and make us sing, which we kind of liked. I hammed it up a little bit.

When did you get your first guitar?

My uncle gave me one when I was twelve years old. It had more than one hole in it.

So does Willie Nelson's.

I think the extra hole in my uncle's guitar was where a pick up used to be.

Your dream was to be a recording artist.

Yeah. That's absolutely right.

Is that desire still there?

No. I would probably been worse than Jones or some of the rest of them, because most of the time I need about a six-pack before I get up and sing.

Two hundred dates a year. That would add up.

Yeah, it would. And in between shows.

You might actually get on a police horse and ride around.

They got a million bucks worth of publicity out of that.

Maybe Tim McGraw and Kenny Chesney should do a duet of "I Fought The Law."

Pay a fine to stay out of jail and they're rocking on.

I opened for Ed Bruce for a year and it was the easiest job I ever had. I just got up and sang about three or four songs before he got out there. I kind of enjoyed that. I didn't have to worry about nothing.

Except getting on the bus.

I always hoped that Ed would fly, because I got the stateroom if he flew and didn't have to sleep in a bunk.

Your first publisher was Ray Baker.

I learned more about writing songs from Ray Baker than I did from any other songwriter. Ray didn't write a lot. But he's got one of the best musical ears of anybody I've been around in my life. He knows the song. He knows about writing. He knows what needs to be changed about it. In that way, he's helped me out a lot.

Ray has always been one of the greatest song pluggers that ever lived. When I signed with him, he only had one writer, which was Dallas Frazier. Of course, that's about all you need. If I'd had Dallas, I wouldn't need no more songwriters, you know?

Did Ray Baker teach you how to write a hit?

I don't know if you can teach somebody how to write a hit, but he knew when it wasn't a hit, I'll put it that way.

A good song editor.

Yeah. He'd say, "Go fix that," or "You need to work on that second verse. It needs to be as strong as the first one."

Did you have any resistance to re-writing?

No, because I didn't know nothing. And people started recording my songs. I was writing; he'd get them cut. You can't argue with that.

I never have been that hardheaded about taking advice, except for these days. I still don't like co-writing. I have a hard time doing that.

Why is that difficult for you?

Because I like to know somebody before I pull my britches down and show my butt. I sat in a room with Vince Gill. I stutter and he's bashful and I'm bashful. We sat there and looked at each other for two hours. There was a guy outside with a jackhammer going. I didn't have any fresh song ideas and he didn't either. Finally, after about two hours, we said, "Hey, we'll just try it again some other time."

And did you all try it again some other time?

No, we never got together again.

What you should have done is said, "Screw it! Let's get our clubs and go play eighteen!"

The guys I play golf with don't play like Vince Gill. I don't want to go play golf with Vince. I'll be looking for my ball while he's putting.

Do you play much pasture pool?

Not really. I used to play a lot. I don't play but about five or six times a year now. I'm going to try to get back into it some.

When I heard you singing "That's The Way Love Goes" at a benefit for Tommy Collins, I closed my eyes and it could have been Merle.

Or Lefty. Lefty and I wrote that together. I had the melody when me and Lefty starting writing on that song. I didn't have a title. I had about the first three lines. The song ain't got but eight lines. But he says, "Let me show you how to sing that." I said, "Yeah! That's great!" He's the one that put all them little curly cues in it.

Johnny Rodriquez went number one with it in seven weeks in '74. His version was only one minute fifty-nine seconds long. They didn't have a turn-around or anything.

Lefty cut it first. He'd just signed with ABC and he cut it on his first session. They were going to put it out second, but it got snuck over to Rodriquez some way. It hurt Lefty's feelings real bad, because he loved that song.

Lefty and I were downtown in Merle Haggard's room one night. I don't even know when it was or why it was, but me and Lefty went down there. Lefty didn't usually go many places, but he wanted to go down there for some reason. And Lefty said, "Hey, Knucklehead, sing Merle a new song." So I sang it in there. Rodriquez was over leaning up against a chest of drawers just kind of quiet, not saying nothing, you know? And Merle said, "Lefty, that'll be my next single." "No, I'm cutting that myself." And I said, "Are you kidding?" I mean, Merle was hotter than a pistol.

Merle eventually cut it.

Yeah.

How did you and Lefty meet?

Well, me and Doodle was riding around one day and he said, "That's where Lefty lives." I said, "What?" I'd been living about a block and a half from Lefty for several months and I didn't even know Lefty lived down that street. I said, "Really?"

Anyway, I did a demo for Ray Baker and the next day I said, "Boy, there's one on here I'd sure like Lefty to hear." I just went down there cold and knocked on his door with my session in my hand. He opened the door. I stuttered and told him who I was. I caught him just right. Alice was gone and he had a beer in his hand.

I said, "My name's Whitey Shafer. I did a demo last night and I've got one song on here I'd like for you to hear." He said, "Come on in. How many's on there?" I said, "Five." He said, "Let's listen to all five of them. You want a beer?" I said, "Uh huh."

So Lefty listened to all five of them and he picked one out called "You Babe." Merle cut that later, too. Anyway, he said, "I'll cut that tomorrow." He was still on Columbia then. He said, "You want to go to the session?" I said, "Sure." I pulled up in the parking lot behind Studio B and I could hear them rehearsing inside. Anyway, he put it out as a single.

What year did you knock on Lefty's door?

Probably '68. I moved here in '67.

Then after Lefty did that, he said "Why don't we write sometime?" I said, "Fine." I had this other song started called "Lucky Arms" and I didn't finish it because I wanted to write with Lefty. So I called Lefty up and I said, "Help me finish this song. I can't finish it." He wrote the second verse just like that and helped out with the chorus, too.

Lefty was always my hero. Always. Since the first time I heard "If You Got The Money, I Got The Time."

Lefty's singing style influenced your singing style.

Absolutely. Not only mine, many, many others.

We went to Dallas's cabin one day and we wrote "That's The Way Love Goes" and "I Can't Get Over You To Save My Life" in the same day. And that's the only time we ever went somewhere to actually write. Most of our writing was done over in Lefty's little house.

There was the big house and the little house. Alice didn't want him hanging around the big house when he was drinking, so he bought this little two bedroom house over on the other side of Hendersonville. The first time I went in there, he didn't even have any furniture. As big a star as Lefty was and he was sleeping on a mattress on the floor.

The interior decorator had not shown up yet.

He had a piece of plywood on the wall where he practiced throwing knives.

Sounds like a camp house.

Yeah, he was camped out.

And you became his drinking buddy.

Absolutely. He was a drinking buddy.

Could you hold your own with him?

He liked vodka, and I never did. I've always been a beer person, but I'd get to where I'd half-sole that beer with a little shot of vodka. But he'd pour out a water glass full of vodka. It'd take him a couple little drinks and he'd have that water glass gone. He drank Popov. He'd say, "A couple sips of this, Knucklehead, and you'll start popping off."

Lefty's death was very unexpected.

Yeah. I was doing a show in Waco. One of my rare bookings. And they called and said he had a stroke. I figured he'd be all right, and then he died that night. They didn't tell me until after the show that he had died. We hopped in the car and came back up here. I was one of the pallbearers. Me and Dallas and Doodle all had a couple of nips before we carried him. That was a pretty bad time.

How did that affect you?

I was kind of in denial for a little while, I guess you could call it. I mean, I didn't cry at the funeral. "I Do My Crying At Night." Me and Lefty and Doodle wrote that. The only thing that bothered me was that before we even started walking away, they started throwing dirt in on him. And that got me, man. Don't let them throw dirt on me. Wait until everybody gets gone before they throw that first shovelful. That's an awful sound, that first shovelful.

Did that bring tears to your eyes?

Yeah, I might have frosted up a little bit. That's the end, when that first shovelful goes down in there.

Did Lefty's death make you start running harder?

I couldn't run much harder. It probably made me slow down a little bit. I didn't have no drinking buddy left. My drinking buddy went away on me.

How did it affect your writing?

Well, he died in '75 and I didn't have any more luck until about '81 or '82. That's when Merle cut "That's The Way Love Goes." And George Strait did "Does Fort Worth Ever Cross Your Mind" and three more of my songs on that album.

I don't know why. I think part of it was because Ray Baker's contract got up with Acuff-Rose and he went away. My song plugger was gone.

And you weren't the type of guy who went out there and pitched his own stuff?

I've never been good at it. Unless I just happened to be around where we was passing a guitar and some recording artist happened to be sitting around. I always liked singing it to them in person. Hank Cochran was a genius at that. I watched Hank in somebody's recording session before. He'd be back there selling somebody a song and a tear would come to his eye. I mean, what an actor. He could do that. Hank Cochran could get a song cut.

I heard he's the world's greatest song plugger.

Oh, he is. No doubt about it.

But you can't take your guitar and play your songs for artists anymore.

If I demo a song, I've lost so much feeling. Except when Ray Baker was doing my demo sessions. Ray knew how to get a song across on a session. You can completely lose a song in a demo session. It don't even sound like what you think it's supposed to sound like when you go in there.

Have you considered going back to guitar/vocal demos?

I don't think it would work, because most of the songs these days are production songs. There's some producers in this town that wouldn't even know where to start if they didn't have something to start with. But I've always thought if a song was good enough, you could do it with you and a guitar, and it'll probably get cut. There's a lot of my songs that got cut, just me and a piano or me and a guitar.

Did you come to Acuff-Rose when Ray Baker's catalog was purchased by them?

That wasn't the reason. I knew Ray was fixing to sell out. And it kind of hurt me in a way. I just kind of quit. The last few years with Ray, we didn't even have a contract. I just wrote for him and he pitched 'em. I didn't write for nobody else.

You were on a draw?

I was on a draw. And we both felt comfortable without a contract. Quick as I could write 'em, he was getting them cut. He was producing Connie Smith. I had three Connie Smith singles in a row. This was after Dallas quit writing.

Ray called me and said he was fixing to sell out. He said, "You ought to go talk to Wesley Rose." So I did.

I almost quit again when Wesley was going to sell out, because I didn't know anything about Opryland. I really didn't know Jerry Bradley all that much. But Wesley talked me into staying, and I'm glad I did. Everything I ever wrote is in this building.

With a thirty-year career, that's very unusual.
Do you have any opinion about the name change from Opryland back to Acuff-Rose?

I was glad they did.

Why?

When I first signed, Wesley took me upstairs and showed me Fred Rose's old office. It's just got such a great history.

Hank Williams. Roy Orbison.
What was your relationship with Wesley Rose like?

It was good, except when I needed money. It wasn't too good then. He was a little tight. Actually, I got in the hole to him about thirty-six thousand dollars. He was worried and I was worried. I wasn't bringing a lot in. That's why it added up. I'd gone back to carpentering to help me get by.

So after Lefty died, you started swinging a hammer again.

I did that when I first came to town. I wrote a lot of songs while I was swinging a hammer. I'd write at night and on the weekends. Drink me a few beers and sit at the piano and bang on it. I need to start doing that again, but I need to lay off the beer. I don't even drink anything compared to what I used to drink. I'm teetotaling now.

I always took my radio when I was working. I was a finish carpenter doing trim work, so I was usually the only one in the house unless there's some painters puttying holes or something. One day "That's The Way Love Goes" came on by Haggard. I was starving back in the early 80s. I wasn't getting anything cut.

Did you wonder if you would ever get another cut?

I thought about that a lot. And also, "I'll never write another song. I don't know how to write." Every time I'd write a song, it was like starting over. And that's the way it's going to be right now, but I've got to start somewhere.

There's something magical about the process of songwriting.

Yeah, it is. There's something from up above. Always has been.

What do you think gives you the ability to tap into that?

I'd say it's just a blessing from God.

Is it still fun for you to go out and play?

I like to do it every once in a while. I just got back from Willie Nelson's golf tournament in Austin. I enjoy going out and singing at places like that once in a while. It feeds my little ego a little bit to have people take on a little bit over me.

I bet if you ran out to Fan Fair today, you'd sign a lot of autographs.

Nobody don't hardly know who Whitey Shafer is. I could walk through that crowd, and nobody would recognize me unless it was Kenny Chesney. Fans don't know what I look like.

That's part of the anonymity of being a songwriter.

I like going in Kroger's without somebody knowing who I am. I don't have to go shopping at four o'clock in the morning when nobody's there but me.

I can go in the Broken Spoke and nobody'll know who I am until I get up there and sing.

"Bandy, The Rodeo Clown."

That came from Lefty. "Let's write one about a clown." I said, "Well, that's cool, man."

Were you writing it specifically for Moe Bandy?

Yeah. Specifically for Moe.

If Moe didn't record it, you could have changed the name to Randy for a Randy Travis cut.

"All My Exes Live In Texas."

That was a true story. I just changed the names to protect the guilty. Changed the towns, too.

I wrote a sequel to that called "Is She Out Spending Christmas In Texas With My Exes Because I've Got A Brand New Ex Mad At Me In Tennessee," but George Strait didn't like it.

It's hard to get a non-positive Christmas song cut. But Christmas is a downer for so many people. It seems like there should be more "cry in your eggnog" Christmas songs.

I always get the blues at Christmas. I always have for some reason. I don't know why. There's a tendency for people to get depressed.

It's kind of nice to hear a song like "Grandma Got Run Over By A Reindeer."

"Please Come Home For Christmas" has a Motown melody. Elvis spiced up "Blue Christmas."

It was pretty sad when Ernest Tubb sang it, though, man.

When did you eulogize your drinking buddy with "Lefty's Gone"?

I don't know what year it was. I really don't. I wrote it in the '80s. I wrote two or three things about him and I didn't like any of them. I can't remember what they were now. I knew that was a good song.

It's acutally a wonder that George Strait recorded that, because we were sitting in the office and Ronnie Gant said, "Let me play you one you can't have." Mel Tillis had already put a hold on it. George came up off the seat and I told Ronnie, I said, "You're just going to have to explain to Mel."

Did you have a great deal of hope for "Lefty's Gone" to be a single?

That's all you can ever do is hope. But I didn't give it much hope. I was just glad to be on the album. When you're on the album, you sell as many as the rest of the people.

I'm still kind of perplexed by your Lefty story. I can't imagine that happening today.

I know.

I've never been one to force myself on anybody or even ask to get backstage. That just bugs me to bug somebody. I just can't do it. I could go back-stage with Merle any time I want. Me and Merle's pretty good friends now. And I don't like bugging him a lot.

What are your thoughts about the current state of country music?

Well, I appreciate Alan Jackson. I really do. He's sticking by his guns and he does country stuff. He's one of my favorites. I never have had anything recorded by him, though.

Maybe you need to call him up to co-write with you and Vince.

I don't know about calling him up.

You could always go knock on his door.

If I had a song, I might. No, he's probably got a dog that would bite your leg off.

Canine security system.

I hate rejection.

There's more rejection in songwriting than sales.

Well, yeah. Rejection is hard, especially if you know it's a good song.

Do you have any major songwriting influences?

Not really. I never did have any major influences. I liked the way Dallas and Doodle wrote songs. But I kind of got my own style of writing. I have a hard time co-writing, too, because I have a hard time getting into other people's ideas.

You find it a more enjoyable process to write by yourself.

I do if I got the right idea. Lately, I haven't been trying much of anything. I've just been confused about what's going on these days. I really don't like the music that I'm going to have to try to write.

I've been laying off for a reason. A lot of writers burn out. They just get sick of it. And I have to lay off every once in a while or I'd be the same way. If I don't just quit for just a little, I would have done been burned out.

Let the well fill back up.

Let the well fill back up and my pocketbook empty out.

The latter is your motivation.

Motivation will get you back down here with a pen in your hand.

It seems like co-writing can be more concerned about the destination than the journey.

Yeah.

I've got some songs down here now that I don't want anybody to hear. Really. We just wrote them because we were going to be together for three hours. "Oh, we got to write a song." And nothing works out that way for me. Publishers want you to produce. Write, write, write, write, write. But I just hate having my name on a piece of crap.

What if one of those pieces of crap got pitched, cut and went to the top of the chart.

If it's making money, I'd let it rock. I'll be the first one to admit that I haven't written just because I want to create something. I like having my stuff played and listened to *and* making money. I just wish I had saved some of it.

We're back to the motivation factor.

I'm getting there now. I'm getting there.

Have your exes in Texas been a part of your financial demise?

No, they never have. My exes don't have any part of any of my songs like they do with most songwriters.

What are your plans for the marketplace now?

I'm kind of starting over right now. I really am. I got the starting over blues, but I'm going to keep writing, because I'm too broke to quit. And I like to write new songs. So I'm just going to do like everything else, I'm just going to play it by ear.

What's your level of enthusiasm?

I don't have the fire in my belly like I used to, but I figure I can get it back. I figure I'm not done. And a lot of that has to do with luck.

Any advice to songwriters?

Don't play louder than you sing.

Photo courtesy of BMI Archives

Don Wayne

You're from Nashville. That's fairly uncommon in the music business.

I grew up in Nashville and lived a while down in White Bluff on an old rocky farm way back in the woods. Little skinny-ass kid.

Did you have black-framed glasses like me?

No, I never did have to wear glasses until now.

I was a lot more mature than most of the young people today. I grew up pretty quick. I've never been all that smart. I always kind of considered myself to be somewhat of a bumpkin. At thirteen or fourteen, I was pretty much earning my own way. We didn't have that much. Grew up poor.

Then you bought into the American dream defined by acquisition.

Yeah, I bought into it. Most hillbillies do. You notice that? They got to have those Cadillacs and those rings and those Rolex watches. I think it's from not having a damn thing when they grow up. Being so poor and deprived. And they think that you got to have all that glitters.

When did you wise up?

Just in the last fifteen or twenty years. I wish I'd a learned earlier.

I started working at about eighteen in a factory—Gray and Dudley. There was a fellow named Irvin Jones. He and his wife was out walking around one day and they come by our place and met me and my folks. He was a shipping clerk at

Gray and Dudley Stoveworks down in west Nashville. I'm sure he felt sorry for me and wanted to get the hoe out of my hand and get me in a factory. So he got me a job making wooden crates to put around these stoves. Then he got me in the tool and die shop. I was still at Gray and Dudley when I went into the service. This was right after Korea in the latter part of '54 and stayed until the end of '56. I was drafted because the draft was still in effect.

Cold war, communism.

Right.

I had already had some songs cut at that time. In '53, I had a song I co-wrote with Vic McAlpin that was the "B" side of a single for George Morgan. My sister, Nellie, got me acquainted with Vic McAlpin. Nellie is the oldest sibling of a family of eight. I'm the youngest. When I was about fourteen or fifteen and started plucking on the guitar and trying to learn a few chords, Nellie started trying to write songs and pitch them to people.

How much older is your sister?

Nellie was seventeen years older than I was. She had children just about as old as I was. She got married real young. But anyway, she got the songwriting bug and she teamed up with a girl named Leona Butram. Leona was a first cousin to a fellow named Hillis Butram. And Hillis Butram was a musician who worked for quite a few of the Opry acts.

I started at a real early age of trying to demo their songs. Neither of them played a musical instrument. Their meter wasn't perfect by a long shot and mine wasn't all together there either. Back in those days, we had to cut acetates.

And you got one shot.

One shot. So I worked with them trying to meter out their songs and then got to co-writing with them. We got our first cut by a fellow named Randy Hughes, who was a son-in-law of Cowboy Coats. Randy cut a little old risqué party-type song of ours and put it on the back of an old bawdy song called the "Birthday Cake." I don't know if you're familiar with that old song, but it's something you wouldn't want to sing to your children.

What was the name of your song?

"Sweetly, Neatly And So Completely." I don't know if it ever got on the radio or not, but it got on the record. It was an awful, awful song. But that was our first recording experience. It was on Tennessee Records.

One of the first songs I wrote was called "My Baby Don't Wear No Drawers." The title was given to me by my Mee Maw. Fortunately, it never made it to tape, so the world was spared that one.

I had an aunt named Frances. When I was a kid I wrote a song called "She's My Two-Ton Fanny With Wrinkles On Her But I Love Her Just The Same." My brother said, "Don, you shouldn't write songs like that and expect to get them recorded. Women don't like to hear about that. You can't talk about fat women in a song."

Unless you're a rap artist. "Brenda's Got A Big Behind" by L.L. Cool was a big hit. Even in the '50s, it sounds like access to the artist was essential.

It's always been that way. People cry and moan about it being politics now, but politics has been there forever. It's just a larger business.

With more lobbyists.

A lot more lobbyists and a bigger buffer zone. You used to could walk in and play somebody something with a guitar. Now you can't do that. They're too busy.

But I regret that somebody didn't take the time to talk to me more about songwriting and the business of songwriting and say, "Hey, you've got a little bit of talent. You need to use it. You need to work harder at it and some day you might have some things in a catalog that will make you money."

I viewed a song as a one-time, one-shot deal. Nell got me to take some songs to Vic McAlpin and we got a cut on George Morgan. On the George Morgan record, the first six months I made about three hundred dollars and the next six months, maybe a hundred or so. But that was a lot of money for '51.

Did you consider songwriting more of a lottery than a career choice?

Yeah. There was no security there.

Was the service your first time away from Nashville?

Yeah.

Where did you go?

I went from here to Fort Knox, Kentucky. Emily and I had been dating for two or three years, so after I come home from Fort Knox, we decided to go ahead and marry. We married on my ten-day furlough with about thirty bucks in my pockets. After the ten-day furlough, I went to Fort Belvoir, Virginia. After about nine or ten weeks there, I was shipped to Germany. Spent seventeen months over there. I come home in December of '56.

A very Merry Christmas. Why Germany?

We still had a lot of forces over in Germany. I worked in a supply warehouse. I whiled away a lot of my free time in the service clubs picking on a guitar and strumming with other musicians. Most of the guys were from the South.

And Emily wasn't there.

No, Emily wasn't able to come with us. I was in barracks, although it wasn't barrack style over there. We lived in a three-story building, four to a room. Had good facilities, we were warm and dry. Didn't have a lot of field duty.

That first few nights down there in Fort Knox I kept thinking, "Oh, Lordy, let this be a nightmare. Let me wake up from this damn stuff." They'd hassle and harass you till midnight.

What happened when you were discharged?

Back to the factory, but I didn't stay there long because things had changed. The economy was bad, but by law they had to rehire me. This was the Eisenhower years.

And the start of the Eisenhower Interstate System.

Right. To get people to work. It was a good thing he done it. But he strictly believed in paying as you go. He wasn't one of these guys that liked to build up a lot of national debt.

Eisenhower might have gotten the interstate idea from the autobahns over in Germany. They had those when I was there. Big wide highways with the exits and entrances like we have now.

It was a well-developed country at that time.

I was an apprentice in the tool and die making at Gray and Dudley when I went in service, and I was still an apprentice when I come out of service. Our job primarily was maintenance work on tools and dies that were built to make those stoves. I worked a couple weeks at Gray and Dudley and got laid off. In '57, I must have worked at four or five different places. It was awfully hard to fit in after two years in service. In fact, I was tempted to go back in service.

Why was it hard to fit in?

I was probably mentally lazy from just working on supply depot. I started trying to work in job shops rather than a maintenance shop. The time limits on the jobs were much tighter than they were at places like Gray and Dudley. They were building new stuff and you were given so many hours to get a job done. All kinds of pressing dies and molds, so it was a lot harder. Plus, the economy was bad. Work was hard to come by. I ended up going to Lexington, Kentucky, in 1959, working up there for six months. I wasn't doing anything musically at that time.

Emily wasn't happy, so we decided to come on back to Nashville.

In 1959, I went to work for Fred D. Wright here in Nashville. And I was still working there when I joined Tree as a staff writer. I went there on the advice of some other people in the business that I had met through Nell. All of my contacts were through Nell. She was working some with a publisher named Gary Walker. Nellie hung in there with me. She was right there when I come out of service. She was there to prod me into getting back into music and trying to do something.

Was she your biggest fan?

My biggest fan. She was a mama just about.

As a songwriter, you became a tool and die maker of sorts. Your tool was your guitar and you were a die maker, because you were killing Mama in a song.

Danny Dill says I kill off everybody. I just kill them off by the hundreds.

Jamie O'Hara might hold the record with over 57,000 for the song he wrote about the Vietnam Memorial called "The Wall."

He's a wonderful writer.

You eventually signed with Tree Publishing.

I signed with Tree in '63. It was really a great place for me to be. They dumped me after ten years.

Join the club.

But it wasn't altogether their fault. I was depressed and drinking a lot more than I should have been. And wasn't turning in a lot of songs. But my relationship with Buddy Killen was good.

At the time I went to Tree, Jack Stapp was running WKDA, which was a pop radio station. Buddy was running the publishing company. Buddy had produced some hits on Joe Tex and was doing a lot of rhythm and blues stuff. And there was a kid there by the name of Ronny Wilkins who co-wrote "Love Of The Common People" with John Hurley.

It was basically just three or four people there when I went. I didn't know Jack Stapp. Later on I come to realize that Jack was the primary owner of the company. Buddy just owned a small percentage. Jack didn't come on board the publishing company until Curly Putman had hit with "Green Green Grass of Home" and Roger Miller hit with "Dang Me" and money started coming in.

So Jack gave up his position at WKDA. I remember him coming and taking the big office that Curly was occupying and moving Curly to an office in the back of the building that wasn't much more than a damn walk-in closet.

Did you hang out with Roger Miller?

No, I never did run around with Roger. Roger traveled in a lot faster circles than I did. I'm pretty much of a hillbilly and I was married. When I first went to Tree, I was pretty straight-laced about even drinking. I didn't drink much and did-n't do a lot of hanging out. I went there and turned in my songs. Tried to keep abreast of what was happening and who was recording.

How did your recording career come about?

That happened through Hillis Butram. I cut a record for Hillis on Work Records in '59. We thought it was going to hit pop. It started making a little bit of noise, but he didn't have the money to promote it. And maybe the record just wasn't there. But, anyway, nothing happened on that.

I don't think I would have been happy as an artist. I don't think I would have been happy living out of a suitcase. I had a regular acoustic guitar and most of the places where you worked they didn't mike your guitar, so you relied on whatever band was behind you. I used to go out and do those one-nighters where the musicians knew all of their stuff and they didn't know yours. And most of them were accustomed to doing that stuff where you're on the one chord and then you go to the seventh and then you step up to the four chord. Then down to the five chord and back to the one chord. That stock country sound.

Three-chord country.

Yeah, three-chord country. And some of my stuff would go from the one chord to the five chord. You weren't able to use the seventh. Then go to the four chord then back to the five chord. They might have rehearsed it one time the week before. We'd send records prior to the engagement. They were never ready, so that was an ordeal to go through. Maybe if I had had a big hit record where I could have hired a couple of musicians it might have worked okay. But I really wasn't obsessed with being an artist like I was being a writer. I was really obsessed with having success as a songwriter.

"Country Bumpkin" was recorded after you were released from Tree. How did that song get to Cal Smith?

I took it to Walter Haynes who was producing Cal Smith.

How successful was Cal Smith's career at this time?

He was a fairly successful country artist. He'd been out a while. He worked out on the coast in California a good many years. Then he got the job fronting for Ernest Tubb. Then he got a record deal with Cap Records. They were owned by Decca. He went from Cap to Decca and then MCA. So he was on MCA. I think the biggest things he had prior to "Country Bumpkin" was "The Lord Knows I'm Drinking" and "I Found Someone Of My Own," which was a pop hit that they put on a country album.

So he'd had a couple of good-size hits. "Country Bumpkin" definitely extended his career for a while. It really gave him an identity. Cal Smith pretty much done my phrasing. All they worked from was a guitar and vocal.

I don't know if you noticed, there's six beats in the first measure. I had been at WSM a few months prior to writing "Country Bumpkin" and was talking with Jim Ed Brown and he said, "I'm going to do some more recording pretty soon, Don, write me a chant. You know what I'm talking about, don't you?" I said, "You want something like 'Morning' or 'Three Bells.'" He said, "That's exactly what I want." So I started writing "Country Bumpkin" and I was doing it that way. Instead of starting with a solid beat, I would just strum the guitar and say a phrase and then strum the guitar again, say a phrase. It came out with six beats in that first measure.

It throws a lot of musicians. They don't like stuff like that. That's out of kilter. It really don't amount to anymore than a split measure. I had a front verse on that thing that I took off. I'm glad I did because the song is more universal now.

After "Country Bumpkin" became a big hit, did you think of going back to Tree?

Well, I thought about going back to Tree. Buddy called me and asked me to come back. I just didn't know if I would ever fit back in there or not. I was hurt pretty bad. It was pretty devastating. I had given ten years to the company and I had not sandbagged a song. I had promoted the company in every positive way that I could. If I was sandbagging, "Country Bumpkin" would have been the one, because I was thoroughly convinced that it would be a hit record if it was recorded right. I could tell it affected people that I sang it for. People were really moved by the song.

How much of a role has Emily played in critiquing your songs?

Well, she just about thinks everything that I do is wonderful.

It's kind of like a mom critique.

That's exactly what I was going to say. You know, Mama's boy can do nothing wrong. And if he's a songwriter, everything he writes is wonderful. I've heard wives of songwriters sit around and go on about what a great song their husband just sung, and I'd know it wasn't a great song. So I don't think they really give a real honest critique. They're biased to you. They love you and they want you to succeed.

I was still working in the factory when "Saginaw, Michigan" was a hit. I had already signed a contract in '63. But if I got something going as a writer and come up with some hit songs, I could become a staff writer. So Buddy Killen called me in March of '64 and said, "How much money do you think you'd have to have?" So I told him a hundred.

How much were you making at the factory?

I was probably bringing home a hundred and fifty, but I had my insurance paid for. I talked it over with Emily and she said, "I think we can make it on that." So we took a chance on it. But I was reluctant even after having a number one recording with "Saginaw, Michigan." I was wanting to see some money coming in instead of a weekly draw.

I hear about people who are having hit songs now and the first quarter performance earnings getting up close to a hundred grand for the writer. God, that's amazing to me. I think the big quarter on "Country Bumpkin" was ten or twelve grand.

Where did your life go after "Country Bumpkin"?

Cal Smith and I started a publishing company in '74 or '75 called Country Bumpkin Music, but it didn't work. Probably the business end of it was taking away from my creative part. I just wasn't coming up with the songs that he needed to sustain his career, and he wasn't finding the songs to sustain his career.

Did you have signed writers?

No. Just me and him. He was financing the company, but he wasn't willing to dump that kind of money into the company. We owned the company fifty-fifty. I was working without a draw, but he was investing the money for the office. We had writers bringing us material.

Have you remained active in your songwriting?

I'm still trying to write. I haven't had a lot of success in recent years. My last thing was a song I co-wrote with Bobby Fisher in the early '80s, "What In The World Did I Do?" It was a Top Twenty record. That's been pretty much the biggest thing I've had in the last fifteen years or so.

Do you consider yourself retired?

No, I don't. I'm on Social Security, but I'm not retired. I'm still wanting to do it. I'm going out and doing showcases. But I made up my mind I'm going to have fun with it and enjoy it. Not be obsessed with it and let it run me nuts. I think it had just about run me nuts at one time.

Where did the idea for "Country Bumpkin" come from?

I was talking to Early Williams and he told me, "We was in a staff meeting a few months back, Killen was talking to Tom Hartman, and said, 'Tom, how's old Don writing?' Tom said, 'Oh, hell, Buddy, Don's writing good. He always does. But, damn, nobody wants to hear about that frost on the pumpkin.'"

So "frost on the pumpkin" hit me, not only as a phrase, but the cutting way he was implying that my stuff was too hillbilly and too down-home to be commercial. That's what he was in effect saying. And I could understand why he was saying that. I was writing a lot of hillbilly stuff.

Early Williams told me that in 1970. And that phrase hung in my mind until the summer of '73. One morning I was driving to Music Row. I got on the interstate and I started writing in my mind this novelty song about a greenhorn songwriter bringing his songs to Nashville and meeting this fat cat publisher. And the fat cat's saying, "Hey, we don't want to hear about that frost on the pumpkin. Take your songs and go back home, country bumpkin."

And all at once I got off on a different tack entirely and in a period of six or seven minutes, almost in the time it takes that story to unfold, I had those three choruses written. Of course, there wasn't much to them, but I was seeing the other stuff happening leading up to those courses. I was seeing the guy walk into the bar and settle himself in and being clumsy and awkward. And I was picturing a guy who was just so green he didn't even really know how to order a drink.

And then the story just unfolded. I thought to myself, "Man, I've stumbled on to a hit song here." But after thinking about it further, I thought, "This could be more than a hit song. This could be a great song, if I write what I'm seeing."

Song of the Year.

Well, I wasn't thinking that big. But I was thinking, "Man, if I can just write what I'm seeing and get the people to see most of what I'm seeing in my mind, this will be a great song, will be around a while." But I'm sure proud that it did make CMA Song of the Year.

Everything really happened fast. We got invited to the BMI awards in '74. It was the CMA Song of the Year in '74. The Academy of Country Music Song of the Year. We drove out to Los Angeles in March of 1975. Had a wonderful trip out there.

Drove out there?

Yeah, it took three days.

My youngest sister lives in L.A. She said, "Now, you guys have got to go back through Vegas while you're out this far. It would be a sin to go back to Nashville without going to Vegas."

That's one way of looking at it.

And she was absolutely right. We went to Vegas and spent one night. At that time, I didn't know how Emily would like it, because she was raised up in the Church of Christ and pretty straight-laced. I didn't know if Emily would take to those cocktail waitresses. She loved it. She couldn't pull that thing fast enough. I thought to myself, "Man, she's gone crazy."

Was she on a penny machine?

Nickel.

She's a high roller.

She still plays nickel machines. She still loves to go to Vegas. She'll go to Tunica at the drop of a hat.

How much of "Nashville" is autobiographical?

You'll notice that I use my older sister Nell in it. And my mother worked at Werthan Bag Mill during the time she was pregnant with me. So this song shows a little picture of the world that I grew up in. I make it ten years after I was born. I was born in '33.

Back in those days, Werthan Bag Mill was a sweatshop. Fourth and Monroe Street is three blocks from where I grew up on Third Avenue in north Nashville. By the time I was two, my mother had divorced my father and remarried, so I grew up with a stepfather.

And an absentee father.

Yeah. My father had from time to time got into a little trouble dealing with moonshine down in Dickson County where they come from, and maybe a little bootlegging here in Nashville. He had had some run-ins with the law, so I threw that in. Then I put my older sister Nell in the trash mill, but she never worked in a beer joint or tavern like that. Trash mill was just a name that I come up with to rhyme with Nashville. I got a homemade guitar from another sister. So a lot of it is true.

I don't know much about David Houston's background, do you?

I know a little bit about him because he was from my hometown.

I liked him real well. He was a down to earth person that I could relate to.

I went to high school with his nephew by the same name. His nephew was a good picker and singer.

David Houston was a wonderful singer.

When you listen to "Country Bumpkin" and "Nashville," the vocal quality on both of those songs outranks a lot of what you hear today.

I got some help on "Nashville." I was out of town at the time they pitched it to Billy Sherrill for David Houston. In the last verse, I had the guy involved killed in Vietnam. And he was dying.

I knew somebody had to die.

Well, the mother's done died.

So Billy Sherrill said, "I really think that's a great song, but that last verse is just too much of a downer. The guy going to Vietnam and dying there before he can make his dreams come true in Nashville. I would rather have it end on a positive note."

So Johnny Slate, who was pitching songs for Tree, knocked out that last verse and ended it with the guy going on stage and singing his songs. Then if they ever called him a star, he'd call the girl that helped him make it big in the town of Nashville.

Johnny wouldn't take any share in the song, but he wrote that last verse. He said there wasn't that much work involved in it and it was a feather in his cap to get a cut by Billy Sherrill.

There's another song of mine that I wrote from my teenage experiences: "Belles Of Southern Bell." When I met Emily, she was still in high school. After she graduated from high school, she went to work for Southern Bell. Back in those days, they'd work a split shift. She'd would go in at ten in the morning and work till two, then two or three hours off, maybe go back at five or six and work till ten. It was a long day, but that's the way they had it set up for some reason. I don't know why.

Might have been the peak calling periods.

Could have been.

Sometimes I would go, especially on Saturdays, and pick her up at two o'clock. We'd go out and have lunch. Then come back at five or six.

But even before then, I had driven by Southern Bell quite a bit and watched the changing shifts, the good-looking women coming up and down the streets in high-heeled shoes. And there was a little old traffic cop down there at Fourth and Church. Almost always the light would be out.

He was unplugging it.

Traffic was murder then. You wouldn't think it would be, but the streets were all two-way and they were even narrower than what they are now. And those lights would be out and this little cop was supposedly there to direct traffic. Hell, he couldn't stay out of a conversation with them girls long enough to direct traffic. He'd be over on the sidewalk running down a half a block talking to them. It was funny.

But I just got to reminiscing about those days at the telephone company and come up with that little old song. Just a matter of being in the right place at the right time.

Bob McDill

What drew you to the art form of songwriting? Why did this become your primary focus of creative expression?

Just loved it. Little ole boys in coastal Texas didn't become a playwright or an opera singer. Not likely. I miss serious music. I started on viola in the fourth grade. Dropped out. My brother stayed with an orchestra and played up into college. I became a guitar bum. Therefore, popular radio was the center of the universe. And, of course, I aspired to be on the radio. If I had grown up in New York in the shadow of Broadway, I would have probably been awed by Broadway and wanted to get up there on the stage. If I had grown up in L.A. in the shadow of Hollywood, I would have wanted to be a movie star.

So, ultimately, you would have loved to sing your own songs.

No. I wanted to tell the stories. I didn't want to be an entertainer. I did some of that in college.

What was your college degree?

English lit.

Was reading and literature a big part of growing up in your household?

It was for me.

Photo courtesy of ASCAP

What did your parents do for a living?

My pop sold real estate. Sometimes successfully; sometimes not so successfully. My mother was a bank clerk for thirty years. Mother was an avid
reader and my brother was a classical music guy. We had classical music going
all the time after my brother got old enough to appreciate it and buy the
records. He was older than I was. But I just fell in love with rock and roll.

How did you segue from rock and roll to country?

In those days, formats were not the way they are today. They weren't
these boutique formats. We had several stations in town. One was pure country. One was all black music. But the other two were called pop music. Everything you could imagine was on pop radio in Beaumont, Texas, in the 1950s.
You would hear Perry Como, Frank Sinatra, the Andrew Sisters, the Mills
Brothers. And then you would hear a New Orleans French record. Then you

would hear a real country record—Brenda Lee and Ray Price. I didn't know it was country. I didn't know it was made in Nashville. It was all on pop radio. The Everlys. Elvis. Nobody knew it was country. Pop radio was so diverse back then.

Your first hit was "Happy Man" by Perry Como. Where were you living then?

I was still in college in Beaumont, Texas, when I wrote that. It was a hit when I was in the navy.

You also spent a few years in Memphis. It's home to a couple of Kings—Elvis and B.B. How did Nashville become King of Country?

The reason Memphis failed was everybody thought so small. Studios wouldn't pay the musicians a full session every three hours. They wanted them to work all night for a session. They manipulated their union scale, and at the same time, didn't want the best musicians working for any other studio so that somebody else could cut a hit record. It was very small-minded. And it's no wonder all the musicians came to Nashville where they could make some money.

Nashville always had a better attitude about it. Part of Nashville's attitude I've always disliked and part of it is good. From the business standpoint, Nashville always had its act together. On the other hand, there's a part of Nashville that's too much business and not enough music. That's the downside of that Nashville attitude.

A few years ago—I won't mention any names—somebody had a grand idea: we'll create a country garage band. They had placards all over town. And the garage band cut a bunch of sides. They had guys in there whooping and hollering and knocking mikes over to make things sound real raw. It never occurred to anybody to go out and find a real country garage band. Nashville's attitude was to record a bunch of slick musicians and then try to make it sound like a garage band.

See what I mean? Top down. Nashville is always very top down. Memphis is more bottom up.

Unfortunately, it went bottoms up.

The Kentucky Headhunters were a bottom up kind of thing, but the band you're speaking of went platinum.

So what? It wasn't real. The Headhunters were pretty real, weren't they?

Yeah. They're family—two brothers and a cousin. They look the way they look. They live geographically and musically close to their roots. They have played together a long, long time. They did go through a breakup, which spawned the Brother Phelps. But if you look at the Headhunters today, what you see is what you get.

They're still the same.

Did you write a lot on Music Row?

Always. Always had an office down here.

Five days a week.

Uh huh.

So you were a classic workhorse in terms of everyday writing. Your peak year, in terms of volume, you wrote forty-eight songs. Some professional songwriters grind out over a hundred songs in a year. Do you think you were much more critical of yourself—rewriting the song and then rewriting the song again—before you presented it?

I think so. I didn't turn one in until I knew it was as good as I could possibly make it. I worked on them lots and lots of hours. I'm not critical of those people who can write five songs a week, but I never could do it that way. I always did it the slow, meticulous way. One song a week was my goal.

It seems like high volume songwriters take a lot of the cookies out of the oven half-baked.

I always thought so. There's a lack of richness and depth. So often there's something else that could be there and it isn't. I've heard some really good things by people who don't do much rewriting, but it was never my way.

I guess it's shotgun versus rifle.

My percentage was really high. It was 50 percent when Bill Hall was my publisher and we were really rocking. And then the percentage dropped, dropped, dropped, dropped, dropped.

Getting 50 percent of your songs recorded is a very high percentage.

Yeah. That was during my peak years.

Did you lament some of the songs that you wrote that are just collecting dust on a shelf?

I have some. Mostly the last couple of years. The last couple years of my career I really reached out and wrote some thoughtful pieces of what I call art. Art versus commercial ditties. I wrote some art songs that nobody would record. But I had a great relationship with Don Williams and then Dan Seals. Both those guys would do songs simply because they liked them. Simply because they wanted them on the album to give it richness. Also, they liked more than just ditties and were always going for something beyond. But then toward the end of my career, there wasn't anybody like that around.

That must have been frustrating, because you live and die by the machine. If you're a songwriter, you definitely need a host organism.

You do. And I guess that was part of the demise of my enthusiasm—knowing that I was not going to be able to get those art things cut anymore.

Were you surprised that "Good Ole Boys Like Me" was a single?

Sure was. Surprised it was a hit. I thought, "The best I'll do is get this on a Don Williams album." But then the disk jockeys started playing it and people started calling. It was an accident. It was not supposed to happen, but those things slip through the cracks.

My fishing buddy at the time was the head of the history department down in South Carolina. A fellow named Tom Connelly. He's deceased now, but he really got me interested in Southern lit. I had just read Robert Penn Warren's *A Place To Come To*, and I thought it paralleled my childhood in several ways. That song just sort of began to happen after I finished that book. Mostly it's just the standard southern themes compressed into three-and-a-half minutes. I got a lot of them in there.

Southern wind, pine trees.

The issues of race.

Religion. Got a little drinking in there.

Dysfunctional family. The father/son thing in the South.

The second verse is autobiographical: when I was in school I ran with the kid down the street and watched him burn himself up on bourbon and speed.

The last verse about growing up reading Thomas Woolf and listening to John R. and the Wolfman on the radio at night is very southern. John R. was at WLAC-Nashville and Wolfman Jack started at WXLR-Del Rio, Texas. Those two stations covered the South. Other kids didn't get that early dose of what was called race music back then. It may have been the beginning of rock and roll. John R. and Hoss Allen at WLAC were playing those black race records at night and millions of white, southern middle class kids were listening to their radios under the covers with a flashlight.

In the '50s?

Yeah. Growing up on black music. I knew Hoss Allen. He was a friend of mine. He died a few years ago. He said, "We never realized we had that audience. Millions of white, middle class kids out there listening to the radio." He had no idea we existed. He said, "We should have been selling Coca-Cola, instead we were selling Baby Chicks and Royal Crown Hairdressing."

To the supposed audience.

The supposed black, rural audience. That's who they thought they had. And they did. But they didn't know who else they had.

I don't guess that would slip past the marketing department today.

No. That mistake wouldn't be made today.

What is your most definitive song?

I am "Amanda" and "Good Ole Boys Like Me." People think of me and associate me with those two. I'm proud of those. There's also another one that I'm very proud of: "Everything That Glitters Is Not Gold" that Dan Seals and I wrote.

Let me tell you, one of the blessings of a long career is that people don't remember the garbage. I spent a lot of years writing a lot of garbage—sex and drinking and cheating songs—to make money during the '70s and '80s. But the blessing is, nobody remembers them. It's as if they never existed.

The songs that are still played on the radio are all things I can be reasonably proud of. The ones that are earning the money are the ones that are really wacky. The songs that still play and the songs that turned into copyrights are the things that were not only not about love, sex, and drinking, but they were the most thoughtful, most arty.

Songs like "The Gambler" or "The Ride" seem to be the hardest to get cut, yet the most enduring.

I'm not the only one who's ever noticed it. Thanks. I'm glad you noticed it, too. I couldn't find any little dumb ditties on my royalty statement after a couple years. They disappeared.

When I first started out at Tom Collins Music, I was slapping on reel-to-reels, listening to the catalog and thinking, "Damn, our best songs are still in the filing cabinets." There was a certain sadness to that discovery. I had not been behind the music business curtain. I had only heard what radio and record companies had fed me. That was quite a revelation, a disappointment, and a shock.

How did that feel as a writer?

That's the tough part.

People may curse Nashville, but it's the same way in any popular art form. You have to be turned into a three-minute jingle writer. For the most part, you can't get on television, rock and roll radio, or any medium doing good art. It's pretty rare.

Did you come to the realization that you needed to write x number of three-minute jingles to be successful, yet x number of art songs to really express yourself?

Yeah. I did both for a lot of years. And I'm glad I did both.

When I was co-writing, I was always trying to write a hit. Co-write and make money. But often when I'd write by myself, it would be because I had an idea that was something more thoughtful or richer.

Did you feel like you sold out by becoming a three-minute jingle writer?

I did to an extent. But I also wrote my art pieces over the years. And I still have them. A lot of them aren't recorded, but they're still there.

What is the value of the art pieces you have written that the world doesn't know about?

Economically, if they're not recorded, the value is zero.

But on an intrinsic level?

My heroes were Johnny Mercer and Paul Simon and Joni Mitchell and people with a voice with something to say. That's what I wanted to do. In the '60s, music was a pulpit, a vehicle to actually say things. Not "she's gone and I'm sad," but to genuinely say things.

Not to merely fill up time between commercials on the radio.

That was what I thought music was growing up. I since found out it wasn't. That was just maybe a blip. But having written those art pieces, I satisfied something deep in me that wanted to do that. I wanted to elevate country music to an art form. I wanted to lift the whole damn thing. I had a mission back then when I was writing that stuff. I wanted to lift country music out of the ooze of cheating and drinking.

"Amanda" was a phenomenon. Not just because Don Williams was a folk singer on country radio. Not just because Allen Reynolds made country music records that you could listen to with earphones and they still sounded good. The song was very different and had something to say.

With "Amanda," you had an inside track because you were friends with Allen Reynolds.

And Don Williams. Don and I saw each other every day. We were both working down there in the publishing company. I was a tape kid and he was a plugger. Allen had brought him here from Texas, because he remembered his voice from the Pozo-Seco Singers. It had that lonesome, windy prairie sound to it.

How did you and Allen Reynolds meet?

I met Allen way back in Beaumont, Texas. Jack Clement and Bill Hall had a little studio there, and Allen and Dickie Lee were writing for their little publishing company. It was right behind the King Edward Hotel. Allen and Dickie would sing at the bar. I had a little group when I was in college and I would sing in the bar. We met that way. Then I joined them in Memphis after I got out of the navy. We all came to Nashville together in 1970.

With no intention of diminishing "Amanda," what do you think would have happened to the song if you took your relationship with Don Williams and Allen Reynolds out of the equation?

Well, I don't know. I'll tell you a story. After "Come Early Morning" came out and it was a hit, they turned it over and "Amanda" was on the other side. And it was a hit. Waylon Jennings called me up and said, "Son, you wrote my life. Why didn't you bring me that song?" Well, when the "Come Early Morning" side was hitting, I took the "Amanda" side over there and put it on his desk and tried to get that gal to play it for him for four or five months. So I said, "I did bring you that. I tried to play it for you, but I couldn't get in to see you." I thought it was his life, too.

"Amanda" went to number thirty-three in '73 for Don Williams, but number one for Waylon Jennings in '79. "We Believe In Happy Endings." Johnny Rodriquez. Number seven in '78. But the duet with Emmylou Harris and Earl Thomas Conley went number one in '88. It's unusual when the definitive cut is the second time around.

Uh huh.

Johnny Rodriquez's "We Believe In Happy Endings" takes on a bit of irony with his murder trial.

I haven't read anything about that lately. What's the latest?

He was acquitted, but it's still a very unhappy ending for Johnny Rodriquez.

It's a shame. He was such a sweet, lovable, nice guy. Talented. Good-looking. Everybody liked him.

I got to know him a little bit when Tom Collins was producing him at the tail end of his career. He was a very likable man. But fate has its twists and turns.

Yeah. I heard he was doing country boy crank the night he shot that fellow and that's pretty hard-core stuff. I think it's a version of methamphetamine.

I was talking to Glenn Sutton and he said that Don Williams—before his career happened—came over to his house and laid carpet.

I heard that.

Don told Glenn he was actually thinking of leaving town. Did those thoughts ever go through your head?

Yeah, it was difficult. Really difficult. My roommate, Jim Casey, and I actually missed some meals, which is a lesson. If you've ever gone hungry, you won't forget it. Most people haven't ever experienced that, but it makes a permanent impression.

Don Williams went on to amass fifty-six chart singles. Twelve were yours. You had over 20 percent of his singles. When you have a string like that going with an artist, you really don't need a song plugger, do you?

No, but I had the best plugger in the world. Bill Hall was a great plugger.

Bill Hall had ownership in your copyrights.

Yeah, he had ownership. But then he sold the catalog to Polygram and sold my stuff along with it. He stayed on as general manager and still did a tremendous job for years and years.

You're the first songwriter I've ever heard praise his plugger.

I don't know what's happened to the plugger. They don't seem to matter. They're not important anymore. They're out of the loop in a lot of cases.

Ever notice how everybody claims credit for getting a song cut?

Oh, I know it. Dickie Lee and I had a song that Joe Cocker covered. We counted ten people who had called us and taken credit for that Joe Cocker cut.

It makes it tough to give out a bonus for getting a cut when a company has multiple pluggers and copyrights split with other publishers.

You can't, because they all would get the bonus. Every time a song was cut, everybody did it in some way. We'd play games and catch them at it.

Would you bust them?

Oh, yeah, sometimes. They'll all take credit. It's amazing.

How much effort did you invest into pitching your material?

Some.

Writers really pitch their own stuff today.

They do. And if you don't, you're sunk.

What are your thoughts on "Gone Country" becoming "Ford Country"?

Ca-ching.

So you approved?

I wrote the ad.

You wrote the ad?

Yeah. Two versions. And quite happy to do it.

What do you think about people who feel that licensing a song to a commercial is selling out?

"Gone Country" is a fun song poking fun at a bunch of silly Yankees. It's not *Porgy and Bess*. Get over it. It deserves to be a Ford ad. It's as good a Ford ad as it was a country song.

I love the line "It sounds so easy, it shouldn't take long."

"He'll back in the money in no time at all."

But you can't write country music looking down your nose at it.

That's true.

What do you think makes country simple and complex at the same time?

The simple/complex phenomenon of country music? I don't know. I didn't get it for a couple years when I first came to Nashville. I was a folky. I could write the folk things, folk/rock things and the country/rock things, but I didn't get real country music. One night, a bunch of guys were riding around barhopping. "A Good Year For the Roses" by George Jones came on the radio. I just had this moment of epiphany. I've got it in that split second. I understood it.

What did you understand?

It's not explainable. You can't explain it. If I could explain it, then anyone could get it and they could go write a hit. I can't explain hardcore country music that only a person who appreciates that art form gets. To everybody else, it all sounds alike.

I don't think the people you wrote "Gone Country" about really get it.

Do you? Maybe they can take a joke or you don't think they get it?

I don't think they get it.

Really? Back that up somehow. Tell me why you think that.

I've never heard any of the recent transplants—and I've met my share—ever take any offense at it or even see it in that light. They say, "That's a great song! It's just like me coming to town!"

They do?

The ones I've talked to. Maybe I haven't polled enough people, but it's as if "Gone Country" went over their heads.

If country music record sales and radio airplay had not increased so dramatically in the '90s, do you think all these Yankees would have cared about coming to Nashville?

No. Hell, no. It's not that I wanted to make fun of them so much, it's more that I wanted to get at the reasons.

The motivation.

The motivation—why they come here. I had heard these comments over dinner with people from L.A. I had heard people say these rationalizations that they used. Like L.A.'s just awful. It's not a good place to raise the kids.

The crime and the smog. All these things that they came up with, because their careers were in the tank out there. They're fleeing to Nashville with all those damn things they use to rationalize it. Hilarious.

Do you think now that so many people without country roots have gone country, that country is gone?

I don't know. I'll tell you, I am not one of these old sticks-in-the-mud who laments, "Well, we're losing the real old country music." I always was for country/folk fusion, country/rock fusion. I love that. I wanted country music to grow and change. I think that's the way it should be.

If those old farts want to sit around and listen to Bill Monroe, great. Listen to Bill Monroe. Listen to Merle Haggard. That's fantastic. But don't try to dictate what a viable piece of popular culture is supposed to be.

The problem with old country music is nobody buys it. People don't buy those records. You can still hear people in town, even guys younger than me, saying, "We need to get back to some of the old country music." Oh, yeah, so we can get back to having hits that sell fifty thousand records, right? I was never one of those people. When I whine, it's not because the music fused with rock or fused with pop. When I whine, it's because the music is without substance.

You're more concerned with the quality of the song.

Yeah.

I grew up on rhythm and blues and rock and roll. I told you my John R. and Wolfman story. I'm not one of these kids who grew up in some little town listening to and worshiping Conway Twitty. I'm a fusion guy.

"Gone Country" was around a little while before it got cut.

Little bit. Alan Jackson's a courageous lad.

Travis Tritt had held "Gone Country" for a couple days and then got scared. I've got a tape of Alan singing that on the CMA Awards show with Travis in the audience. He looks like "I can't believe he got up here on network television and insulted all those powerful Yankees."

The people in Nashville were afraid of it because you can't do that. And I think the reason is we as Southerners are so used to being made fun of, that there's really some sort of fear about Southerners making fun of others. We love to make fun of ourselves. And we don't mind others making fun of us. Outside Nazis, white Southerners are the most made fun of and violated people in modern culture. And yet we just sort of take it and yuk along.

Southerners are very uncomfortable with making fun of L.A. or New York or Las Vegas. I'm not even sure why, but we are very uncomfortable with that. Maybe it's because that's where the boss man is. That's where the people that own everything live.

When I first heard "Little Man" on the radio, I thought, "I bet Bob McDill wrote that," which is a huge compliment to Alan Jackson.

Why, does it sound like something I'd write?

Sounds like something you would write, but Alan wrote it 100 percent. I thought it was very well written. It was a real slice of life, real Americana.

I know Alan, and I think he's a great guy. Two of the twelve songs on *Under The Influence* are mine. I think he grew up liking my songs the way I grew up liking Paul Simon and Johnny Mercer. And I think he sort of feels he owes me a little something because he has patterned some of his songs after some of my formulas. Of course, I got them from somebody, too. He doesn't owe me a thing. I'm the one who benefited by it. He's paid me back a hundredfold.

But do you feel a sense of satisfaction that the torch has been passed?

Yeah. I feel very complimented that he was influenced by my music growing up.

I heard Pam Tillis say she thought you and Dean Dillon each took two Midols and channeled "All The Good Ones Are Gone."

That was my idea. I can't say it was mine. I grabbed it out of the air. I heard several women use that phrase. I had to hear it five times before I said, "Yes, okay, it is a title." I sat down with Dean one day, and he came up with the first two lines just like that.

I read in some reviews that a lot of women were actually angry that two guys had written it. Sort of like a lot of black authors were angry at William Clark Styron, Jr., for writing a Pulitzer Prize winner about slavery, *The Confessions of Nat Turner*. They were angry because they didn't write it. They said, "Who are you, a white man, to try to explain the soul of the southern black." But he really did a damn good job of it.

How did "All The Good Ones Are Gone" get cut?

Dean got that cut. He played it for Pam almost immediately.

He's a great writer, isn't he?

Yeah, he is. Smart lad.

Do you think a man could have sung that song as effectively?

I don't know. Pam did an awful good job.

She's got the voice for it.

Yeah. Real torchy.

"Everything That Glitters Is Not Gold." The vanilla line in that song is the title line. But the story that leads up to that line is phenomenal.

The title is a well-known cliché, which is an old country trick. One of the reasons I love it is every line has its own integrity. Every line is a gem. I wouldn't change a word.

You and Dan Seals wrote a quintessential three-minute western. That would translate to the silver screen as well as Jon Voight, Ricky Schroeder and Faye Dunaway in The Champ.

I wish it had.

So what about adapting "Everything That Glitters Is Not Gold" into a screenplay.

I don't want to write it. Let somebody else write it.

You know why the daughter is named Casey?

No.

Because Casey Tibbs was a great rodeo star and all of those damn guys used to name their kids Casey—girls and boys.

Did you follow the rodeo?

I went to a lot of rodeos when I was a kid. Grew up in Texas.

Dan and I wanted to write the definitive rodeo song and, damn, we didn't miss it by far. We just sat down to do it.

Another favorite rodeo song of mine is Sterling Whipple's "Silence On The Line" by Henson Cargill on National Records.

Which didn't help it.

Independent labels do have a tough time getting airplay.

I remember that song. That's a good story. An O'Henry kind of payoff.

They made a video of "Everything That Glitters Is Not Gold," but how do you make a video of a song that's already the video?

I know it. I saw the video one time. It was made way after it had been a hit. And I was so disappointed. The song says that Ol' Red stumbled because he is old. In the video, Dan Seals walks up there and shoots the damn horse.

Shades of Old Yeller.

He comes back with a big six gun smoking. And he's just shot Ole Red. But in the song, he can't bear to send him to the soap factory.

As bad as that is, isn't it even worse to show the horse stumbling? Now they have characters in the video pantomiming the lyric.

On a literal level, in the event last Saturday at the rodeo when he came out of the chute to bulldog or rope that calf, Red missed a step.

And I may need a new horse.

Yeah.

I don't see him shooting the horse.

He says he can't bear to. And yet they shot him in the video.

Poor Red.

And he still sees the mother of his daughter. They're still on the rodeo circuit together. The fans see one thing and he sees another. Everything that glitters is not gold.

Did that take a long time to write? Did you and Dan have to get together several times?

Took forever.

Dan and I would get a whole bunch of it, and then he'd go on the road and I would work on that damn thing. The first two lines took us months to write. I was stuck. I remember sitting up in my den and finally taking a page and writing out everything that's got to be in these first two lines, every bit of information to make this thing work. Find a way to get it all in there. Squeeze it in—background, scenery, fame, the West, passage of time. It took a lot of work.

You have no idea how much information is in those first two lines. The amount of information in there is phenomenal and every bit of it has to be there.

You had the title though.

Yeah. We had the title in storage.

And you knew the framework of the story.

Yeah. What was great was then Dan would go to the studio and just make these phenomenal records.

Great records. He and Kyle Lehning.

Folk/country fusion.

A great record can certainly enhance a great song.

Oh, yeah.

I heard you were one of the last holdouts on doing full-blown demos. You stuck with the guitar/vocal demo.

Possibly. I don't know. As long as I was getting them cut, I continued to do it. When people were no longer willing to cut anything from a guitar/vocal demo, then I had to start doing studio demos. I knew the time had come.

This was when?

Late '80s. It's not that I used to just sit down and sing a thing through. I used to spend a day or two with the guitar/vocal demo. I'd do harmony parts. I'd do lead parts. I'd do an arrangement.

How many tracks?

As many as eight. I'd do them all.

But there got to be a point where people were afraid of those. At some point, it changed so that producers wanted to go into the studio with not only the song, but the arrangement.

Yeah, because they were producing ten acts. Who has the time to arrange a hundred songs?

And they didn't know how. It's a pretty terrifying thing for a young cat who's never really done anything except A&R, and he's never played in a band. He doesn't play and he doesn't really know how all of this stuff works. But he knows one thing: he can take something in there and say, "Copy this." He knows the musicians can do it.

Also, the amount of money that we began to spend on records. It gets pretty scary going in there and asking a bunch of guys to poke around and play until they find something while the clock's ticking.

But if you have a thousand-dollar demo.

You know it's going to come off if it came off in the studio once.

And the same guys might have played on the demo.

Possibly, yeah.

If a songwriter produces a great track and the record producer cops it, why isn't the songwriter the producer?

I don't know. It's the top down. Too much business, not enough music. It's easy to get caught up in your cash flow statement. I'm talking about people cutting a lot of acts and spending very little time with any of them.

So much money gets spent demoing songs that are never going to get recorded. It's great for studios and pickers, but not so great for songwriters and publishers.

I remember the first studio demo I did in the late '80s. We did some great arrangements. And I hadn't been able to get them cut before.

You did full-blown demos of songs you had previously pitched as guitar/vocal demos.

Yeah. We did two dates. I think we did six hours and six sides. Three of them got cut immediately.

Because people could suddenly hear it.

Yeah. I re-demoed "Baby's Got Her Blue Jeans On."

Did they copy the electric guitar lick on the record? It's pretty infectious.

They did.

You have been honored as ASCAP and BMI Country Songwriter of the Year. That's kind of like winning the Cy Young Award in both leagues.

Do you think American songwriters would benefit from one performance rights organization, as most other countries have?

Oh, no, we don't want that. If we only had one organization, we'd be getting paid whatever they wanted us to be paid. However they felt about it. And that's not the American way. Free enterprise, competition. The ASCAP board would never have been swept clean a few years ago and the whole thing revamped from top to bottom if it hadn't been for the competition from BMI.

The exodus of songwriters.

Yeah.

ASCAP got competitive again. Now, if there had been no BMI, ASCAP wouldn't have had to get competitive. Never would have gotten competitive. And the same thing's true of BMI. If there were no ASCAP, BMI wouldn't be competitive with anybody. They'd just pay us what they want.

Why have you shifted your creativity away from songwriting and into sportsman's fiction writing?

Just tired of the music business. Tired of the songwriting business. After thirty years, you ought to be tired of it.

You want to explore other art forms instead of writing another verse and chorus that rhymes.

Exactly.

Are you writing Pat McManis-type stories with hijinx on the camping trip?

Well, he's a humorist. I'm not as overtly funny as Pat McManis. But there used to be a lot of fiction writers like Nash Buckingham. It's about gone. *Gray's Sporting Journal* and *Shooting Sportsman* are the only ones left that do fiction. I have a relationship with *Shooting Sportman*, but it's a very small niche.

When I was a kid growing up in the '50s, they all had fiction. The articles now are called "how to/where to." I went here and we caught this fish and here's what we used, as opposed to a fictional story.

Would you be satisfied being a monthly contributor to an outdoor publication?

Possibly. I've got this fictional duck camp—The Old River Rod and Gun Bloody Mary Society and Gentlemen's Club.

I've written three stories about it. I got a great letter from Ralph Stewart, the editor of *Shooting Sportsman*. It said, "I love this story, it's funny, but we don't do this."

Were you writing stories throughout your songwriting career?

I wouldn't let myself think about too many other things. I was pretty focused, pretty driven. I felt having an opportunity to be successful at songwriting was a great blessing, whether I had created it or not. So I took full advantage of it. I wouldn't let myself get distracted very much for that thirty-year period.

If a song idea comes, are you reshaping it into a sportsman's fiction story?

I haven't had a song idea in a long time.

And you're comfortable with that?

Oh, yeah.

Do you still play guitar?

Haven't picked it up since May of '98.

If I leave here today and a song idea hits you, will you shrug it off or will you pick up your guitar?

Give it to somebody if I think it's good.

You've stopped.

I'm through. I have no desire. In fact, I was sick of it before I quit. I made myself do it longer than I really wanted to.

Do you feel a sense of freedom in saying that?

Yeah, man.

What about a novel some day?

Who knows? I have no idea. It took me a year to get my computer skills up to level.

Are you into the Internet?

Yeah.

Any thoughts on what you see that doing for music as friend or foe?

I don't know enough about it to have an educated opinion. I just hope we continue to get played. I hope our organizations keep up with technology and the laws can keep chasing the technology.

There's a lot of free downloads out there.

It's dangerous, isn't it?

What do you see is the greatest threat to songwriters today?

Bad taste in clothes.

Sonny Throckmorton

You're what we call off the beaten path.

Really? I thought the world was off the beaten path and I was sitting at the right place.

How did you land in Brownwood, Texas?

My dad had retired here and had got in ill health. I wanted to be with my father. I got to spend seven or eight years with him before he passed.

I had burned myself out writing. Just got tired of the music business. Actually, got where I was just sick of it, to tell you the truth. Didn't like to hear songs. I never ever heard anything good, it was all bad. I said, "Wait a minute, it's not the music, it's you." So I came back here on a vacation and never went back to Nashville. I've been down here on a ten-year vacation.

I thought many times of going back, but I haven't made it so far.

Are you still writing?

Yeah, I'm still writing. But for a long time, I didn't even like music. Maybe it was a depression. I really got to where I hated music. Then I cut an album, so I had to write something for it. And I come back to where I like music. I like to play a lot. I still like to write. And I love to do the studio thing. I'm just not sure that I'm ready to ever jump back in that dogfight. If you get the cut, everybody hates your guts. And if you don't, you

Photo courtesy of Sony/ATV Music Publishing

starve to death. I don't know if I like that world. We don't have none of that down here.

Did the business side of the music business taint your enjoyment of music?

I had about three or four lawsuits. That didn't help me a whole lot. I got sued on "Last Cheater's Waltz." I got sued on "She Can't Say That Anymore." I got sued on "Temporarily Yours." I went through a divorce and just a lot of shit in my life.

The main thing, I didn't like being number one. I didn't like that. I felt like a hog in the trough. I was getting it all. And I would look around and see all my friends that weren't doing that well. I had been there and I knew how bad that was. Until I was thirty-five years old, I was in with the portion of the people that didn't have it, you know? I know how tough it is. How hard it is to go home and tell your folks, "No, I hadn't had a hit yet. No, I'm not crazy. Some day this is going to pay off. Just hold on. You all quit laughing now." That's what happened in my family and I'm sure it happened in a lot of other families. You're thirty-five years old and you still haven't really done anything to speak of.

It's the grocery store syndrome. Your parents don't want to run into anybody they know at the grocery store out of fear someone will ask about you.

That's right.

When I lived in Nashville, I'd be out working in my yard and my neighbors would come around and ask, "What do you do?" I'd say, "I'm a songwriter." And they'd say, "I'm a songwriter." Everybody in Nashville is a songwriter. Most of them had jobs, but they were songwriters.

I just got burned out on it. I cut an album for Warner Brothers, which I put a year of my labor into. I was really proud of it. I really thought I had finally done an artistic thing.

Through a mix-up, which was my fault, I missed an appointment with the Warner people in Dallas and the album was stopped. Then Don Gant died. He was my best friend. All that kind of added up to a big sour taste in my mouth. I come down here on vacation and never did leave.

So you check your mailbox quarterly.

Yeah. Got that mailbox money coming in.

I'm thrilled with the whole deal. I'm in awe of it. I'm still getting royalties on songs I wrote twenty-five years ago, and I don't know why I've been that lucky. I'm damn sure not smart enough to do it. I would sit down and write, and a miracle would happen.

I believe the old Chinese proverb, "He who knows when enough is enough will always have enough." What is my purpose in life? Is it to be the top songwriter in America? I don't think that's my purpose. At one time, I was the hottest country songwriter in America. And that surprised the shit out of me. What more could I ask for than that? I'd be greedy to ask for more than that. There's too many other writers that are standing around the trough starving to death.

You weren't finding fulfillment in writing hit songs?

I was finding fulfillment, but I was also finding guilt. There was too many friends of mine who were starving. It made me feel guilty.

Everyone was drilling for oil and finding a dry hole. Then suddenly you struck oil.

Yeah, that's a good way to put it. All the years I lived in Nashville before that, I had one record that went number four called "How Long Has It Been?" I had another song that had gone fifty-eight. That's all I had. Then all of a sudden, I couldn't write them fast enough. Everybody wanted them. It just got crazy there for a while. And thank God, I was having hits. Lucky me.

How long were you in Nashville before you got hot?

I moved there in '64 and it really busted loose about '75.

Were you on a draw during this period?

That was one of the things that had slowed me down. I wrote for little bitty publishing companies that didn't have any political pull. I didn't get with Tree until about three years before I broke out. When I signed with Tree, they put me on a draw.

Buddy Killen called me in his office. He said, "You're in debt to us $17,000. I don't know what to do." I said, "Buddy, obviously you don't want to hurt my feelings. If I'm in debt and you don't know how you're going to get your money back, you need to let me go." So I left.

I was gone from Tree for six months, and it was during the period that I was gone that I got hot. So Buddy called me and said, "Sonny, you need to get back up here, we can't keep your songs on the shelf. Everybody wants a Throckmorton song. What have I got to do to get you back?" I said, "Just promise me you won't let me starve." He said, "I promise you." I had moved back to Brownwood, so I loaded up and went back. That's how that all started.

So, you had created the material, it just hadn't been cut.

Actually, they were cutting my songs, but it was by Tex Nobodies and Joe Blows. They can't get you number one records. I had a song that I had written called "Knee Deep In Loving You," and it had been cut during that period of time. When it got cut by Dave and Sugar, it had been thirteen times. Roy Drusky went to number seventy-five. I can't think of other artists. Dave and Sugar cut it and took it number one

I would never have made it if it hadn't have been for Curly Putman. Curly's the one that believed in me. When I wasn't there, he just kept on telling them, "You got to get Sonny back. He's a great writer and I feel like he'll be big for you." And he constantly harped that night and day until somebody heard him. He's the guy, really, he and Don Gant. I was lucky enough to be in their presence when I needed somebody to get my songs cut.

Was Curly still pitching and writing songs at that time?

Yeah. He was writing and pitching every day. He had an office, but it was a writer's office.

He lost his office when the corporation took over. It was a changing of the guard and a sad day in Nashville.

Well, I didn't want to stick around and watch none of that. That made me sick to my stomach. When I was at Tree, everybody was pulling for everybody. We'd sit around at night and listen to everybody's demos. And we'd listen to other people's songs around town. We were constantly doing music. We lived, ate and drank it. That might have been another reason why I burnt out. We put a lot into it.

I hated to see the corporate thing, because I had seen it in California, and I didn't like it. That's why I didn't stay in California. That's why I went to Nashville.

I went to Hollywood first. Within three days, I had a writing contract and a recording contract. And within seven days, I had my first record out. But I didn't like the feeling of it. So I left and went to Nashville. It was such a laid-back, wonderful, musical kind of a place. I don't know if it's still that way or not. I'm not there.

But what led you to choose L.A. over Nashville?

I lived in San Jose at that time, so it was the closest place to go. I went down there and took some of my recordings that I'd done in San Jose.

What style?

Between country and pop — what they're doing now.

Maybe you can fish ... sor ... -reels.

I've got a song ... ll It Country, I Call It Bad Rock And Roll."

Is this a recent song?

Yeah.

Your tribute to the state of country music?

I was just telling it like it is. It's heck to grow old, because you start hearing stuff you heard before musically, and it's never as good.

What kept you going through the lean years and the disappointing chart activity?

That's a great question. There were two things that kept me going. There was a certain amount of people that would come and say, "What have you written lately? Let me hear it." And, "Oh, I just love that song." And then there were a few assholes that were telling me that I ought to give it up and go home. They didn't live in Nashville. They lived in Brownwood and places like that. I was kin to them. Those two things kept me really focused—the belief and the disbelief. Oh, man, they honed me right into where I was going.

They were both motivators.

Damn right. Both of them are strong motivators. Somebody really telling you they believe and somebody saying, "That's dog shit."

Why do some people try to rain on your parade?

I don't know why they do it. I think some of them are trying to help, but you're already touchy about it, so whatever they say you're going to take offense to it. You've already got enough doubt going already. You've got kids that need feeding. You've got enough of that shit already on you. I don't know if they're trying to help or hurt, you know? But the end result was I always thought, "Well, I'll show you, you asshole."

Can you succeed with belief or disbelief only?

I don't think so. I think you need both of them.

So the naysayers are an important ingredient to success.

The snickering.

And there will always be the snickerer and there will always be the prover. Life's that way. It's always going to be that way. So anybody who succeeds, if they're honest, that's part of their motivation.

It seems like they should put chalk stripes around Music Row like it was a big football field. If you're not on the field, you're not in the game.

Don Gant always said, "You must be present to win."

The exceptions to that rule are far and few between.

In ten years, I've probably been in Nashville five times. I pitched songs one time. I went in and played some songs for Tony Brown just to see if I was totally out of it. I guess I was. He held two or three of them, but they didn't cut anything.

How important is the buzz that gets behind the writer?

It's extremely important. Nothing succeeds like success. People were wanting to cut my songs.

Suddenly your old catalog becomes buried treasure.

Well, mainly, mine was new. Stuff that I wrote after I got to Tree the second time.

It is said you haven't really made it until you are sued. How did your first lawsuit affect you?

A lady had come into United Artists when I was recording for United Artists, and she had a song called "The Cheater's Waltz." I remember her playing me the song and I told her, "The way you got it wrote ain't no good. It's not a hit." I was always trying to help. I said, "If you want to, I'll sit down with you and try to rewrite this song, and get it right so we can get a hit on it." She didn't want to do that. So she walked across the hall and signed the song with Frank Sinatra's company. Then they demo the song. She brought us the demo and played it for us. I hated to hurt her feelings, but it was really a piece of shit. And I never thought more about it.

Many, many years later I was writing a song called "The Strawberry Waltz." "Watch how he holds her as they dance to the strawberry waltz." Then it dawned on me that if they were dancing to the last cheater's waltz, it would even be better. At that point, I wrote "The Last Cheater's Waltz."

She didn't sue me for stealing her idea. It's not the same idea at all. Mine is "The Last Cheater's Waltz," hers is "The Cheater's Waltz," where they're getting together and dancing and having a fun time cheating. You being a writer, you definitely appreciate the difference.

She sued me for breaking a verbal contract with her. For telling her that I would write it with her, if she ever wanted to rewrite it. And since I didn't write it with her, I had broken the contract, which is bullshit because she immediately went and signed it. There's no contract if I tell you I'll sit down and rewrite it, and you walk across the street and sign it with somebody else.

But that wound up into a wasp's nest, because every time I'd kick her ass, she'd want to take it further. She was going to take it to the Supreme Court. It wasn't the regular "I'm suing you because you stole my song." This was a precedent case.

So, finally, we got ready to go to court and I had the best lawyers in the world. I had the best lawyer in New York. I had Nashville lawyer, Harlan Dodson. They come in and said, "Sonny, she wants to settle." I said, "Tell that motherfucking bitch to kiss my ass. I ain't settling. Fuck her." He said, "She wants $15,000." I said, "Harlan, why are you even telling me this? You know I'm not going for this shit. I'm not going to settle with that bitch. I told her I'd write it with her, then she left. Fuck her. Many years later I write a different idea. You know this isn't right." He said, "No, it isn't right. But how much has the song made?" At that time, it had made close to a hundred thousand dollars. He said, "We're going to go to court. We're going to win. It's going to cost you about $35,000 or $40,000. Then she's going to take it to the District Court. We're going to win that, too. That's going to cost you another $30,000 or $40,000. And they're going to take it to next court. You're going to win that one. We're going to finally wind up at the Supreme Court. And you're going to win it. But, what have you won? By the time you do that, you've spent more money than the song's ever made. And you've got all the aggravation of going to court five times." And I said, "Well, shit, what would you do?" He said, "I'd settle."

And it wasn't the money. She was a real rich lady out of New York. The bitch wanted to have her name on a hit song, which she had nothing to do with. That was a bummer, you know?

So her name is on the tune?

No. Fuck, no. She's got nothing to do with the song.

Lucky me. I didn't get a regular lawsuit. I get a precedent lawsuit. Can you believe that?

Another song I was sued on was "Temporarily Yours." It was the melody. They had sued and settled out of court on that melody two or three times. Just before we was getting ready to go to court, I met the songwriter that wrote the song it was like. I said, "Do you think I'm on your melody?" He said, "Yeah, I do. And I don't have a bunch of hits. It's the only hit I ever had." I said, "Give him his half and let's go on. Let's don't go to court. If he thinks it's on it, then it's on it. He ought to know, it's his song."

If we got his melody, we got it. That's possible. It can happen. Melodies come to me in my head. It's a unique experience. I sit there and bam, here they come. I don't know where they come from. I just pray they're not on somebody else.

How much do you write now?

Only when the spirit moves me. When I was hot, I was coming to town every day and staying late.

Earlier you mentioned it wasn't your purpose to be the top songwriter in America. What do you consider your purpose to be?

To be a spiritual influence on people that they might get something more out of life than the hoggish culture that we live in today. I've always hoped that people would just slow down a little bit and get more focused on people than money. Being the top dog, that's so unimportant. It means so little in your life when it's said and done. Big deal.

My wife's fighting me right now. She wants to hang a couple awards in here. I don't want no awards. I don't want none of that. I got all my awards in trash barrels up there in the barn. I've got two or three barrels full of BMI and ASCAP awards. I don't care about that shit. I don't want to impress nobody.

I do want them to come to my concerts. If there's some way I can get them to come watch me play, now I'd like that. But so far I hadn't been able to. It's hard to get them to come out and hear dog shit.

A close friend of yours, Rock Killough, lives here.

He lives on my ranch outside of town about fifteen miles.

Did you all do much writing together?

No, we've written about three or four songs. We're buddies. I never have done a lot of co-writing with anybody other than Curly. Me and Curly probably wrote thirty or forty songs.

Rock didn't realize the same type of commercial success that you did.

No.

What was the difference?

Rock was always such a great artist. He was always torn between being an artist and a writer. Before he come to Nashville, he had played on the road and he's really a wonderful entertainer. He's a great songwriter and he's a great entertainer. Rock will be playing until he's eighty years old. He never would sit down and focus. When he lived in Nashville, he had a band out on the road playing all over. I think that's what really slowed him down. That old "must be present to win."

What I didn't hear you say was quality of material.

No, he has great songs.

I was watching on the news today. They have cloned pigs. They all look alike and they're all in a pen together. They're all doing the same thing to each other. It was kind of funny. And I thought, "If you turn those pigs loose, which one of them would find the corn on the cob the quickest? If there's only one corn on the cob, which one of them would survive?

They're all the very same. It gets back to circumstances. And my circumstances was that I was lucky enough to have people in my life like Curly Putman and Buddy Killen and Don Gant. I had people like Pete Drake that believed in me enough to bring me to town. I was just lucky. I flunked out of college and I didn't have anything else I could do. I had to make it. I was like the kid they threw out in the lake and said, "Swim." I had to do it. It was either swim or dig ditches. And I didn't like digging.

Did you have a time line of when you would throw in the towel?

I had set a limit that when I turned thirty-five if it hadn't happened for me, I would call that the realistic point of stopping and doing something else. And when I got let go by Buddy and moved back to Brownwood, I had just turned thirty-five.

All luck, man. It's just all luck. When I hear people say, "This guy's better than that guy," I almost want to puke. Without luck, nobody's good. If there's ten of you just alike, one of you is going to get the corn on the cob and nine of you ain't.

When I moved to Nashville, them old-timers would say, "Sonny, you're really good, but there's a lot of people that are really good. But Nashville will be good to you if you pay your dues." I didn't know who you paid your dues to. I was always asking, "Who do I pay my dues to?" But I finally discovered what paying the dues is. That's when you stay in town so long that the people that you used to hang out with down at Linebaugh's drinking coffee—because you couldn't afford nothing else—are cutting records or running a record company. He's a lot more receptive to my songs than that guy was fifteen years or twenty years before when I looked like Johnny Come Lately.

Where did the idea for "The Way I Am" come from?

I was doing a lecture at a college this last spring in Athens, Texas. It dawned on me during the lecture how "The Way I Am" came about. It occurred when I was kid, actually. I didn't know it when I wrote "The Way I Am," but it's what happened.

We left Dallas, Texas, when I was eight years old. We went down through Louisiana going to Biloxi, Mississippi. Dad was going to pastor a church down there. Back in those days, the highways would be cut right down through those bayous. There would be green algae and beautiful cypress trees and cypress stumps on each side of the highway. But you couldn't pull off. There was not shoulders, just water on each side.

And I remember coming out of dry Texas and telling my dad, "We ought to stop and fish. That really looks like it's got some good fish in it." And Dad said, "Oh, man, don't you know that would be loaded with fish. But we can't stop, son, I got to get on to Biloxi."

That's the way "The Way I Am" came about. That was the bayou. I was on a road to Mississippi.

I thought I wrote it, but I didn't. God wrote it many years ago. I don't write the songs. God writes them. I'm not a creator. I'm not a writer. I'm a reporter.

The last part of the song was the way I was feeling about my career. I was getting tired with the whole deal, because I didn't like people looking at me as number one. I'm not a good winner. I'm a terrible winner. I'm a lot better loser.

What happens to you when you win?

A lot of people that treated you like shit treat you nice. You have a lot of people that used to treat you nice that are afraid to talk to you anymore. I went to one party and a bunch of old friends was telling me that I had changed and I wasn't helping none of them. I proceeded to tell them all to kiss my ass, that I wasn't helping me, that I was just lucky. If it had been my help, I wouldn't have got nowhere. All those years, my help wasn't worth a shit. People don't understand.

What denomination was your father?

Pentecostal.

How did that shape you?

It gave me the freedom to pick up a guitar in church and learn how to play. They sang real loud and I played real low. It finally got to where I played real loud and they sang real loud. And it also enabled me to sing. I was always singing. Dad would preach revivals and me and my sisters would do trio stuff. We was part of the ministry, you know? It gave me the freedom. I didn't feel shackled in my religion, so I also didn't feel shackled in writing.

Do you think it gave you a spiritual foundation that made you receptive to creativity?

Yeah, I do.

When I was really having my streak, Sterling Whipple come to me and he said, "Man, you must have read every book that Hemingway ever wrote. You've got his style." I said, "Well, if I did his deal, it ain't because I read him. It's because he writes the same way I write."

I've never read any of Hemingway. I've never been a reader. The only thing I've ever read was *Reader's Digest*. I'm not bragging; I'm actually ashamed. When you say that, it marks you a total idiot.

Hemingway was a reporter. He can put his name on it and call it fiction if he wants to, but he saw it happen somewhere. I believe all the great works are that way. When you hear a song and it's dog shit, then you can walk up and shake the man's hand and say, "Congratulations! You wrote that song!" But if it's great, you can shake his hand and say, "Congratulations! You're a good reporter!"

I've just always been more for letting it come from the heart. Let it be real. That will burn you out, too. That's like pouring your soul out on paper. You don't have to see any psychiatrists, though.

Did your father understand what you were trying to do?

He did not understand it at all. Even after I made it and moved back here to Brownwood, he'd come over and have dinner with me. And he'd laugh and say, "Well, I went to the barber shop today and this lady down there cutting my hair asked me, 'Are you any kin to Sonny?'" And he said, "Yeah. I'm his daddy. And she told me all these wonderful songs you wrote. She knew a whole bunch of them. I never heard of none of them."

And they were all hits. That was just so revealing. But it wasn't a slant. He was into God. Toward the end, I always told him, "You know, Dad, I learned to write songs listening to you preach, because your theory always was that you wanted to preach the word where a twelve-year old kid could understand it. If you'd have been a songwriter, you'd have been a great one." That was always the way he taught. And I tried to write songs the same way, where you don't have to strain yourself to understand where I'm at emotionally and what I'm trying to report to you. But he didn't understand it, just like I didn't understand his deal with the preaching.

What about your mom?

My mom died when I was very young, so I had a stepmama. She was with Dad, pretty much. Whatever he thought.

Now the tables have turned. You're the father with a songwriting child.

Debby's my younger daughter, who got bit by the same thing I was bitten by at her age. You like her?

Yes, sir. She's real grounded, has her head on straight.

Well, thank you. You couldn't pay me a higher compliment than that.

She sat on the front desk as receptionist paying her dues.

I know it. And I don't know what to do. I don't want to push her in people's face. I want them to like her because she's good. So it's been really hard for me to sit back and try not to get involved in her deal. It's really hard. As a father, I want to jump in there and say, "Listen you all. Listen to this girl." But you can't do it. I hope I'm doing right.

I think you have to make your own way. She had a short career pitching songs, but if you're really a songwriter, you can't be a plugger. You are more concerned with your own songs than others. She told me, "I just made a decision that I'd rather starve if that's what it took to be a songwriter."

I told her, I said, "You made the right decision. And that tells me that you're doing what you're wanting to do. It's speaking loud and clear."

Does she come to you for advice?

She comes to me for advice a lot.

On critiquing songs?

Everything. When she gets the blues, sometimes she'll call and she'll be so discouraged. She's a great actress and comedian. She's funnier than hell. I told her, I said, "Don't give up. Do both of them. Keep your comedy going and write." She's just finished a two-man play that her and another girl have written. She'll do all right. She's got what it takes. That drive. She's not boy crazy. She's not there chasing boys, thank God. I've seen so many girls come to town that just said they were writers. She's there for the right deal.

Now we've got a lot of second generation legacies in country music, and a few third generation. Those legacies that have chosen the business side seem to have an easier go of it than those who choose the creative side.

There's a book right there. What you're saying there, that's something that ought to be followed in a book.

There seems to be more to live up to on the creative side, just like those sons and daughters who follow parents of athletic prowess.

It's sad, because they never should have to. I got a tape on Roger Miller. Sounds like shit. I'm not kidding you. It's not good stuff. You can tell the talent's there and you can see where he's eventually going to make it, but he ain't there on that stuff. So why would you expect a kid of mine to be there until she's there, you know? I tell her, "Well, honey, when you get the blues, go home and write a song. And try to talk to enough people to get a good idea of something you can write about. But write. Because you're going to have to really stun them. You're going to have to walk in there and knock them down with your stuff. And the only way you can do that is write a lot."

But it just breaks your heart. You think, "Crap, looks like they would give my kid a break." But then you think, "I don't want nobody giving her a break. I want her to be so good, they have to sign her."

Her last name probably helped her get on the front desk, though.

Yeah. I'm sure it did. It got her into the mix.

When the Tree building was renovated, everybody took one last look at all the ceiling panels just to see if anything was missed.

And they found twenty pounds of the greatest marijuana in the world, right?

They came up empty, but not for lack of trying.

I don't think it's a sin. I think it's like drinking coffee. It's no big deal. But I think cocaine's a big deal. If anybody's on heroin, that's a big deal. But smoking a little marijuana, I've just never seen that as a big deal. But also, I don't see it as something that I would want to tout.

You could walk in the building and you would smell it. It constantly had Buddy Killen wringing his hands. He would say, "I got on the elevator this morning and I could smell it all the way up." There was smoking in every office. There was all kinds of different things going on. There was cocaine. It was a party house. But that was part of the secret, too. It was a loose run thing where everybody there was having a good time and doing music. And I think Gant had the good sense not to step on it and let it go.

It was generating copyrights.

Big ones. And that's why Buddy put up with it. That's exactly right.

Did you see the use of marijuana as a window to your soul?

I did. I wrote my greatest songs straight, but I wrote "The Way I Am" when I was stoned.

"If We're Not Back In Love By Monday."

Glenn Martin and I wrote that. I think that's one really good song. Merle Haggard cut it first. And then the guy that produced Millie Jackson heard Merle's record and decided it would make a great R&B record.

Any inspiration for "If We're Not Back In Love By Monday"?

Glenn and I was going out to write. Dallas Frazier had a little place in the woods. Him and Doodle Owens would go write there. And Dallas said, "You all go out there and write." I never had been there, but Glenn had a key to it. We made up our mind we was going to go out there until we wrote a hit, then we could go home. I took my pickup and Glenn took his car. He had to stop and get some gas, so I pulled in behind him. I walked over and he was putting the gas in his car, and he was singing the hook line. And I said, "Hey, don't write no more of that. You wait until we get over to the cabin before you finish that." He said, "I won't." But when we got to the cabin, he already had the words and the chorus.

We sat down and I helped him finish that one. I always felt like I got in on that one.

That works both ways. Bobby Braddock was talking about getting in on one of your ideas, "Thinking Of A Rendevous," where he wrote the second verse.
"She Can't Say That Anymore."

I like "She Can't Say That Anymore." I didn't like the lawsuit. I got sued on the melody. I wound up giving half of it away. He thought it was part of his, so I gave it to him. I thought the lyric was a little cleverer than I actually was.

"Friday Night Blues" really hits a nerve.

It was about my life. It was about my wife. I wrote the first verse and the chorus. And I run into Rafe Van Hoy and played it for him. I said, "You want to help me finish it?" So we sat down and about thirty minutes later we had finished it. It was directly from seeing what life was doing to my wife.

If you look at it, ain't that reporting? I've never, ever claimed to be anything more than a reporter. I just couldn't do much more than that. I wasn't smart enough to create it.

When did you write "Middle Age Crazy"?

'75 or '76.

You weren't quite middle age.

No, I was approaching it. I was seeing my friends go through it. Bobby Braddock and Glenn Martin and different people was changing their wives.

But sometimes even though you see the lesson, you have to live it to learn it.

Well, I think I was going through it, too.

"I Wish I Was Eighteen Again"

A guy at a antique shop, about fifty-five or sixty, said, "You wish you was eighteen again?" I was thirty-five or forty, having a good time, I said, "I never thought about it." He said, "Man, I wish I was eighteen again."

"Trying To Love Two Women"

I lived on a farm. My neighbor was out in his yard, and he asked me, he says, "Did you hear us partying last night?" I said, "No." He said, "You ever hear us down here?" I said, "No, I don't ever hear you all." Shit, he was pretty good ways from my house. He said, "Well, if you ever hear any shooting down here, will you call the law?" I said, "God, yeah, what's going on?" He said, "Man, I'm trying to love two women." But that's just reporting. That's all that is.

I consider "A Little More Like Me" one of your most important songs.

Well, thank you. I wrote that one Easter morning. Everybody had gone to church except me and it was really cloudy outside. The skies were gray, looked like it might rain. That's what I saw and that's what I wrote. The day after Christ had been crucified, as I understand it, there was a darkness that fell upon the face of the Earth.

The person is uncomfortable with Jesus' commitment because of what it requires from him.

Yeah, for him to be a little more like me, instead of me having to be like him.

Mickey Newberry got me that cut on the Kenny Rogers *The Gambler* album. It sold about twenty million copies. The sales have just been incredible. I often wondered if people ever really heard that song, because it was the tenth side on there. It's a long way to listen to get to one song, but I reckon they did.

Did "A Little More Like Me" enjoy any success in the contemporary Christian market?

Never been put out, except on that one album.

The Oak Ridge Boys cut it.

I believe they did. There's so many of those cuts, when you add them all together. The other day, I run across an old tape of Ray Price singing one of my songs I had forgotten he had ever cut.

I also wrote a song during that time that I like just as good called "Safely In The Arms of Jesus." I don't try to preach in my gospel songs.

I've been here two hours and you haven't called me Puddin' once.

Well, that's because I remember your name's Philip. If you hung around, you'd get Puddin', I guarantee. I'll always Puddin' everybody.

Where did Puddin' come from?

Whitey Shafer nicknamed me Puddin'. I nicknamed him The White Man.

He was always Whitey, but down in Texas, he'd become The White Man.

One night we was just acting crazy down in Texas at a party. And we started saying, "I beg your puddin', I never promised you a really good 'un." We kept on acting silly with that and next thing I knew, I started calling everybody Puddin'. And they called me Puddin'. We was all Puddins.

Harlan Howard

You were born in Harlan County, Kentucky. Is that where the name Harlan comes from?

That's not true. I was born in Detroit, Michigan, on September 8, 1927. I did an album for Capitol about 1960, '61. The gal that was going to be my manager suggested I make myself two years younger, because I was thirty-two. You know, thirty. In Hollywood, you change your name, this and that. And she says, "You got a good name, but we can't have you born up in Detroit, not and be a country songwriter." I said, "Well, I've got some kinfolks from Kentucky that come up twenty, thirty, forty years ago. I think my ancestry's from there." So we picked Lexington. That's all BS. I think it's laughable now, because when I die, they'll get the wrong information. I'm seventy-two, and I've been fighting a false bio for forty years.

We'll do our best to straighten that out. So your name Harlan did not come from Harlan County. Where did it come from?

There's a Harlan Steed on my mother's side of the family, whose grave I've been to in Ironton, Ohio. I don't know if he was named after Harlan County. It's not that far away, so that could be. But I'm named after him, and I've got the tombstone to prove it.

You wrote an interesting song called "Be Careful Who You Love."

Oh, I love that. That's one of my favorite songs. I'll tell you the truth, I'm

Photo courtesy of BMI Archives

not surprised it wasn't a hit. I actually wrote this about a guy, Arthur Q. Smith, who did everything in the song. A bunch of people sang his songs and claimed they wrote them.

Arthur Q. Smith named himself that because there were two other Arthur Smiths in country music that were popular. One was Arthur "Guitar Boogie" Smith, which was his big hit. And then there was another one that had something to do with a country show that was over in North Carolina. He lived all of his life in Knoxville.

Did you ever meet Arthur Q. Smith?

No, he died long before I even knew about that story. Chet Atkins told me about him. One time I was having a little party at my house and I got Bill Monroe alone and I asked him about Arthur Q. Smith. He said, "Yeah, I know him. He was a wonderful writer." And I asked him, "Did you ever buy any songs off him?" He said, "Yeah, I bought four. That was quite common back in those days, Harlan. It wasn't anything fraudulent. Somebody's got something for sale, and you buy it and it's yours. But I got four from him. I recorded all four of them." And he named them, but "Blue Moon Of Kentucky" wasn't one of them, I assure you. Then Bill said, "They were twenty-five dollars apiece. I gave him a hundred dollar bill and he wrote me a little receipt."

But, anyhow, that's when I wrote the song. Once I pinned down a singer who acknowledged that he had bought and recorded songs from Authur Q. Smith.

Although it was not fraudulent, I find it unethical. I thought "Be Careful Who You Love" was a great tribute to a fellow songwriter.

I sent it to his widow and she had a couple grown-up sons, and they enjoyed it. Chet Atkins asked him one time, "Man, you know what you're doing? You're selling these wonderful songs for twenty-five dollars apiece. These guys go on and make thousands and thousands of dollars and own them the rest of their life. How can you do that?" And he said, "Chet, you don't know how many I wrote." I thought that was a great answer about quantity. If you sell enough, you get rich.

Sure, but I bet at twenty-five dollars a pop, he didn't. It probably went back into the bottle.

The deal is, he liked to drink and he liked women. I've liked that a little bit in my life. As soon he got that twenty-five, fifty bucks, whatever, he'd be heading for the bars. He was an alcoholic, but evidently, a very gifted guy.

You were a U.S. Army paratrooper. I would be like the paratrooper when asked many times he jumped replied, "None. But I got kicked out ten times." What's a bigger rush, jumping out of an airplane or writing a number one song?

Writing. You don't even have to have number one. The hit songs will fall in place, and other people have to help you. But writing a really good song is absolutely the most wonderful thing I've ever done. And jumping out of an airplane wasn't natural, so I never really got used to it. I wasn't jump happy.

You were happy to be on terra firma.

I wouldn't do that again for ten grand.

Jumping into the music business isn't natural either, is it?

I don't know. When I was a little twelve-year-old boy in Michigan, I heard Ernest Tubb on the Grand Ole Opry. And man, I was blown away with his rich baritone and those wonderful sad love songs he'd be singing. I got hooked. It was a hobby for years and then when I was thirty-two, I finally come here and turned pro.

When you got a false bio, it screws you up. I was thirty-two when I got here, actually. But we changed it to thirty just in case I was a big success, I'd be younger. I didn't realize this gal didn't know what the hell she was doing. It didn't matter if I was forty at that time. Video wasn't in, and if you could sing, you could sing.

So the fudge factor had more to do with being an artist?

Yeah. She was trying to help me get my background more country for liner notes. You shouldn't be a hillbilly songwriter and born in Detroit. I mean, that's Motown.

How did your recording career come about?

Buck Owens and I were buddies, and we had written several hits together. He liked my singing, and by that time, I had moved to Nashville. Buck told Ken Nelson at Capitol in Hollywood, he said, "Man, you ought to do an album with Harlan. He don't sing bad and he's a hell of a songwriter." So Ken Nelson called me and said, "You want to do an album for us and see what happens?"

I knew immediately this was twelve paid-for demos. I was very much a Music Row writer. I didn't have to go any place. I didn't have to perform. It wasn't necessary back then. So he came in and we did twelve songs. It was fun. I was a little nervous. I hadn't been out of the factory very long, and here's Floyd Cramer and Grady Martin and all these wonderful first team guys. And they're all sitting there staring at me thinking, "What in the hell's he doing here?" And I was wondering myself, because that wasn't really my forte.

I did some pretty good cuts though. Especially, two or three years later when Chet Atkins let me do two albums for RCA. Out of five albums, those were the best I did.

You married a lady named Lula Grace Johnson who later became Jan Howard.

We arrived in Nashville in June of '60 in a new Cadillac we'd bought. We just motored on in here and she got on the Grand Ole Opry, thanks to Bill Anderson's help. She had worked on the road with him. We were married for several years after we moved here. We've been divorced since '65.

I wrote her songs. Helped her get a record deal. Helped her get her first hit on Challenge Records. Then wrote her a couple hits. Got her off of Challenge and on to Capitol for a while. Had several good records on there. Then that fizzled out. Got her with Owen Bradley. I gave them a hit song called "Evil On Your Mind," and they cut the hell out of it.

Jan has said publicly that she wanted to cut "I Fall To Pieces."

No. Bless her heart. Time changes things and it makes a good story. I did a fifteen-song demo for Pamper Music in three hours. That was my habit. I wrote them all myself except one, and that was "I Fall To Pieces," which Hank Cochran and I had just written. It was his idea and I helped him.

Anyhow, Jan sang all the girl demos when we'd do a demo session. I mean, you know, we're husband and wife. So she sang three or four songs that day out of fifteen. We got Anita Carter to come down and sing harmony with us, and so forth. We took this fifteen-song tape back to the office and started pitching it.

One day shortly after that Owen Bradley called Hank and said, "Have you got anything that you think is a hit?" Hank said, "Well, Harlan and I just wrote one called 'I Fall To Pieces.'" And Owen said, "Bring me a copy." So Hank pitched the song several days after we wrote it.

Jan had demoed it. She didn't ask for it, didn't say she loved it. She was selling more records than Patsy at the time. That's the deal. Hank and I, mercenary sluts that we may be, would rather at that time have had a Jan Howard record, believe it or not, than a Patsy Cline record. Patsy hadn't had a hit since "Walking After Midnight," and that was a long time before "I Fall To Pieces."

It's just a sweet little ballad. It had a great feel to it. Patsy sang the hell out of it. And it was a hit for about a year. It just worked out for her. There's some things that are hit records, and she just nailed one. Of course, she was a hell of a singer. Anyhow, the deal is, Jan could have had "I Fall To Pieces" in a heartbeat just by asking for it.

You share a birthday with Patsy Cline. Did y'all have other similarities?

Her and Jimmie Rogers, I might add. I always thought, "Wow. That's good company." No similarities at all except she liked to hang out, smoke and drink.

She liked songwriters.

She liked songwriters and I was one of the gang. And a lot of them like Hank Cochran, Roger Miller and Mel Tillis are funny guys. Very humorous. So on Saturday nights in between songs, she liked to come over and seek out our table because they were her buddies. And I'm sitting there just listening, because I'm not funny. She did love the songwriters.

Did you hang out much with Roger Miller?

Oh, yeah. God, night after night. In fact, every one of us got divorced from that. It was when I was still with Jan. I just couldn't seem to leave Willie and Roger and all these guys and go home at dinnertime. The day's work is over and you've busted your butt, but that night, man, go down to Tootsie's and get a cold one.

We always hung out upstairs. The truck drivers and everybody would hang out downstairs. We only used the downstairs once in a while. That's where the jukebox was. If I had a new Buck Owens record or something, we'd come downstairs and play it a couple times and judge it, and so forth. But except for that, we stayed upstairs. Sometimes they even had us a bartender up there. That was our little hangout. The steel players would set up their steel guitars and we'd have a guitar. But all of us guys should have been single, because we were so much in love with music.

You eventually were.

Yeah. But the thing is, you could have done that up front if you knew about life. Looking back you know a lot. If you're married to music, it's tough to follow the rules that a decent woman would expect you to follow. Why in the hell should you be home for meat and three? You can get a hamburger at

Tootsie's and just hang right in there. So, in other words, it's hard to follow two mistresses.

Absolutely. What's the value of a good watering hole?

Writers have changed a lot. They don't hang out and drink and party like we used to. And I guess this is healthier for them. But I don't hear as many great, down-to-earth country songs coming out of this town like I used to. Or records.

You can get a lot more feeling, usually, out of a sad song than you can a happy song. The American people have a 51 percent divorce ratio. So that's the side of the coin I write for. They need songs, too. Lately, it's a problem getting them recorded because these guys are young and I don't think they know a hell of a lot about it. They all want positive, happy, and that's what I have the most trouble writing.

To borrow a phrase from you, they're juvenile delinquents. When did you start using that term?

At some barroom conversation, I'm sure. I read it in a magazine. And then I did use it quite a bit. I still do once in a while. But, man, I'll be seventy-three in September and it's amazing how I feel. Even though I'm sitting here twitching around because my arthritis and my back are bothering me, I still wouldn't want to be young. Because I would have missed the great era of country music, which was the '50s and '60s and '70s. I'd say up until maybe 1980. It started backsliding, I think, during the Urban Cowboy thing. That definitely changed things. We started getting platinum albums and country pop things, and so forth. Once that happens, everybody sees where the big bucks are. And record labels, especially.

So they started getting producers a little rock-and-rollish, more popish, and so the music changes. And when it changes a certain amount, it'll never change back. It's over. So why would I want to be younger and miss Lefty Frizzell and Wynn Stewart and Ernest Tubb, all these wonderful people I knew and wrote songs for?

The '80s are a forgotten era of country music.

I had a hit or two in the '80s, but I don't remember what. I had slowed down a lot from my heavy-duty writing, getting records and all that stuff. But I don't remember, musically, much about what happened during the '80s. I think after 1980, we lost it, except maybe for Randy Travis. He did a great job of reviving country music.

Years ago in an interview, you were talking about Elvis Presley's records being rock and roll. Then you mentioned "Crazy Arms" by Ray Price and you said, "That record, to me, is the key that brought us all back together and put country music back, really, where it kind of belonged." Now you speak of Randy Travis reviving country music. Do you think a country revival will happen again?

I don't know. I really like the Dixie Chicks, and they do really good songs. They're also wonderful on stage and delightful the way they dance around. They also are well-versed musicians. They're exciting. They're selling. And they're country. So, in other words, that's the positive news.

There's nobody I know of that's really as country as Lefty Frizzel or Buck Owens or some of those guys that's hitting right now. If there is, I'd like to hear them. You never say never, but country music could never be as country as it was in the '50s, in the '60s. There's too much country pop stuff going on and it's lucrative. If it's a great song and record, I may even like that. If it's great, it's great.

Who influenced your songwriting?

I'm a fan of the great old Tin Pan Alley writers. It isn't just Hank Williams and Ernest Tubb. I love the classics and how well they were written. I learned a lot from Irving Berlin just studying his songs. My God, they're simple.

To me, "White Christmas" is the same structure as "I Fall To Pieces." So in other words, I was studying where they put titles, how they used words and phrasings. I learned a lot from the Tin Pan Alley guys.

Irving Berlin was also very prolific like you.

And he pretty much wrote alone.

Do you think co-writing killed the need to hang out together?

No. No, that didn't do it at all.

Mel Tillis says, "I'm going to be a star." And I said, "Are you sure? Man, you're a damn good writer and you don't have to get on those buses." See, I never liked that. He said, "I think I can do it." So anyhow, he went and got a record deal and, by God, a couple years later I had his first number one record, which was "Life Turned Her That Way." He was Entertainer of the Year three years after he started out. So there went one drinking buddy. Willie sold the pig farm and went back to Austin, so there went another one. Hank Cochran bought a big boat.

Roger Miller got with Jerry Kennedy on Mercury. Jerry set him on a stool with a small group and that's when he cut "Dang Me" and those little fun songs. And so, hell, the next thing you know, Roger's a big country pop star. And he's gone. Dallas Frazier became a preacher and quit drinking. I see him now and he looks real happy, so it worked out for him.

I'm not griping about all this. It's just that things change. I've been here forty years. June 6 was my Normandy day when I landed on the beaches of Nashville.

Fortunately, you didn't have any German publishers shooting at you.

I've been sick for a couple years, so I ain't been out and about. Now I'm starting to get out a little bit at noon and have a few drinks. I love to sit around and BS with my friends and laugh a little bit. But it's hard to find drinking buddies anymore. I've got several from the younger crowd, but most of them are so businesslike and official—accountants and lawyers and blah, blah, blah. Honest to God, I don't think they're having any fun like I had. And I think radio reflects that—well-crafted, carefully written songs, not too much originality.

You praised Randy Travis for reviving country music. And yet a few years after he hit, you sued him over "Better Class Of Losers."

I not only sued him, but I also withdrew it because we talked on the phone. He kind of hurt my feelings.

How so?

Something about you can't copyright a title. Well, I know that, but I had an original title. And that was the name of his song. We sent my song to him several times for a couple years. Whenever he was recording. He's a wonderful singer. What really upset me more than that was Mark Chestnut had just recorded my song. And my song had been recorded by Ray Price and what's the guy's name. These two guys in a pickup truck. TV series.

John Schneider.

Schneider had a really neat record on my song.

I had a Mark Chestnut record already cut. Mixed. It was going to be his first single. And they were fixing to rush Randy's out, which they did. My song was seven or eight years old. It wasn't new. But we finally got the record on it that I was wanting from the start. Plus, I'm really a big fan of Mark Chestnut's, and I was excited about getting a hit with him. It was so embarrassing. We had to change the title of our song to something else to get it on Mark's album. I mean, that's degrading to go through.

But looking back now, I don't think Randy stole it. I think he probably heard it. Things can register in your subconscious. Our song had been played a hundred thousand times. Logged at BMI. And that's a lot of play. So you could have even got that title off the radio. But it never was in the charts. It's just that it had two good records and they were played that much.

But I was hurt about that. I still like Randy Travis. Alan Jackson got kind of sideswiped because he co-wrote that song with Randy and it was Randy's idea. Except, I thought it was my idea. And you know what? Randy's a good guy, and I doubt very much he would ever knowingly steal anything from anybody.

When the record come out, I called Donna Hilley and said, "Donna, I'm not going to go to court and pursue this, so you might as well tell your lawyer to drop it, because I shouldn't be suing songwriters. It's not what I came here to do. I've never been sued and what is all this crap? These are two decent guys and I'm a decent guy."

Your breakthrough song was "Pick Me Up On Your Way Down." I know three things about Mae Boren Axton: She co-wrote "Heartbreak Hotel" with Tommy Durden and put Elvis Presley's name on it. She gave birth to Hoyt. And she was forever bitching that she wrote a song called "Pick Me Up On Your Way Down" and Harlan Howard was getting her royalties.

Patsy Cline did her song about four or five years between "Walking After Midnight" and "I Fall To Pieces." She was under contract to a manager in L.A. that owned Four Star Music. He also had the right to choose her material. He gave her "Walking After Midnight," but then he dumped, oh God, thirty or forty quite mediocre songs on her, including Mae's version of "Pick Me Up On Your Way Down." But, see, I never owned a Patsy Cline record in my life until she cut "I Fall To Pieces." I didn't buy records, for one thing. I was a factory worker. It was just an album cut, so I had never heard her song.

I don't think she was saying that you stole her song. I think she was saying that through clerical error, when her money would come in on the Patsy Cline record— because your song was bigger—it would get credited to you.

Well, the deal is, it wasn't by mistake, because I had the hit. I'm the one that was getting the airplay. And she and I, well, she's gone now, and bless her heart, we were good buddies. But it was just a joke between us. And she did gripe and bitch. She wasn't really a songwriter. She was actually more of a managerial person. She had great stories to tell and that was one of them.

I met my wife at a Harlan Howard Birthday Bash.

Really? Isn't that great?

It was put out to pasture several years ago, so recent transplants have never had a chance to experience one. Any chance of a revival?

Well, I don't know. Back in our younger days we used to have big parties. In fact, it would be the night of the ASCAP banquet, because there was hardly any country writers at the time that wrote for ASCAP. So, I'd have my party, and I'm talking about five hundred people. I had this big house up on a hilltop. I had this big glassed-in room and you could see downtown Nashville. I'd get two of those shuttle buses. I'd always invite about thirty, thirty-five writers. I had a few guitars, so around ten or eleven o'clock after we got sloshed and everybody got unwound, somebody would start singing. To make it move along, I would be refereeing and so forth. Everybody played two songs, just because I wanted to be fair. You got two chances to be funny, to be serious, or pitch your singing. I didn't want somebody to grab the guitar and sing all night. It really wasn't a show.

It was a guitar pull.

Willie Nelson got a record deal one night. So did Linda Hargrove. Willie and Linda got on Atlantic Records the same night. The guy that ran Atlantic at the time was at the party. I always invited a lot of people who could help people. The core of the thing was the songwriters.

Then time went along and somebody suggested a benefit. On purpose. Someplace. So, anyhow, we did one. It was kind of hodgepodge—Hank Cochran and a bunch of buddies. It was in the BMI parking lot before they put that new building in.

And that turned out real good. It wound up being a benefit for the Songwriters Association Hall of Fame building, which I don't know if there'll ever be one. But that's where the money went. And we'd make them thirty, thirty-five grand a year from tickets and so forth. You remember; you were there. A bunch of bars set up. Chili dogs. And people just loved it.

In fact, Tony Brown and a bunch of the producers would all come there and stay backstage and have a few drinks and hear the writer sing something they had recorded on one of their artists. And that might be the first time they ever made the connection between the writer and the song.

I thought it lost something intimate when they added the band.

Well, the second year we did that. Part of the show was acoustic. Four or five people would do their own picking. It was great. But if you are a mediocre rhythm player, which I am, just very ordinary, a band can make your buddies feel better. So what the hell? We got to hiring this band and the day before was a bitch. Twenty-five, thirty songwriters rehearsing two songs apiece. But I don't think it lost anything. I just know it made the songwriters more comfortable. And most of them don't get to sing with bands very often. So it was make 'em sound good, make 'em shine. I've always wanted the writers to shine.

You said something very interesting in an interview one time: "When you screw up, you pay for it. That's the Lord's way and I swear it's the truth."

Well, yeah. I said that in conversation. What's wrong with that?

Nothing's wrong with it, but why is it that way?

I believe in God, Jesus. I'm not a preacher and I don't dwell on it. But I believe there's a supreme being. So feeling that, I also believe in karma. You cheat on your wife and you get caught, you get divorced, you lose your woman, you lose your children, you lose your money, you lose your home. You rob a bank and you get shot or something. In life, people pay for the wrongs they do. Usually they pay for them here on earth. But if you don't, you're going to pay for it later. I really believe in karma. I'm not a saint, but I certainly don't ever want to hurt anybody. I care about their life and I don't want to cause them any sorrow or any problem whatsoever.

The other side of the coin would be that the good you do is returned to you.

Well, yeah. In fact, that's why I dropped that lawsuit after I calmed down a little bit, got over my hurt feelings and said, "Man, I shouldn't be doing this. I wouldn't want this done to me. What the hell's one song? I've written hundreds. And I had many hits."

See, that's part of the process of that thinking. I knew Wynn Stewart and Lefty Frizzel and Tex Ritter and Johnny Bond. My God, these were all buddies of mine. All the fun I've had from this gift. I shouldn't be doing anything negative. That's not what I was sent here to do. I sure as hell shouldn't be suing a songwriter. Just forget about it and move right along. It was just one song. God has been so good to me.

My favorite song of yours is "I Don't Know A Thing About Love."

Yeah, that was fun. My writing buddies—the ones that know about me—that's their favorite song that I've written. I think it's the last hit I wrote alone. Could be, I don't know. It gets confusing after forty years, but I think it was. Plus, I originally got Conway Twitty with Owen Bradley and helped him get his country record deal. I wasn't a manager or anything. I was just his buddy. And he had a great country career. Finally, I wrote him a hit song and he cut the hell out of it.

As I was saying, you did a good deed and it came back around.

Yeah.

It was pleasant for each of us, because we liked each other so much. Conway cut several album things that had already been hits—"Keys In A Mailbox" and "Above and Beyond." But I never had a single by him until that one.

Who were the people that supported Harlan Howard?

Ray Price, Buck Owens, Chet Atkins and Owen Bradley about covers it.

They recorded your songs. What about people that weren't as well known?

Then you'd have to go to the Tootsie's crowd. My best friends and the people I know the most to this day are songwriters, would-be songwriters, over-the-hill songwriters. It don't matter.

Beyond the songwriters, the next people I get along best with and enjoy are the creative producers of Nashville. I think record producers, if they're good, are about as creative as songwriters are. And there's still a few of those around, like Paul Worley and Tony Brown. Blake Chancey's getting awfully good. They're enthusiastic. They're gifted. So it's a pleasure to get a record by one of them, because you can have high hopes.

You wrote for the two greatest country music publishers in Nashville: Acuff-Rose and Tree Publishing. Was Fred Rose at Acuff-Rose when you signed?

No.

I had a deal with Wesley Rose. He kept bugging me to come over there, so I went over there and signed the first exclusive contract I ever signed in Nashville. It was a five-year deal, but I had a clause in there: if I wasn't happy after six months, I could inform him and the contract was null and void.

Well, anyhow, I exercised that. I just didn't feel that comfortable settling down writing for one publisher. I wrote too many songs to write for just one publisher. I loved to have two or three of them competing against each other with my songs. I mean, how could I lose? But the biggest hits I got with Tree, they bought from Pamper Music. That's the company.

And what was Tree's Jack Stapp like?

Wonderful. Wonderful. He and Buddy Killen were partners. Jack was the one that was more fun. He was basically the silent partner, because Buddy was the music man. Jack had managed the Opry. He was a fun guy and just a really good guy. He liked the ladies. He liked to have a drink. I've missed him quite a bit.

What's next for Harlan Howard?

I've got two or three appointments next week with young writer friends of mine. I've got about six or eight people I like to write with. Most of them are strong on melodies. And I want to write a few more really good songs. I don't have any big drum beating thing I want to do. I don't want to save country music. If I could make a little dent in it and write a brand new great country song as good as "Pick Me Up On Your Way Down," that would be really great.

You're truly blessed to have found your passion and to have followed it. Thanks, Harlan.

Thanks, pal. Good luck on your book. You've done your research. See, when you work hard, you deserve blessings. Just keep on doing it.

Jerry Chesnut — Side A

I first met you back in 1982 when I was working the front desk at the Hall of Fame Motor Inn.

Boy, that used to be a live wire. I knocked two guys down in there—Hal Bynum and Faron Young. Hal never knew who hit him.

Now he does. Who was the drunkest?

Hal. Faron didn't have to be drunk to start trouble. It came natural with Faron.

I've never seen you without your hat on.

Everybody at one time wore a western hat. I collected Civil War stuff. One day I put a little cavalry cross sabers on one of the hats. Nobody paid much attention to it. I had one of these big Civil War eagles. And just for meanness, I stuck it on a hat. And everybody said, "God, man, that's beautiful! Where did you get that eagle?" One day I didn't wear it and somebody said, "Hey, where's that hat, man? You don't look right without that hat." It just kind of became a trademark without me intending for it to.

My wife's sister had known me for at least twenty years. She worked for *Music City News*. She told my wife, "There's a new product out. I thought Jerry might want to try it. But I didn't want to tell him about it, because I

Photo courtesy of Sony/ATV Music Publishing

thought he might be self-conscious about his hair." And Pat said, "What in the God's world? He gets his hair thinned every time he goes to a barber." She thought I was bald. She had never seen me without a hat on, I reckon. I go a lot of places without a hat. But any time I go to a music function, if I don't have it on, nobody don't know me. They know the hat. They don't know me.

I watched Sling Blade *without knowing Dwight Yoakam was in it.*

My wife told me that.

You didn't know it was Dwight?

No.

This guy had a baby and all it was was just a head. A great ol' big boy's head. So he named him Head. He took him everywhere he went. He was proud of him. And on December the fifteenth, the day Head was twenty-one, his father took him to a bar and set him up on the bar and told the bartender, he said, "Head is twenty-one today. I want to buy him a drink." And the bartender said, "You got a birthday right here at Christmas. Head, are you looking forward to Christmas?" And he said, "Oh, God, not another hat."

I read where you did some cattle rustling.

I was railroading, playing music on weekends and broadcasting in Saint Augustine, Florida. I was very poor, and just about everything I ate was wild meat. Hunted all the time. I killed wild boar. We poached deer at night with a light. People used to pay me to pull alligators out of the canals. They'd be up in the shallows that hadn't been dredged. Hunters would shoot 'em and then they'd pay me to jump in and get 'em out before they got to that deep water. And they'd just beat my legs black and blue. But I'd do anything for a dollar.

I was coming home from railroading one night, and I took a back road to see if I could see anything on the side of the road to hunt the next day. I guess it was five miles from any house. Just a barren place between Jacksonville and Bayard. When I came around this curve, this black angus heifer—I thought—was standing in the road a pretty good piece off. It turned away from me and started down the road. There was swamp and so forth on both sides of the road and nowhere for it to go. So I thought, "I'm going to get me a cow. A heifer. I'll kill that thing and take it home."

I was driving a '51 Chevrolet. So I pulled up on the cow and it was running down through there. When I got right next to it, I hit the gas and run right up on its hind legs and I guess broke one of them. Anyway, it went down and I jumped out with my knife and cut its throat. I waited a minute or two until it died and quit kicking and carrying on. Then I decided to load it. I drug it around behind the car and in dragging it around there, I discovered it was a full-grown black angus cow. And God knows what the thing weighed. Half a ton maybe. I got it around there, opened the trunk and started trying to get it in the trunk. I'd get the front end in and when I'd go to load the back in, the front end would flop out. I'd get the front end in, then the back end would flop out. It was just limber, you know?

I finally got one end in and the other one about half in. I was having trouble getting it in while trying to keep that other end in with one knee. I don't remember it too well. It ain't something you want to remember. A car came around the curve and the headlights hit me. It was probably a mile away and I had plenty of time, but I panicked. I knew I had to get that thing in there. So I grabbed hold of it with both hands and both legs and leaned forward and just come up and flipped that thing in there. Just through panic you can do a lot of things. But when I did my back went out.

When I got home, I fell out of the car. I couldn't get out. My back was tore all to pieces. All the vertebrae in the bottom of it was just ripped. I fell out of the car, crawled in the house and got my wife to drive. We drove out to a swamp and I decided to just throw that thing in the edge of the swamp. But before I did, I took my knife and cut one hind leg off. Hide and all.

I've had back trouble and surgery all my life. I'd buy that guy a herd of cattle if I knew who it belonged to.

That was some expensive beef.

Lord.

I done worse stuff than that back then. I paid thirty-two assault fines in one town one time. I used to rather fight than to play music or anything. I thought I could shape up every smart aleck in every bar that I went in. I never shaped up none of them. They'd just swear out the warrants and I'd have to pay fines. Never helped none of them. They probably died just as ignorant as when I met 'em.

Did you hang up your gloves at some point?

No gloves. It was knuckles.

Have you mellowed?

Yeah. I finally just decided that it wasn't doing any good. An old man told me I had to move. I said, "What do you mean I got to move?" He said, "Everybody in this town's afraid of you and that's dangerous. Somebody will kill you." I got to thinking about it, and I got scared. I moved up to East St. Louis.

Boy, what a wild place that is. You can get killed there in two minutes. The thing that saved me was it was wintertime and I had just gotten out of the Air Force. There was no work. My family was about to starve to death. They couldn't pay the fines to keep me out of jail. So I moved to Florida where it was warm. Got a job down there plumbing and then went to railroading. Got to broadcasting down there and then moved to Nashville to get in the music business. Came up here and everybody was doing rock and roll. Webb Pierce and Faron Young was trying to go rock and roll. Buck Owens said he wanted to go pop and somebody told him he couldn't go pop with a mouth full of firecrackers.

Country music had had it. They was fixing to close the Opry in '58.

They came close to tearing the Ryman Auditorium down.

Every business in the world is based on one thing: a product that's needed and wanted. I started writing songs when I came to Nashville. I didn't come here to be a songwriter. I came here to be a star and play guitar. Webb Pierce was the first one to tell me, "Son, we don't need no stars. We've got them. We need somebody to write hit songs for 'em. Can you write?"

Everybody started telling me this. The only security you've got on earth is to be needed, so I started writing. And people need to figure where they're needed.

Where do you feel you're needed now?

Now? Probably talking to you.

Good answer.

And ten years later I started having hit songs. What Nashville needs today is hit songs for the stars just exactly like they did in '58. You've got to have a good product that people want and will go out and buy. It all hinges on selling that product. For example, several artists, like Razzy Bailey, just got played like crazy. And then after about ten Top Ten records, RCA drops him. He goes in there and says, "What's going on?" They said, "Man, you ain't selling no records."

Bill Anderson come to me for hits and I said, "The man with the golden pen is wanting a hit from Jerry Chesnut?" He said, "Jerry, I'm out on that road signing autographs, talking to these people every day. You can't write songs with all that going on."

Alan Jackson and Vince Gill cannot write enough songs to keep the supply going for their albums. Nobody can. What they need to be doing is putting out the very best that can be found in Nashville. Not the best of what can be found in their den. And that's what's happening. Labels are putting out what they've got publishing on. And they're hiring these—what do you call them?—they've got a name.

Consultants?

Yeah. Consultants.

The other day, me and Jimmy Dickens went fishing in the Grand Ole Opry Tournament. They told us not to worry about a thing. They was going to have a guide with us and he'd have the boat. Don't bring nothing. He's got everything. We got out there and I asked the guy, I said, "How long have you been fishing Old Hickory Lake?" He said, "I've never been here before in my life." And he's supposed to tell us how to catch fish there.

He started to cross that lake and there was floating logs everywhere and he's running wide open. It's a 250-horse motor. I said, "You got a kill switch on?" He said, "I don't even have one in the boat."

And that's what's happening with Nashville. It's been running wide open, run by consultants that don't even know what Nashville is. Don't know what country is. Everybody says, "We're not going back to the old twang." Now they're not talking about country music. They're not talking about Merle Haggard. They're not talking about George Jones and Conway Twitty. They're talking about Roy Acuff. They're talking about Jimmie Rogers and the old three-chord twang and no drums, no bottom whatsoever. It was just kind of noisy. It was old, like old cars wasn't nothing like they are now. It was great for the day, but there's no twang to country music now. It's got bottom. It's got drums. It's got piano rhythm. It's very sophisticated and great. You can't call that twang.

What kept you plugging away at the music business for ten years without success?

I didn't plug away at it. I did it like I had done music when I was a kid. I just enjoyed it as a hobby and played with it in my spare time. I didn't go down and pitch songs and all that. I went to work and started a sales organization over three states and just got out of the music business more or less. It was just a hobby.

What were you selling?

I had a product called Filter Queen. It was made at Oak Ridge. Then they made it into a cleaning machine and it would filter air in a house. I had a distributorship with it. I'd write songs on the side and piddle with them.

Ed Hamilton was working with Monument Records and he told me, he said, "Put down about three or four of the best things you've ever wrote. Just you and a guitar. Let me take them to Bob Beckham at Combine Music and see if he can do anything with them." There was one song in there called

"Miles From Nowhere." Beckham liked it. He told me he was going to demo that song that night and wanted me to come down there. I got excited. It motivated me and I started writing more.

Was this your first studio experience?

Yeah. Beckham told me to write some more things and bring 'em. "Don't let anybody else hear 'em till I do." So I started writing more.

My back couldn't go no more from the cattle rustling days. They told me if I would lay down on the floor on a rug and just sleep and eat there, just lay flat for about six months, my back might go back in place and might heal. I tried that to keep from having surgery. While I was laying there, I didn't have nothing to do, so I'd listen to country music. I listened to what was happening and who was happening.

I just laid there and listened to this all day long. Haggard and all these people had become part of me. Then I started writing kind of in that vein, kind of in that bag. Not the same things they were saying, but just kind of in that zone.

Then Beckham went in and did a session on me and Dolly Parton. I had written three songs and she had written three and he wanted six on the session. Beckham introduced me to Norro Wilson. Norro was running Screen Gems and thought I could be an artist. He wanted to try to get me on MGM. Norro told me, he said, "Listen. Take three or four of the best songs you've got written and go ahead and do a demo session and I'll get Screen Gems to pay for it. They'll publish it. But we'll dress this thing up like a master and see if we can lease it to some label and get you a record deal." I said, "Fine."

So we went in with "A Dime At A Time" and "Another Place, Another Time" and did it. And about a month after we did it, a girl that wrote some songs for Sandy Posey, it might have been Martha Sharp.

Warner Brothers' Martha Sharp?

I think so. I believe it was Martha. I'm not sure. But anyway, some girl that wrote a couple big hits for Sandy Posey told Screen Gems—supposedly, now this is all hearsay, but the way it happened, I guess it's true—that if she could run that company, she'd write for it. Or they had told her that they'd hire her if she would write for it. I don't know how it happened. But anyway, they fired Norro and hired her. Well, that left that step hanging out.

So Norro told me, he said, "Listen, we're going to have to do something about that session. I guess I'll just have to go ahead and send it to New York and let them pay for it." I said, "Then they'll have it up there. They don't know how to get no song cut." He said, "I know it. But we got to get the session paid for and get the musicians paid." So I said, "How much is it?" He told me how much it cost and so forth and I said, "Why don't I just pay it? I'll pay the musicians and I'll pay the studio and everything. Then it won't go to New York and nobody will own it. We'll have it here." So I did.

Norro liked "Another Place, Another Time" so well that he played the piano and sang it on the Ralph Emery Show one day. Del Reeves was also on and he heard it and said, "Whose song is that? Has that been out?" Norro said, "No, a friend of mine wrote it. Jerry Chesnut." Del said, "The next time I record, if you'll get that to me, I'd like to listen to it. I may do that."

I was in Norro's office, and now he's working for Al Gallico, running his company. I'm sitting in there. Norro and I shooting the breeze. The phone rings and it's Del wanting to find out how he can get "Another Place, Another Time," because Del's having trouble finding anything that they like at all. Norro said, "The guy that wrote it's sitting right here. You got a copy of that session?" I said, "Yeah." He said, "I'll send him over there." So I went over to UA, and Del and Bob Montgomery was setting in there listening to material.

I knew the song on there for Del Reeves was "Two Dollars In The Jukebox A Dime At A Time." Up-tempo and just made for him. Del said, "Which one is it on here?" I said, "It's number three, but play number two on there before you do, because that's the song for you." Del said, "Well, now, I'll play a little bit of it if it's no good, I'll just tell you." I said, "You ain't heard it have you?" He said, "No." I said, "Well, I have. If it wasn't any good, I'd know it." He looked at Bob and Bob looked at him and Bob said, "I think you ought to just play it." So Del played it and the demo kicks. It's up-tempo more than the record. Boy, it was kicking.

And, you know, with a new writer, everybody's sitting there waiting on him to run out of something to say and just start repeating himself and it fall apart and all that. Del and Bob kept waiting on it to fall apart and it never did. It just kept getting stronger. When they got done, they said, "Oh, God!" Then they played the other one. They said, "We'll do 'em both." And then Del said, "Who's the publisher?" I said, "There ain't none." He said, "What!?" I said, "There ain't none." He said, "You wrote them all by yourself?" I said, "Yeah." He said, "Who paid the musicians and the studio and everything?" I said, "I did." He said, "Well, why don't we just start a publishing company?" And we did right there on the spot.

And it was called?

Pass Key Music.

They went in the studio and Del cut a hit on "A Dime At A Time." It was in the charts five months. Then he come right back with "Looking At The World Through A Windshield" and "Good Time Charlie" and just kept going. "Wild Blood." He just had one Top Ten record after another.

Porter and Dolly wanted a song and they cut "Holding On To Nothing." They was the Duo of the Year with that.

Eddy Kilroy was working at Mercury and had heard "Another Place, Another Time" on Del's album. Smash Records, supposedly, had give them until Saturday morning for Jerry Lee to come up with a hit or they was going to drop him from the label. At that time, Jerry Lee just couldn't buy a hit. He was at the bottom music-wise and personal-wise and everything.

I got home one night about midnight and the phone rang. It was Eddy Kilroy. He said, "Chesnut?" I said, "Yeah." He said, "I'm down here with Jerry Lee Lewis and we're trying to find him a hit. If we can't find one, they're going to drop him from the label." They had booked a session for Saturday morning. And back then, if you booked a session on Saturday, and you wanted to cancel, you didn't have to pay the musicians. That was a union rule, I reckon. So they booked this session on Saturday. If they didn't come up with a hit, they was just going to drop him from the label and cancel the session.

This was midnight and Eddy said, "The session's tomorrow morning at ten." Done had the musicians coming. He said, "If you'll bring 'Another Place, Another Time' down here and teach it to Jerry Lee, I believe we can cut you a hit on it." So I said, "Well, that's fine. When do you want me to bring it?" I thought he was going to say tomorrow. He said, "Right now." I said, "Where you at?" He said, "I'm at Mercury Records." So I said, "All right. I'll be there in a little while."

I turned right around and back down to Nashville I went. See, back then, everybody was looking for hits. That's the answer.

But how do you gain access? That's the question.

I had over fifty-two releases a year for three years in a row. That's over one a week. I don't think RCA Victor ever done that. Nobody has ever called me and said "We need a 'B' side." Or, "We need an album cut for so and so." "Hey, man, I need a hit."

That's all they was looking for was hits. Today they're not going around looking for hits, and that's the problem. The product. They've got great artists.

What are they looking for?

Whatever they can have all of. And all of nothing is nothing.

Del Reeves started a company with you when it was worth something.

Well, we started a company together. It was a convenient thing. Then I had a vehicle and it started rolling.

Nobody in Nashville I don't think, with the exception of one or two maybe, like Buck Owens that didn't even record here. Nobody in Nashville from George Jones to Tammy Wynette to Loretta Lynn. Nobody in the world dreamed of doing a session without calling Jerry Chestnut and Ben Peters and Dallas Frazier to see if they had a monster hit for them that would sell a bunch of records. If you didn't have a good product out there and wasn't selling records, you'd get dropped from the label.

And publishers have signed everybody that they thought may possibly ever be in a crowd where a song was written and get part of it. Seriously. I used to go to the BMI Awards and they'd say, "'Another Place, Another Time,' written by Jerry Chesnut, published by Jerry Chesnut Music." And I'd walk up and get two awards. Now, they have to have a van to carry the awards to three stages. I mean, there's five writers, four publishers.

You think the stage is going to collapse.

Yeah. It's unbelievable. Columbia printed a songbook one time called *Top Country Hits*. And it was twenty-three of my songs. You open it up and on about the third page is said, "From the pen of Jerry Chesnut." Nobody cared who Jerry Chesnut was, but these songs. When they started seeing "Holding On To Nothing," "Another Place, Another Time," "A Good Year For The Roses," and "They Don't Make Them Like My Daddy Any More." And it just goes on and on and on. They see all these great songs and they buy the book.

Sure.

Merlin Littlefield came to me and he said, "Before you sign with BMI again, I want to take your catalog and showcase it to ASCAP and just see what they'll do, see what they'll offer you." I said, "Okay." He said, "How would you say to do this?" I said, "Well, here's a good start." And just handed him that book.

Merlin looked at it and turned through it and looked at all them titles and he said, "My God! This has to work. Tell me something, because I want it on there, who published all these songs?" I said, "Me." He said, "Who else?" I said, "That's all."

He said, "All right. Tell me about the co-writers. How many co-writers are there on each of these songs? I want to write it down, because they'll want to know." I said, "'It's Midnight.' It's co-written. Me and Billy Ed Wheeler wrote that together." He said, "All right. What else?" I said, "That's it. That's the only co-writer in the entire thing."

I got up at four o'clock in the morning and wrote songs. They were hits. I don't know how. It's a God-given thing.

It's hard to find a co-writer at four in the morning.

Yes, it is.

Unless they're just getting in. They're not going to get up and come meet you.

No.

I think the brain is like the back. Right now, there ain't no way I could write a hit song. But tomorrow morning at four o'clock when I get up, my mind is fresh. And if I turn it loose and let it create, it will.

You're coming out of your dream state.

Yes, sir. Anything that comes out, I write it down. And you won't believe what it will do. A lot of people sit and say, "Well, that don't rhyme." Or, "That don't make sense."

If I'm writing a song about driving a truck, a trucker driving down the road and he's running a hundred and fifty mile an hour and a tire blows out. He runs over a ninety-year-old woman and kills her. "Why, you can't put that in there!" I don't do that. I'll write it down. You can always mark it out. And then when you mark all the bad stuff out, you wouldn't believe the stuff in there. You say, "Lord, where did that come from?"

"T-R-O-U-B-L-E" and "Woman Without Love." All these double rhymes. And people said, "What caused you to do that?" I have no earthly idea what to tell them, because that came out of the air at about four o'clock in the morning. Me about half asleep sitting there drinking coffee, smoking a cigarette and just letting my mind drift and create. You can't harness the mind. If you do, it can't run.

I'm just not an early riser so it's hard for me to understand. What made you get up at four in the morning?

I was needed at four o'clock in the morning to write hits, because nobody was looking for "B" sides or something that just rhymed. I had to get up and create at the time that I could.

What was special or unique about the time frame?

I've written some of the greatest songs that you'll ever hear in your life at ten o'clock in the morning. Or nine and ten o'clock at night. I have never had a Top 40 record in my life that I wrote at that time. Everything came early. That's what people can't understand. That's the difference between a hit and a great song—a hit comes from God.

Do you read a lot?

No. I've read two books in my life. *Elvis, What Happened* and *Call Of The Wild*. I don't read. I didn't finish high school. I can't read music. I don't know the name of chords on a guitar. I can make them all and some that nobody even knows what they are. It was meant for me to write hits. I don't know why.

Willie Nelson put it great. He said, "God fills the air with beautiful hit songs and gives a few people the talent to reach out and get one." Going to college and studying music, there's people that do that. I can't even read sheet music, but I can write a hit song. It's a talent that God gave me. And I don't know why he gave it to me and didn't give it to all these people with all these big music degrees.

Jerry Chesnut — Side B

You seem to have a great amount of life energy.

Everybody used to ask me, "You smoke pot?" I said, "No." "You take bennies?" "No." They say, "How do you write all these hits?" They thought you had to have a upper or something to write a hit. I have taken Valium in order to clear my head and get a good night's sleep occasionally. I have never lit up a joint. I have never taken any kind of uppers. I just never needed it.

How much do you sleep?

That depends. If I get to thinking about something, I can't sleep. I go to bed or go to sleep watching a ballgame about eight o'clock and wake up about three-thirty or four and make coffee. Get up about five.

So you get a good eight hours.

I think the body will tell you when you need to go to sleep. A lot of people try to go to bed at a certain time and then they wonder why they can't go to sleep. They're not sleepy. If you're not hungry, nothing's good. But if you're hungry, everything's good. You can go to Kroger, and if you're hungry, you'll buy everything in the store. But gorge yourself on a bunch of shrimp and go to Kroger, and you won't buy nothing.

Photo courtesy of BMI Archives

How did your association with Elvis start?

I never did really understand Elvis and all that leg shaking and stuff. That wasn't no part of country music, really, when he started. I admired what he was doing, but I didn't particularly care for it. Never bought one of his records or nothing.

Lamar Fike was working with Hill & Range and he also worked with Elvis. I don't know how much work he done, but he was there. And Hill & Range went out of business. Or they went out of business with Lamar, let's put it that way. They agreed to disagree. So he had some time on his hands when Elvis was in town.

Lamar needed a place of business, so he rented an office in my building. And I started paying him so much a week to pitch songs for me. He'd been working with Hill & Range and Dallas Frazier pitching songs, and I figured he'd get some songs cut. He got a cut by Tanya Tucker and a couple people.

Elvis was cutting and Lamar asked me if I had anything for Elvis. I sent three or four songs down there. One of them was "It's Midnight" that Billy Ed Wheeler and I had written. Lamar called me that night and he had lost the lyric to it. So I gave him the lyric over the phone and he said, "They're running it down now."

Lamar called back and said, "Elvis said, 'That's my next single. That's a lock standard. That song's going to be around forever.'"

If Elvis got to listening to your music as a writer and liked it, then he would kind of get glued in on you. When he cut, he wanted to hear what you had. So when Elvis was getting ready to cut he would tell Lamar, "See what Jerry's got." He wound up doing six or seven of my songs in no time. Lamar pitched everything Elvis ever did of mine.

Lamar and I went to Graceland and went to a movie with Elvis. I got to know him and we'd go out to dinner and everything. If Elvis liked your song, he never changed anything. If he liked the demo, he did it just like that.

One of Elvis's last hits was "T-R-O-U-B-L-E."

I wrote "T-R-O-U-B-L-E" about David Wilkins. He used to play in Ireland's. I had watched him perform. Get up there and shake, rattle and roll, and them people just having a good time and him up there just burning his ass out trying to entertain 'em. And he did it from about nine till one with one or two musicians. He sounded like twelve people going.

If you've ever been in the bar and seen a fight start over a girl, then you know what the hell "T-R-O-U-B-L-E" is all about. You can associate with it. I played enough joints to know when a good-looking woman by herself walks in the door, it's trouble. There just too many men on the prowl, and it's going to be hell. Just matter a of when and where. Whether it's in the parking lot or in there, there's going to be some brawls over that.

Someone's going to Fist City.

Travis Tritt had a hit with "T-R-O-U-B-L-E" in the '90s.

Boy, that girl in the Travis Tritt video. I thought that beautiful thing had to come out of L.A. as a model. She took her girlfriend to try out for this video. The girlfriend didn't have no way there and she took her over there and was sitting out by the office waiting on her to try out. One of the producers started to lunch and seen her sitting there. He said, "Are you here to try out?" She said, "No. I'm just brought a girlfriend." He took her back in there and went and got the other guys and said, "Boys, come here and look what I found sitting out there waiting on one of these other girls."

He had found T-R-O-U-B-L-E.

So they just dismissed all the rest of them. I don't think her girlfriend ever spoke to her again.

That was a long ride home.

Boy, that's a beautiful video.

A beautiful song is "A Good Year For The Roses."

"A Good Year For The Roses" is about some roses I had. The buds fell off before they ever opened up. And I called this guy, I said, "What's wrong with these roses? The buds are falling off." He said, "Jerry, we've had a wet spring. This is just not a good year for roses."

So later on I get to thinking. What if it was a good year for roses, but everything else went to hell? What if a man's wife was leaving, the baby's crying and everything in the world's going to pot, and all this crap? But the roses are just blooming like hell. I wrote that thing before you could turn around.

Tom Collins gathered his people before they started writing one day and played them "A Good Year For The Roses." Made them listen to it. He said, "This is the way a song's supposed to grow, build, be written."

My first job in the business was working for Tom Collins. I think people underestimate what a good song guy he really is.

He told me one time, he said, "If you ever write a song and don't know what to do with it, give it to me. I'd just love to peddle one of your songs." And I thought, "What a great compliment." He's had some good writers. A great track record. Done some great things.

He's developed some good writers. Publishers don't much do that anymore. They just hook them up to co-writers.

Describe your writing process.

Nine times out of ten, I never had a hook or an idea. It was just a feel. I'd take the guitar and just pick around on it a few minutes until I heard some words coming out of it. If it felt good, I'd write it down.

I don't know how in the world people put a tune to words. How does anybody take a poem and put a tune to it? I've tried. I've had hundreds of people say, "I'm a songwriter and I've got a lot of songs, but I need somebody to put a tune to them." That's ain't a song. If it don't have a tune, it's not a song. It's a poem.

To give you an example, Bobby Hardin gave me two melodies. Beautiful melodies. I heard words in them and wrote two songs that just knocked me out. I can sit and hear a piano going "da-da-da-da-da," and I'll think "What we gonna do?" I can hear something in that. It may be good, it may be bad, but I'll hear some kind of words in this music from somebody just sitting play-ing the piano. But I can read four thousand newspapers and the entire dictio-nary and never start whistling, never hear a tune.

"Da-da-da-da-da." You might say, "Will you marry me?" You might hear a proposal in that. But if you say, "Will you marry me?" I don't hear no tune in that.

You wanted to sing your tunes. Talk about the experience of becoming an artist.

I would be cutting the stuff of mine that nobody else was cutting. The instant leftovers. And it wasn't all that great. And I definitely didn't want to get a bus and go out on the road. I had been with Del Reeves on a few trips, and I knew I didn't want that. It interfered with the writing.

The last record I had out was "I Don't Want To Be Lonely Alone." It was a good record. It was played a lot of places, but you couldn't buy it on a bet. UA didn't stock records. Back then, they kind of played with the record busi-ness here.

Built a high-rise and left town.

"I Don't Want To Be Lonely Alone" had thirty-eight picks and forty heavy plays, but it didn't sell nothing. And it was very disgusting to me that they didn't even care. Scotty Turner was head A&R man at UA, and he called me in one day and said, "What are we going to release next?" I said, "What have we got better than that last one?" He said, "Nothing." I said, "What are we going to cut better than that last one?" He said, "Nothing." I said, "That's what we're going to release—nothing!"

I said, "If I ever do want to be an artist and be on a label, the more things we've put out that didn't work, the worse shape I'm in. And I don't need that." So I resigned. Something that very few people ever do.

Jeannie Riley was my secretary when she cut "Harper Valley P.T.A." When she went out on the road, people said, "I'll bet Jeannie don't even call you anymore, does she?" I said, "Hey, man, Jeannie is out on that road run-ning. She ain't got time to call me." But I had an accident, got hung in a trac-tor. They was wanting to take my leg off. I was on morphine and everything. I opened up my eyes and all I seen was a big white hat and there was Jeannie Riley with big tears in her eyes. People don't forget. But in this business you get so busy in your world, you can't run everybody else's. You've got to under-stand that.

You spent a few years in the cast of Hee Haw.

Roy Clark told me about how much fun we could have on *Hee Haw*, so I got on it.

What did you do on Hee Haw?

Act stupid. Put overalls on and fall over bales of hay.

You'd go out there and they'd rush you out there. Kind of like the army. And then they'd say, "Well, Buck showed up, so we're going to have to do him first." He may be out there three hours and you're sitting there waiting. Then when you finally get there, they put you in a room by yourself. They've got you on monitors. They'd say, "Look to the right." And you look to the right, and there's a wall. Then they said, "Say, 'Sunshine, you beat it all.'" And then you'd say, "Sunshine, you beat it all." They'd say, "Now, look to the left and laugh hysterically." And they'd dub it in on jokes that people are telling.

Then they told me, said, "Listen, we're going to leave town and we'll be back in about six weeks. In the meantime, you just write you up a bunch of stuff to do." I got to writing crazy stuff like a boy chopping up his mother's house and selling it for kindling, selling it for twenty cents a bushel. Hee haw! And blah, blah, blah.

It was just the craziest thing I ever done in my life. This is not creative songwriting. It's just another world. It got in the way, too. And I got out of that.

Archie Campbell taught me that laughing is contagious. You just start laughing, and in a few minutes, you can't stop. It's absolutely great. He helped me more than anybody on there. He was a jewel.

People would come to Nashville expecting to see bales of hay everywhere just from watching Hee Haw. *A lot of the talent was Opry stars.*

They're trying to bring all this young talent on the Opry. That's not going to work for one simple reason. The audience that comes to the Opry is not interested in seeing some fifteen-year-old boy that they've never seen before. They want to see Bill Carlisle, Porter Wagoner, Jimmy Dickens. They want to see the old stars that they've been raised with. That's that audience.

They sign a baseball player for ten million and then they raise the price of hotdogs. When they finally get them up there so high that a man that works in a factory can't afford to take his little boy on Saturday to the ball-game, it's over. I don't care how many million dollar players they've got. When them seats are empty, it's over. The fan is the important person. The important people at that Opry is them people sitting in them rows out there. It ain't that stage. And the important people in country music are the people that buy records. It ain't these consultants and program directors.

The program directors have no choice. They play the best of what they get. But they're not getting the best product possible. They're getting the best product possible that the consultants are supervising or bringing out.

What would change that?

If people quit buying records.

When you were writing hit songs were you disciplined about writing every morning?

No, no, no. I may wake up at seven o'clock and get up and write. I may wake up at six and write a few minutes and nothing's happening and go get on the tractor. Run a Bush Hog. Had a cattle farm in Springfield.

I'll tell you something else that I think should be said. I didn't waste a lot of time on songs that were not hits.

How so?

That sounds awful conceited or misled or something, don't it? Let me put it this way. If I started working on a song, and I got four or five lines written, or maybe a verse, and it was a song and it was rhyming, but it just didn't knock me out. It wasn't a hit. I wouldn't get no cold chills or nothing. This was just another song. I quit. I'd just stop. Didn't waste my time on it. I'd go fishing or something. But when I started writing "A Good Year For The Roses," I knew I had a smash going.

A lot of people sit and write song after song after song and just rack their brain and none of them are hits. It's a funny thing. You can take those same people and take thirty songs and put one hit in the thirty. Play them the thirty songs and say, "Do you hear a hit in there?" "Yeah." And they can pick it.

Why can't they take thirty of theirs and do that. If I had a ugly kid, I'd know it. I'd love it, but I'd know it was ugly. Bless his heart, he can't help it that he's just homely as mud. They ought to know he's ugly, but they don't. If you've got a beautiful kid, you know it.

If you're writing a beautiful, wonderful, commercial song, work on it. Go with it. Play with it. If you're not, can it.

You didn't do a lot of co-writing. Why?

There was no sense in it. I was writing hits. Getting them cut right and left. I'd look and I'd have three in the Top Ten and five in the *Billboard* chart at one time. Why go hunting a co-writer?

What do you think created the rise in co-writing and what do you think it has done to songwriting?

A lot of times, rather than a man trying to really develop his talent and really get in a groove and get to where he can do something to be proud of, he's leaning on somebody else. For example, from everybody that I ever talked to that knew him, Hank Williams was a great motivator. He would get with Fred Rose and just start humming a song and telling him about this song and get it motivated and Fred would about half finish it for him. But he was a motivator of this. I don't know what happened when Hank Williams was doing all this. I was alive, but I wasn't there. But some people can motivate somebody to write.

When I see two people has written a song, I think very seldom did they have equal input to this song. I think one guy wrote a song and another guy put a few lines in. Or maybe he was a better musician and put in a few chords and maybe helped out with the melody or something.

You remember the song "Near You" by Frances Craig? You're not old enough to remember the record, are you?

I've heard it.

Great record. The songwriters' wives were in New York at a big show. They were getting awards and so forth and somebody looked over at this one woman and said, "Are you a songwriter?" She said, "No, my husband wrote 'Near You.'" And this lady across the table said, "I beg your pardon. My husband wrote 'Near You.' Your husband wrote 'da-da-da-da, da-da-da-da, da-da-da-da.'"

Cat fight. But if someone writes a melody and someone comes along and puts a lyric to it, you can say they've equally contributed.

Yes, you could.

They've each brought their special talent to bear, like offense and defense on a football team.

When I played football, you played both. If you played defense and recovered a fumble, you didn't go to the sideline. You stayed out there unless they carried you off. The same way with songwriting. When I get a song going, I don't want nobody around, man.

Let's say it's six o'clock. I started writing at four or five and I've got something really going. I'd hear a commode flush in the other end of the house. And I'd think to myself, "I wonder if that's Linda or Barbara." You just wonder which one's up. It's over.

If you get a line of thought going, you got to keep it. The mind will not create a hit song when you're wondering who's flushing a commode on the other end of the house. That's why a lot of writers go off to a fish camp or somewhere miles from nowhere—so they won't be interrupted.

Like Dallas Frazier's place.

Yeah. Great writer. He used to be my challenge. When I started, Dallas was just the greatest country songwriter around and had more songs out than anybody. I used to try to get more songs in the charts than Dallas.

So you were competitive?

Oh, yeah. And Dallas didn't even know me. I finally got to where I'd have four or five songs on the charts and he'd have two or three.

I remember I went to Frances Preston at BMI one time and I said, "Frances, I need an advance of about ten thousand dollars. I want to open an office and so forth." She said, "Now, Jerry, we give advances to people that's been around for years and are established. But new writers we don't." I said, "Well, you know, in Kentucky they take care of those old racehorses that they've got out for stud. But the one that won the Derby yesterday, he ain't going hungry. They're looking out for him, too. He may be more important than that old stud. I've got five songs in the *Billboard* chart. You show me any writer that you've got that's got five songs in the *Billboard* chart, and I'll forget it." She said, "Give me a couple days, and I'll cover you." She gave me the check.

And back then, BMI kept up all the publishing companies and writers. We'd all have starved to death if it hadn't been for them. They was our biggest ally and our biggest asset. And as Tom T. Hall once put it, "also our biggest threat and our biggest enemy."

Because?

You got so dependent on them you couldn't live without 'em. When it come time to negotiate, the only way you could talk to them about the next deal or the next advance was to resign. You would send them a letter of resignation. It was a formality that everybody did. When they got it, they'd call a meeting. Then you'd go in and meet with them and you'd negotiate.

ASCAP was your bluff?

Yeah. They never did sign none of us, I don't think. Somebody one time said, "You know Ed Shay?" And I said, "Yeah. Ed can say, but Ed can't do." Frances Preston could tell you something and do it. But at ASCAP, whoever they had running the place always had the power to say no. None of them had the power to say yes. If you asked them for an advance or told them you wanted a deal, they could say no. But they couldn't say yes. All that had to come out of New York.

You owned Pass Key Music. Why weren't many other songwriters becoming their own publishers?

Okay, let me say something. I was a businessman.

You were a salesman.

And then I became a hit songwriter.

Many of your most talented people that I love in the music business don't have enough business sense to know whether it's raining outside. They have to call the dog in to see if he's wet. But they're great talents.

Jerry Lee Lewis is no more a businessman than nothing on earth. Elvis wasn't. George Jones is a lovely friend of mine. I love him. But he's not a businessman. Any business you see going with his name connected to it, somebody else is doing it. And Haggard's not a businessman. The greatest talents on earth are not businesspeople.

You've got to be a businessman to run a publishing company. You can write a hit song on a piece of toilet paper and sing it to somebody and you ain't got nothing. Somebody's got to put out lead sheets on that thing, do a demo session on it. They've got to send it to Canada. They've got to talk with Harry Fox and license that thing with the labels. It just goes on and on and on with what you've got to do as a publisher. That's why most of these people didn't start publishing companies. They weren't businesspeople and they didn't want to be tied down that deep.

Why did you sell your catalog?

Very simple. I had an office on Music Row. Pat was my secretary. Had been for sixteen years.

Your wife for sixteen years?

No, no. She was my secretary for sixteen years. She's been my wife about fifteen. She copyrighted all the songs, typed up the lyrics, filed all the forms. I wrote the songs, did the demo sessions, pitched the songs and all that. And the two of us in this office for three years in a row licensed over fifty-two releases a year on major labels.

George Jones would call from the Ramada Inn and I'd go down and sing him "A Good Year For The Roses." And he'd say, "That's what I'm looking for." Tammy Wynette would be in working on her hair and I'd sing her "The Wonders You Perform," and she'd say, "Would you do that again?" And I'd do it again. I'd say, "I don't know who in the world would ever cut this song." She said, "I will if Billy Sherrill will let me." And she cut it. Waylon Jennings would come to my office and sit down and he'd say, "I want a song just exactly like 'A Good Year For The Roses.'" And I'd buzz Pat and I'd say, "Get Waylon a copy of 'A Good Year For the Roses.'" He said, "I don't want that." I said, "Well, that's the only one like that." And I'd play him four or five songs. He'd say, "I want them two right there. That's my next two singles." Loretta Lynn would say, "I'm fixing to cut, have you got anything for me?" I'd written "They Don't Make Them Like My Daddy Anymore" for Merle Haggard. But before Haggard got it, she cut. I took it over to her. Bingo! Number one single for her. Nobody cut without calling and looking for hit songs.

When I was having all these hits, songwriters wrote songs. Publishers published songs. RCA started a publishing company one time. And the anti-monopoly law got so tight on them that they gave it to Boots Randolph to get it out of there. You see what I mean?

And all of a sudden, everybody quit coming to me and everybody started doing their own thing. They'd go to Hawaii and pick material. You sent it over there. Well, hell, it never got there. I don't think. I don't know. But all of a sudden, nobody's coming to your office anymore for music. Everybody is trying to write, publish, produce, manage, record and buy a label, I guess. Do it all.

I don't believe there's an artist out there that continuously can write the song, publish it, produce it, record it, promote it, play the road, manage, book and run the label.

And I thought, "There ain't no need in me sitting down here on Music Row with a big building that I own and nobody coming." So I sold the building, sold the copyrights, and retired, more or less, at fifty-five years of age in 1980. And made up my mind for the rest of my life I wasn't going to do nothing except what I wanted to. It's beautiful to be able to afford that when you come from a coal mine camp.

You know the good thing about being successful? You don't have to do nothing. If I wanted to be in Africa right now, I could be there on safari. If I wanted to be in the Bahamas laying on the beach, I could be there. I could do anything I want. But I'm sitting here talking to you, because there's nowhere in the world I'd rather be. And that's a good feeling.

I was nominated to the Songwriters Hall of Fame. Went in on the twelfth nomination. You know why? Nobody in the Songwriters Association that have joined in the last fifteen or twenty years had any earthly idea of who Jerry Chesnut was. Probably didn't know who Eddy Arnold was.

I visited with Sonny Throckmorton in Brownwood, Texas, right before South by Southwest in Austin. I was telling about a half dozen twentysomething country music business employees at major record labels and publishing companies where I had been. Only one of them knew who he was. That's not a slight on Sonny Throck- morton. It's a disgrace and an embarrassment to the industry.

I bought a publishing company from Sonny Throckmorton one time. Him and Bobby Hardin and Ralph Davis had a publishing company. Ralph Davis came to me and said, "I want you to buy this publishing company. The songs in it ain't worth a hoot. They ain't no good at all. But we need to sell it. We need the money and you need to buy it." I listened to all that stuff and it was the awfulest bunch of crap I ever heard in my life. And they knew it.

There was one song in there by neither one of them. By some girl, I think, called "Lead Me, Don't Drive Me Or You'll Drive Me Away." A song about a man singing to his wife. Boy, I fell in love with that song. I thought, "God Almighty!" I gave them several thousand dollars for their publishing company just on the strength of that one song.

And later on, it got to a point to where Tree would bring you a Sonny Throckmorton song and if you didn't cut it, you was ignorant. He just got so hot it was unbelievable. I told him, I said, "Boy, there wasn't nothing that hot in that stuff that I bought from you all." He said, "No, I was sober back then."

What advice do you have for songwriters?

I can sit and listen to song after song and I think, "How in the God's world did I ever do that?" But it wasn't me. They were out there and I'd just reach up and pulled 'em out. You can't tell nobody how to write songs.

The only thing that I tell new songwriters—and I think it's very impor- tant—is I play golf, but I'll never be good enough at golf to be a professional golfer and make money at it. But I still enjoy it and I'm not a failure. And the fact that I'm not a pro and haven't won a major tournament on the tour don't make me feel like a failure. It's something I love to do and I'm going to enjoy it till I die as long as I can swing the club.

The same way with fishing. I'm not a professional fisherman. Wouldn't want to be. Boy, that's work. I know a guy that had three hundred fishing dates in one year. That's only sixty-five days off. He's got these idiots out there that don't even know how to tie a hook on the line trying to catch a fish or they're going to be mad at him. Isn't that horrible? And he hates the sight of a lake.

I know a guy that works on motors and outboards. I said, "What do you do on weekends? Do you fish or anything?" He said, "I don't even want to get within a hundred miles of a boat on a weekend." It's like a plumber watching a commode run over on a weekend. You just get to where you hate it.

I love to fish, I love to play golf, but I'll never be able to do it for a living. People who love to write songs ought to keep it that way. If they ever get great and somebody starts cutting their songs, wonderful. But if they don't, keep writing them, have a good time, sing 'em to your mother, enjoy it. Don't feel like a failure if nobody ever cuts one.

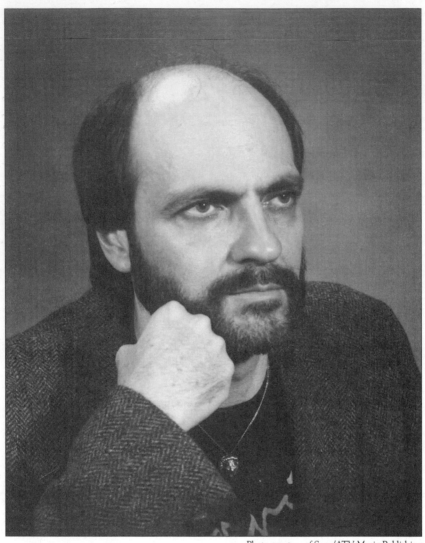

Photo courtesy of Sony/ATV Music Publishing

Bobby Braddock

You've written your share of great songs, but I've always been impressed by your humility.

I see some people who get so stuck-up and become devoured by their own ego. And I think it's sometimes sad, sometimes funny, and sometimes disgusting. Some of the greatest people I've seen aren't that way. Kris Kristofferson's success made him even nicer.

What led you to songwriting?

When I was a kid, I used to substitute my own words for the songs that I heard on the radio. And I didn't know then that that was a symptom of being a professional, full-time songwriter. It was just something I did. And by the time I was eleven or twelve years old, I would hear songs on the radio and think, "Well, I can do that."

I didn't know any songwriters. I wasn't even sure that anybody wrote songs. It was just something I wanted to do. I was in my early twenties when I came to town. I was a rock and roll musician for a while.

Did you have an early appreciation for country music?

It just sounds awful, but when I was about ten years old, my brother listened to country music—Hank Williams, Carl Smith. They called it hillbilly music. And I didn't like it very much.

When I was in junior high school, Ray Price came along with "Crazy Arms" and Marty Robbins was singing the blues. That's when I fell in love with country music. I really liked it about as much as rock and roll.

When I was in high school, I started writing songs. I'd send them to Nashville, and they'd be rejected. I came to Nashville thinking, "Well, I know I can make a living as a piano player." I wasn't sure that I would be able to make a living as a songwriter. I thought, "I can give it a try and support myself by playing the piano." So I gave my notice to Big John's Untouchables, which was the rock and roll band I was in, and came to Nashville.

What year?

That was 1964.

Were you writing songs for the rock and roll band when you moved to Nashville?

No, I was writing country songs and sending them to Nashville. Big John's Untouchables was a really good cover band. I was making a decent living at it, but something told me I had to come to Nashville, so I did.

Your father was in the citrus business.

My father was a citrus grower. He grew oranges and grapefruit and tangerines.

That didn't have an appeal to you? No pun intended.

I knew that I didn't want to be in agriculture.

Was your father a landowner?

He was. Auburndale, Florida is a small town. At one time, my father was the mayor, city manager, and city judge—all at the same time.

I'm sure you spent some time picking fruit.

Well, usually the people at the packinghouse that buys the fruit come in with their crew to pick. I spent a lot of time pruning off dead wood. Working in an orange grove in the Florida summertime, that's really a lot of fun. Snakes, humidity, heat—none of which appealed to me.

That was incentive to move to Nashville.

Yeah.

Was it humble beginnings?

I was just really excited about it. I was playing in a band in Orlando and I had just gotten married. My first wife was very jealous of anybody that I had ever been out with before, so she was all for moving to Nashville just to get away from all these girls that I used to know. If there was one thing she was ever supportive of, it was that.

I didn't hardly know anybody and there was an excitement about it to me. There was a mystique, even in the sounds of the street names. Franklin Pike. Old Hickory Boulevard. I was lucky enough to get a job playing piano with Marty Robbins after I had been here just a few months. Then Marty cut two of my songs. I thought, "Well, gee, maybe I really am a songwriter."

After playing on the road with Marty about a year and half, I came to Tree Publishing, before it was Sony/ATV Music Publishing, and played some songs for Buddy Killen. He let me know that he didn't usually sit down and listen to people's songs off the street. He usually had somebody else do that, but in this case, he had heard the Marty Robbins song that I had written. It wasn't a big hit, but he had heard it. So he met with me, he liked my songs, signed me up, and that's it. I've been here ever since. Is the interview over?

Not hardly. What year?

1966.

More than thirty years with one publishing company is extremely unusual.

That's right. I spent most of my adult life in one publishing company. My God! I like to tell people that I signed here when I was nine years old. Actually, I was twenty-five.

Your breakthrough hit was "D-I-V-O-R-C-E."

I had four things that were in the Top Ten in 1967. "D-I-V-O-R-C-E" was my first number one.

When did you write "D-I-V-O-R-C-E" and was it autobiographical?

I wrote it in 1967. I was thinking, "This song is kind of old for me." My daughter was a baby and the protagonist in this song had a four-year-old child. We pitched it to everybody without much luck.

Curly Putman was Tree's only song plugger at that time. He managed, I might say, to be a really good song plugger when you consider he was a great songwriter. He was really good about pitching other people's songs. I said,

"Why do you think this song has not been cut?" He said, "I think the melody is a little bit too happy for such a sad song." So I said, "What would you do?" He picked up a guitar and he altered it a little bit, but what he did made a vast difference. It just sounded a lot sadder. And I said, "Let's put it on tape like that." He didn't want any of the song. He said, "I'll get all the credit, because I'm an established writer and you're the new kid in town." I wanted him to have half of it and he didn't want any, so we compromised. He took a fourth of it. He took the song to Billy Sherrill, and he cut it on Tammy Wynette within a week or two.

Is that one of the major ways that you have seen the business change? It used to be a short turn around time from written song to cut song. Whereas today someone co-writes a song, they wait around until they have enough songs for a demo session, then the song gets into the hands of song pluggers, then it goes through a system of gatekeepers in a sometimes futile attempt to get it to the producer or the artist.

You said it very well. When a person writes a song now, usually they'll wait until they have enough songs to do a demo session. So they may wait two months after they've written it before they demo it. Then it gets pitched to an A&R person or a producer who is maybe going to record an artist four months down the road. So you have another four months to wait. But that could be after pitching it around for three or four months. Now you've accumulated ten months. Then after they cut it, the album's not going to come out for another few months. If you're lucky enough to get a single, it could be the fourth one on an album. So you could conceivably wait two years from the day that you wrote a song until the time that you hear it on the radio.

Which is somewhat of a best-case scenario. Most songs are never recorded.

That's true. I wrote a song with Rafe Van Hoy called "Golden Ring." We did a little work tape of it the day after we wrote it. It was pitched to Billy Sherrill, and before the week was over, Tammy Wynette and George Jones had cut it. About two weeks after that it was playing on the radio. That was fast even for the old days in Nashville. That's the best-case scenario, but it won't happen now.

What gave rise to the demo becoming much more professional, much more sophisticated—overdubbing, background vocals, intense mixing—instead of a simple guitar/vocal?

Well, the records are more sophisticated now, and in turn, the demos have become more complex. There are so many different ways to make a record. So somewhere along the line we started making demos to sound like records, which they had been doing in the L.A. pop music scene for a long, long time.

I heard a demo of "Like A Virgin," and there was a guy singing it, but he sounded like a girl. The Madonna record was almost exactly like the demo. When I write a song, I write an arrangement. A lot of the cuts I get are just like my demo. Some of my earlier demos were pretty raw. Now I take a lot of care, because that enhances a song and your chances of getting it cut. A person needs to cut a good demo today, because they're competing with good demos. They're competing with a lot of the demos that sound like records. Frankly, a lot of the records don't sound as good as the demo.

We couldn't talk about your career without discussing "He Stopped Loving Her Today." To me, it is one of country music's definitive songs. And one of only two songs to win CMA Song of the Year two years running.

I didn't think it was all that great a song when Curly Putman and I first wrote it. We wrote it way before it got cut in the summer of 1977. Curly says I brought him the idea. I don't remember. I remember we wrote on it, and I took it home and finished it that night. When George Jones recorded it, Billy Sherrill wanted another verse in there. So Curly and I got together about two years later and put together a verse that Billy accepted. The record came out in the spring of 1980.

I kept a journal, as I do now, and I would apply a number between one and ten for how good I thought my songs were. And I applied another numerical value based on what I thought the reaction was from other people. By "He Stopped Loving Her Today," I put a seven and a seven. I thought it was an okay song. And I thought it was being perceived and received that way by other people.

Curly and I went over to Billy Sherrill's office to hear the George Jones cut and, as I said, I didn't think it was all that great or unusual a song. But when Billy Sherrill played it, I knew then that it was something really special. I honestly think that the performance by George Jones and production by Billy Sherrill made "He Stopped Loving Her Today" what it was. There was more to the song than I realized. In the hands of somebody else, it probably wouldn't be perceived as the standard that it is.

Was Billy Sherrill one of the best song men you knew?

The best. Great producer. He really defined what country music was from the late '60s to the early '80s. A lot of people criticized him for being smaltzy because of his orchestrations. But when you look back on it, the truth is, he cut some of the best records by the greatest traditional country artists of all time. They were great records. The strings on "He Stopped Loving Her Today" actually made it a lot better record.

Billy Sherrill was an engineer, a songwriter, a piano player. He had all the components of being a really great producer. And he was an excellent song man.

Billy Sherrill never won any popularity contests. Never tried to. He was not a glad-hander or a schmoozer at all. He was kind of a recluse with a sort of Don Rickles sense of humor. I liked him. I thought he was funny.

I was very fortunate to get in to see him, because there were a lot of people who couldn't.

Billy Sherrill cut a great record on "He Stopped Loving Her Today," but you don't receive any writer royalties from it.

You mean after selling my catalog to Buddy Killen?

Correct.

As I look back on it, I had gotten myself in so much debt with the IRS that I really had no choice but to do that. And I think my catalog was worth more than what I sold it for. But I have to say that it was a need I had at the time and Buddy filled that need. I don't have any problem with it. It saved my butt. It bailed me out. It just barely got me by until the hits started coming again a few years later.

I think other people lament it more than I do. It is sad in a way, but it's a choice I made. It's something that's done, so I've let go of it. I look to the future rather than the past.

When you say you sold your catalog, you were selling your writer's share, because you didn't have any publishing share at that time.

That's right. I never even had co-publishing on my songs until the past couple of years. When it came time to re-sign, I was always so needy for advances. So everything I wrote before 1989 still has my name on it, but I don't get any money off of it.

It was like starting over from scratch. It's like I came to town ten years ago and started writing songs.

You said you got in trouble with the IRS. Obviously, you were behind on taxes, but why was that happening?

When God gave me a right brain, He didn't give me a left brain.

It starts with my first marriage. I'm not blaming my first wife for it, because it was my fault, too. Neither one of us had any sense. If I was making $12,000 a year, we'd live on $15,000. If I was making $20,000 a year, then we'd live on $30,000.

A lot of debt accumulated. If you get behind on paying the IRS, the penalties and interest and fines are staggering. So I got to the point where I actually owed the IRS twice as much as I would have owed them because of the interest and penalties.

The best feeling in the world was a couple of years ago—for the first time in my life I was totally debt free.

If I had anything to do over in my life, it would be financial things. If I have any regrets, it's what I did with my money. I wouldn't change any of the relationships I had with anybody. My first marriage was awful, but I got a wonderful, beautiful daughter out of it, so I wouldn't even change that.

I feel like I'm very lucky to have been able to make a living doing something that I really love to do. My vocation and avocation are the same. The only thing I would change is I would take better care of my money.

That's good advice. But there weren't a lot of people giving financial advice to songwriters in the good old days.

That's right. Of all the self-employed people in the world, songwriters are atypical, because most people who are self-employed have some business sense. Creative people don't seem to have as good business sense as say accountants, for instance.

Maybe that's why they are doing debits and credits and you're doing music and lyrics.

I'm sure there are some songwriting accountants out there, too.

Tim DuBois.

That's right. Tim DuBois has a good left brain and good right brain. He has been doubly blessed.

Did you see the Tennessean today?

I haven't seen today's paper.

On the front page it says, "T-Shirt Not Enough? Make Jones Record. Buy His Lexus for $20,000." The headline refers to the selling price of George Jones's recently wrecked Lexus. George said, "Maybe they ought to keep it until I die, it might be worth more."

Do you think he sang his own eulogy with "He Stopped Loving Her Today" and that it was about Tammy Wynette?

First of all, I think the character in "He Stopped Loving Her Today" is a terrible role model. I think he should have gotten a life. He was obviously co-dependent. That's pretty pitiful—a person who pines their life away over somebody that they lost. So the character in the song is not a very good role model.

Is George that character? I don't think so. I've been around George and his wife occasionally. Not a lot, but every once in a while. And I have the feeling that they're pretty solid. Obviously, George and Tammy were this great, legendary country music love story. I think he really did love her. I think he eventually got over her and that he really loves Nancy now.

There's a little story that L.E. White told me. L.E. was at the session when George recorded "He Stopped Loving Her Today." L.E. White is pretty reliable, so I take his word. Somebody else substantiated the story, which I only found out a few years ago.

Back then, they cut everything pretty much live. They cut the lead vocal performance and the background vocals along with the instrumental tracks. Billy Sherrill continued to do that after a lot of people stopped doing it that way.

George Jones had done one take on "He Stopped Loving Her Today" and it wasn't quite right. About that time, George Richey and Tammy Wynette, who had not been married very long at that time, walked into the control room. Tammy sat down behind the console next to Billy Sherrill, and the light illuminated her face. So when George sang "He Stopped Loving Her Today"—take two—he was looking right at Tammy. That's the performance you hear on the record.

When he sang it, he probably still had strong feelings for her. But it seems like Nancy Jones has sort of saved George's life, so I don't know if it was his eulogy or not. It is the stuff that legends are made of, though.

You were a big part of the George and Tammy duo career.

George and Tammy and Billy Sherrill were a big part of my career. I was really fortunate, because for hardcore country music, I don't think there's anybody better than George Jones or Tammy Wynette. They were absolutely the best.

Let's talk about your recording career. You're not one of Billboard's "one-hit wonders," because you had four singles spanning from 1967 to 1980.

I was on five major labels, which shows you how easy it used to be to get a record deal. I was on MGM, Mercury, CBS, Electra and RCA. If I had ever had a big hit, I don't think I would have survived the road.

But you did the road as a recording artist, didn't you?

Not much. Mostly promotion. I never had a big enough hit to justify me getting a band together and run out there working. I had several things on the charts, nothing really big. I don't know if I had the fire in the belly for it. I always had it in my head that I could do like the Beatles—just make records and not have to tour.

As I listen back on my records, I think a lot of them are just awful. The later ones were certainly better, but the MGM records were just hideous.

Not the songs.

The songs were pretty sucky. The whole thing sucked.

Even the shrink-wrap?

I didn't have shrink-wrap until I made albums. The albums on Electra I did with Don Gant were probably a little melodramatic, but they weren't bad. They weren't awful.

The best album I did probably was a little thing for RCA called *Hard Core Pornography.* I produced it all myself and it was fun. I look back on it and think, "Yeah, well that made sense. That was kind of funny."

You should have put "Mother Funker" on it.

Oh, my God! I can't believe I wrote that!

These things follow you.

You can't take back a fuck and you can't take back a bad song.

I've heard that "Love Bomb" was autobiographical.

That's true. It really happened.

My second wife's brother and his wife were over at the house. We were drinking and they got in a fight. And my wife and I drove them back to Alabama in separate cars. It's absolutely true.

In the second verse of "Love Bomb" you talk about drinking with friends. Everyone was Caucasian, with the exception of one African-American. The group was kind to his face, but talked behind his back after he left. You equated this racist behavior to Hitler's treatment of the Jews.

The second verse absolutely happened. It happened in the late Don Gant's office.

There was a black writer who wrote at Tree. Being a small-town southern boy and being brought up with a lot of racist attitudes, I just got beyond all that myself. I think I got beyond it before some of my friends did. And it disturbed me. So I guess instead of lecturing everybody, I put it in a song.

Another song of yours is quite interesting, "The Kute Klux Klan," which is a play on Ku Klux Klan, where you take the liberty of using the "N" word.

I guess I thought I could be Randy Newman. He makes himself the bad character in his songs like somebody playing a bad character in a movie.

Randy Newman expounds on social issues by putting the bad guy in the song in the first person. And he is a genius for that. That's what I attempted to do there by using the "N" word.

Of course, the song obviously was an anti-Ku Klux Klan, anti-racism song. But when the album came out, somebody from the record label misread it and thought it was a racist song. They thought that I, myself, was using the "N" word. So it caused a little bit of controversy.

"Kute Klux Klan" is a satirical song. You clearly come from a point of unity. You're putting down racism. Is it frustrating when people miss the message? Does that disturb you?

Oh, yeah.

I try to write concisely and clean. When I say clean, I'm talking about making sure that the song is tight and well written and easily understood. Because, ultimately, if the song is misunderstood, the blame is going to have to go back to the songwriter.

Words go by rather quickly when they're on the radio. A person listening to it might be carrying on a conversation with somebody else. It's easy to miss. I think it should be crystal clear, as terse as can possibly be. You have to be careful with the double meanings.

I think the mark of an amateur songwriter is somebody who has written something that they thoroughly understand in their own mind, but they have not articulated it very well. That's an important thing in writing a song, a book, a poem, instructions, directions. Just because you understand it doesn't mean the other person's going to understand it. Don't assume that I know half of it. Assume I don't know any of it.

So in a song, I try to make it as clear as I possibly can.

It seems the radio tends to be the lowest common denominator because people are doing other things—driving down the road, talking on the cell phone. Music is being played in the background at a party or in the workplace. In your journal where you self-graded your songs, do you find many of your tens ending up on the radio?

I have very, very few tens.

I can't imagine you writing anything under a seven, so let's talk eights and nines.

Oh, I have twos and threes. I definitely do. I have a song that's never been a single. It should have been. George Strait recorded it. It's called "The Nerve." I would self-grade that a ten. That's the best song I ever wrote. I'd say "Time Marches On" is a really strong nine. That's probably my favorite song that I've ever written that became a hit.

"Time Marches On" really demonstrates the economy of the country lyric. You traverse several decades in a short amount of time. It was all very clear and the listener sees the timeline.

It also breaks a lot of the rules. I was surprised that it was a big hit, because the song was just chock-full of things they tell us we can't write about—drugs, alcoholism, dysfunctional family, mental illness.

You mean you can't write about the American lifestyle?

They're just supposed to be nice, innocuous little positive love songs. That one somehow slipped by. Matraca Berg and Gary Harrison's "Strawberry Wine" is another one. You don't see "a five-minute waltz about a girl losing her virginity" as the kind of song they're looking for on pitch sheets. But that song got through.

The advice I would give writers is write stuff that you love. I think you should listen to radio, because if you're going to write left of center, you need to know where the center is. You don't want to get so far out there that you can't communicate with people. You can speak the best Latin in the world, but I won't understand it.

After you've been in the music business for a while, you realize there are so many factors that go into getting a song on the radio. Why do you think "The Nerve" didn't get picked for a single?

Three words: promotion got scared. And the answer to that is three other words: it was different.

I've heard a lot of great songs that never make it to records, much less the airwaves. There's a certain sadness I have that people don't get to hear these wonderful works of art. If people didn't buy the George Strait record, "The Nerve," which is an incredible song, may have escaped them. It seems like country radio should be playing those kinds of songs for the public.

I almost wish I hadn't written "The Nerve," because the talk initially was Song of the Year. Then the label changed their mind about it. Another artist cut the song several months ago and was enthusiastic about it, but his label killed it. It didn't even make his album. I still have other plans for it.

Maybe as a producer?

Well, I can't even get my own artist to do it.

Maybe we'll have to rev up your artist career again.

Some of the best songs in this town are never recorded.

Don Henry songs are a classic example.

Don Henry is a genius and I don't toss that word around very much. But he is absolute genius, and sadly, his songs don't get cut very often. But he's far from the center.

He's over the centerfield fence. He knocks it out of the park.

He definitely does. Brilliant songs.

Speaking of brilliant, did you spend any time around Roger Miller?

One of the reasons I came to Tree was Roger Miller had left and gone to the West Coast. And I thought, "Okay, here's this company that's just become the top publishing company. Roger Miller has gone. Maybe that would be a good place to start. Maybe they'd be interested in some new young talent."

Of course, Roger came back and I eventually got to know him. I just really loved him and I still miss him. He was the quickest man I ever met in my life. I never seen anybody that could come up with a line so quick.

Roger was down in the studio one time and there was this girl who worked here who talked pretty country. While we were standing in the studio, she said, "I think I'm going to get me some warter." And Billy the engineer said, "Is there an 'r' in the middle of water?" And Roger said, "Well, if there's not, there ourghta be."

And he was just like that. He never missed a beat. He was always on. I remember he met somebody one time and the guy was so nervous he tripped over him and immediately Roger said, "Did you enjoy your trip?" He met John Hyatt, he said, "I like your hotel."

One liners. He could have played the Catskills.

Absolutely. I would sometimes foolishly try to keep up with him. I was never able to, but it was fun trying.

You've been around the business for thirty-something years. You've got to have a few favorite stories up your sleeve.

Let's see. Stories that can be told.

That can be reprinted without any libel suits.

The very best stories have to go untold, because if the person the story is about is alive, he could kick my ass. And if he's dead, I don't want to tell it out of respect.

I can think of a Harlan Howard story I can't tell. A Curly Putman story I can't tell. I've got some funny Sonny Throckmorton stories I can't tell. I don't know if I'll live long enough to be able to tell some of these stories. Most of these stories, you understand, don't have to do with the actual writing of songs.

Maybe I could tell one without using the guy's name. A well-known songwriter was with a bunch of people smoking dope. He seemed to have a proclivity for smoking a lot of marijuana. He was supposed to meet a real estate man and he was an hour late meeting. When he got there he told the guy, "I'm sorry I'm late, but I had to do some paperwork."

I heard Rafe Van Hoy and Don Cook bartended at a party with their pants off. They had their shirts on, but they were behind the bar butt naked.

I got into a birthday cake with my pants off one time. Rafe Van Hoy peed in Buddy Killen's aquarium.

Did he have a compelling reason?

It was there.

The biggest thrill for me was when Buddy Killen brought Paul McCartney in. Because I was a big Beatles freak, I told Buddy it would really mean a lot to me to meet Paul. One evening, Buddy was taking Paul and Linda and Chet Atkins out to Loveless Café for dinner, so he asked them to come by early. He said, "There is somebody that really wants to meet you and I want you to meet him." They came by and hung out for a few minutes. And Paul was such a sweetheart. He and Linda were both so nice.

As they started to leave, Buddy got in the car and Paul says, "Bobby, you're going with us, aren't you?" And I could see Buddy was about to shit in his pants. He did not want one of his songwriters tagging along to a dinner with Paul and Linda McCartney and Chet Atkins. So I immediately said, "No, no, I'm not going. I just wanted to meet you guys." And I thought, "Damn it, Buddy, couldn't you have let me gone along?"

The thing about the oral tradition though . . .

Did you say oral tradition?

The oral tradition. The telling of stories.

That brought to mind another story.

The old Tree elevator?

Otis. Going down on Otis.

Years ago, when I was at Tom Collins Music, Johnny Russell dropped in. Johnny is a consummate storyteller. And it was the first time I had sat in the presence of someone telling insider entertainment industry stories. I thought, "My God, I've arrived!" That element seems to be missing today.

It's a lot more impersonal and certainly a lot more corporate. When I think back twenty years ago, I think about songwriters and their wives or girlfriends or boyfriends or husbands—most of the writers were male—sitting around in Don Gant's office drinking wine, smoking dope and listening to each other's songs. There was a lot of camaraderie then.

When I look back on it, though, I think there was a lot of misspent energy, too. That's another thing, if I had it to do over. I don't think I was ever addicted to marijuana. I smoked marijuana two or three times a week. They say it kills the brain cells, so maybe I smoked it more than that. It was fun at the time, but I could not imagine doing that now.

How much material did you create under the influence of marijuana?

I was never able to create while I was smoking marijuana. Never. The only song I ever wrote while I was smoking marijuana that did anything was written with a guy who smoked a lot of marijuana. He wrote so many wonderful songs and he was stoned, I think, during every one of them. And they were great songs. It's an individual thing. It's however that substance affects you. I don't think I ever wrote much that was worth a hoot while I was drinking either.

But I don't see the young people partying. I see them very, very serious. They approach this like a business.

A lot of them have college degrees.

They come in here and it's a nine-to-five job. Back then it was pretty wild.

Certainly there's a lot more money on the table today than there was back then.

Absolutely.

Today, you can make more off the mechanical royalties of an album cut than you might have made on a hit single twenty years ago.

That's true. The big difference back then was there were not as many country radio stations. Not nearly as many. Of course, our numbers may be going down now with this boring stuff on the radio. And deservedly so.

But "Please Remember Me" gives me faith in music in this town.

What a wonderful song. In my opinion, that's maybe the best breaking up song ever written.

Why do you think that?

For one thing, it's so generous and so loving. He's wishing her the very, very best. And makes it sounds like something out of somebody's life.

He doesn't want to be forgotten.

That's right. He doesn't want to be forgotten. I think that it's pure musical and lyrical genius. And the killer line is that little extra line at the end of the bridge. Good God! That is perfect. That's as good as it gets.

I think it's great to hear you appreciate other people's songs.

I can get as excited over somebody else's song as I can my own. And I can hate somebody else's song as much as my own.

I always thought one of the best breakup songs was "New Way Out."

I have to agree with you. That's a wonderful song. A new way out that you're not going to hurt the person.

We're talking about a song that wasn't a hit and I could not understand why it wasn't a hit. Was that Karen Brooks?

Yes. It was written by Randy Sharp.

Funny you remember that song, because I love that song. And it didn't get very high on the charts.

Some of my favorite movies weren't big at the box office and it's the same way with songs. The public, for the most part, never gets to hear some of the greatest songs.

What inspires your writing?

I write a lot of autobiographical songs. I write semi-autobiographical songs and quite a few biographical songs, too. Like "Time Marches On." That was fiction based on what I've seen. That's the way it is with a lot of songs. "Texas Tornado" was inspired by somebody. I was hanging out with a really nice person, but the relationship was a little stormy. She was originally from Texas and she liked tornadoes. That's where that came from. So there's some truth, some fiction.

Do you ever intend to pursue writing something other than songs?

I've got a big closet full of journals and diaries that I've been keeping for many, many, many years. The first thing I'll do is just sit down at the computer and edit. The first one will begin when I started keeping this series of diaries, which was in 1971, and it will end in 1983—day my divorce became final on my second marriage.

It's not that I think that my life is so fascinating that people would be interested in it. I think, maybe, I'm a halfway decent observer and I happened to write what I saw. The pages would be populated with some pretty interesting people in the music business. Also, I chronicled the continuing downhill slide of a very, very bad first marriage and the effect that it had on my daughter. The second marriage was really a big love story that was a lot of fun. But it had a tragic, sad ending. I would call this first book *D-I-V-O-R-C-E: A Nashville Diary*.

Was your second marriage the love of your life?

I'd say it was one of the three loves in my life.

Do songs still come from that source?

Oh, no. I got over that a long time ago. I'm not like the guy in "He Stopped Loving Her Today." I've been pretty seriously in love a couple times since then. And she and I are very good friends. We're good buddies. I'm good friends with her husband and long, long past that.

There was a group of people a hundred years old-plus on TV one time from varied backgrounds. They all had one thing in common: the ability to let go. And it's important to let go to survive. That's why I say the character in "He Stopped Loving Her Today" was a very bad role model. He's the opposite of what I want to be. Past loves, they're over. It's something that's gone and you have to let go of it. Like my old catalog. I had to let go of that. I can't dwell on it.

Is there anything you consider a secret to your songwriting that you could share?

Then it wouldn't be a secret anymore. No, not really. I just look around me. Look at life and make it meter and rhyme. Put a melody to it. It's a strange way to make a living, but that's pretty much it, really.

Photo courtesy of BMI Archives

John D. Loudermilk —
Bonus Track

In today's interview, you have heard me speak of Ernest Moon, the classical guitar player with white paint under his fingernails, who turned me on to classical guitar. Now I'd like to tell you about the person that turned me on to this philosophical bent that this whole thing has taken today.

As soon as I got my first royalties from "A Rose And A Baby Ruth," I bought my folks a house and went to college. Total waste of time in college. I wanted to go see what the kids were listening to so I could write songs for them. I didn't give a shit about learning anything, because if you're not self-educated, you're not educated. If you have to go sit in college and read the stuff that they tell you to read, then you're industrially educated. You're not personally educated. A reading list is all you need.

I had to take Spanish in order to go to Campbell College in Williams Creek, North Carolina, because I worked in high school and didn't take my foreign language. The first day in Spanish class, a little fat woman in her fifties with big eyes said, "Would Mr. Loudermilk come by my desk as you all go?" All we did was sign our names on a piece of paper and give it to her the first day in school. So I went by and she said, "I can tell from your handwriting that you need to be a special student of mine." I said, "How do you know that?" She said, "It's not important, but I can tell. How badly do you need this credit?" I said, "I need it very badly." She said, "Okay. If you'll come to my room when I invite you and you read what I tell you, I'll give you the questions to the exams." This is in a Baptist school in 1957. I said, "You got a deal."

She was a dorm mother of the girls' dorm. So the first night she gave me two books. One was *There Is A River*, a life history of Edgar Cayce, and *Philip In Two Worlds*, about a guy dying and going over into the hereafter and not knowing he was over there. A lot of them don't know they're dead for a long time. They still think they're living.

So I read those things and she said, "I'm a spiritualist. I'm going to teach you some stuff that goes much further than Spanish." I said, "Well, I have written 'Sitting In The Balcony.'" It had just come out. She said, "You're a songwriter." I said, "Yeah." She said, "Okay." So we sat down in chairs across from each other with our hands on our thighs.

This is beginning to sound like a Penthouse *letter.*

She said, "I want you to envision your record going around, the disk jockey putting the needle on the record. It's going around and around and he's saying, 'Here's the number one hit of the day,' and then forget it. Go on to the next thing now. I want you to think a picture of a kid putting a dollar across the counter at a record store, then handing your record to him." We had four images that we sat there and we thought about.

This "Sitting In The Balcony" took off. We couldn't understand why it was selling so damn good. And that started a relationship of reading what she gave me to read. It was all about Edgar Cayce. So I read everything on his life that was available.

Then I read a collection of channelings that were done by an unknown person at an unknown time. A group from India put it all together. I don't trust a lot of that shit, but back then this was the only thing that was being channeled. It was another version of the Bible. Another way of looking at the creation story.

This led from one thing to another thing to another thing to another thing, and has been a direct reason for this interview today taking the slant that it's taken. These things come through us from an unknown place. Hank Williams called it God. Everybody else calls it one thing or another. I don't know where the hell it comes from. But it does not come from me. It comes from somewhere else.

I have gotten the same song that a fucker in France got at the same time. We were on the guitar strings that go around the world. We hooked on the same string. He in France and me over here. He wrote the same song I wrote about the same time that I wrote it. I have had that happen in my career.

There's a scientific level of understanding and tools that our five senses cannot identify. There is a science that has yet to be developed. A musicologist in Jerusalem that is moving stones with music. This is not just some hillbilly out in the woods in Tennessee talking.

You're a perpetual student.

Well, hell, yes, you've got to be. What's the alternative?

I spent seven thousand dollars on books last year. The IRS guy just couldn't understand it. I got a receipt for every damn one of them.

Do you have any interest in the Internet?

My wife does. She wastes a lot of time on that damn thing. Anything I need to know, she can find out. She's traced her family back to 600 AD. That's before last names. She's got her family in France. All of it on the Internet.

In one little town in France where there were thirty families, one of those families in 1300 was Loudermilk and one of them was Chalet, her maiden name. Now the synchronicity of that is startling. It is astounding. In a town of thirty families we had ancestors that close together.

I would reckon it would even astound Art Bell. I don't know him personally and I don't want to know him personally. I never want to be friends with somebody I admire. Eddy Arnold and I bump into each other at parties. And I turn around and avoid him. He asked me about it one time, and I said, "Eddy, I don't want to know you. You're such a star in my mind. I just want to love you and respect you and admire you." He's the best star I've ever known. He's upheld a standard that I continue to try to climb toward. Getting to know a star brings his ass down on the floor. He's off of the box.

You got to have him on the box if he's going to be a star. I've got all his records. He's been the greatest drive in my life as far as stars. He's just like Chet Atkins. Chet has set standards that I have struggled to attain and never have. And I want that. I love that. I don't want to know stars. Every time I know a star, he ceased to become a star.

It's like the moon. They fucked up the moon in the '60s when they went up there. It's ceased to be a romantic thing. Nobody writes songs about the romantic moon. Now they're fucking up Mars.

And you can't really write a romantic song about Uranus.

Well, depends on your sexual proclivity.

We've lost seven spaceships in the last twenty years to Mars. Nobody knows why. NASA says it's just accidental. But Richard Hogland, an ex-NASA scientist, couldn't stand being in the box. Got out of the box. He's the one that saved the stone circle down in Miami. Have you heard about that? The wooden circle down in Miami. They tore down a hotel to build a bigger hotel and found a circle of holes where wooden posts used to be with alignments back forty-thousand years ago where stars and celestial bodies rose on the horizon. They can go back now with computers and find out what rose there then. And he personally saved that damn thing. He kept the hotels from building on top of it. He got fourteen million dollars out of the Florida legislature to preserve that place.

There are wonderful heroes now that are happening and they're out of this genre of literature. I go see them speak. I get their autographs. They don't know who the hell I am. I don't want them to know. I just want their autographs. I had dinner with this Jacob guy I was talking about. The one that said the aliens are after our planet. He's the head of a damn department with tenure and everything at Cornell. And the son-of-a-bitch is so smart, he looks down on me as being a clod, a songwriter. And I look at him as being a professor that I take a course under.

I bought his goddamn dinner. And he would not even eat food. You know what he did? He pulled out a sandwich and ate at this restaurant that goes a hundred dollars a person. He said, "I'm on a diet." I later found out he thought I was a CIA guy. He was afraid to have dinner with me, afraid I'd poison his ass. There's intrigue going on in this genre that is incredible. It's the most interesting thing I've ever gotten into.

If you ever get a chance to go down in March to Gulf Breeze, they go out and see flying saucers every night of the damn convention. And there's a guy now, a Dr. Greer from North Carolina I told you about, who is leading little groups of fifteen people. They go to where there's recent activity and they sit there and meditate with big strong lights and sound that's been recorded from other flying saucers. They amplify the damn stuff up into the sky, and the fuckers appear. They've got them now flashing three lights to them. They're communicating with these damn aliens. On demand. It's called encounters of the fifth kind, because humans have instigated the thing. Now they're waiting for it to land. And eventually they're going to go on the damn thing and be taken for a ride. That's Dr. Greer's goal.

Have you been to Gulf Breeze?

No. I'm reading his book now. It's brand-new. And I'm going to do that. I'm going to do that. But I've got to change my fear. My fear is keeping me from seeing. Out here I watch stars all the time at night. I spend a lot of nights out in the wintertime. Last year we waited for a shower and I saw one come under the cloud cover. Things the size of houses that come in. I've seen them break apart over this property. So I'm a big star watcher. I love to watch the stars. I have telescopes and things. Matter of fact, I'm one of three who are watching a certain crater on the moon for movement. Things are moving on the moon, Phil. There's a guy in Louisiana and a guy in Ohio and me. We're triangulating the movement and we can tell how big it is and how fast it moves by our CCD cameras on our telescopes. It takes a picture and then five minutes later or however long you want to set it for, it takes another picture. You can go back during the day on the computer and tell if anything moved.

There's a twenty-one mile long deal up there that's cigar-shaped that is moving. I haven't gotten into that project yet, but I'm lined up.

Seismic activity on the moon?

No, man! It's something moving on the surface. Something man-made or somebody's made it. It's not natural. Something is moving.

And they found a twenty-one mile high tower on the moon. Twenty-one miles high. That's staggering. New science is just blowing me out of the water. Shit, I've met a lot of the guys that are heroes in this movement. I've sat in UFO conventions, where I know the government's highly represented. Matter of fact, at these UFO conventions, there's no pyramid hats there. You find mainly teachers, writers, psychologists, psychiatric people. Because they wonder what the hell this all is. Is this coming from inside us or is it coming from outside us? A lot of medical people. A lot of retired military people.

And a lot of people say, "The army sent me." Or, "The air force sent me." And, "I'm here to try to tell them what the hell you all are doing." And they're all welcome.

Ten years ago at Gulf Breeze, they had a flat, a flying saucer down there. It's the first place the triangular craft had been seen. And I believe, and a lot of other people believe, that they have reversed-engineered some technology from a craft and they're testing it down there at Eglin Air Force Base.

Art Bell said that he and his wife were out in their yard. They live in Parumph, Nevada, just north of Las Vegas way out in the desert. And they saw one that took up most of the sky. Blocked out all of the damn stars. And said they could tell the shape of it, because there was a triangle of no stars.

And said if he had had an arm about fifty feet long, he could have touched the damn thing. He was that close to it. That's about one-and-a-half telephone poles. And he said he could see the way the thing was put together with rivets. Said it was riveted. So there are some very exciting things happening right now, man.

I know I take up a lot of your time talking about that shit, but it's all pertinent, it's all relative. It has to do with songwriting. It damn sure has to do with songwriting. Whether songwriters know it or not. And Nashville's a good place to talk about this shit. Did you know there's more psychics in Nashville, per capita, than any other town in America? Did you know that there are seven religions based in Nashville? Why do you think songs are so important in Nashville? Where do they come from? Why are they centered there?

New Orleans had the chance to get the recording business. And they didn't get it because the goddamn people were so greedy they said they wanted scale to start with and we here said, "Give us a little bit more than we're getting now, and if we sell records, we want a raise." And that's why the music business came to Nashville. It was all planned.

I heard the same thing happened in Memphis. Greed killed Memphis.

Oh, yes, that's right. Exactly right. Jack Clement will tell you that, and Sam Phillips will tell you that. That's the truth. But this town has been blessed. It's a magical place. If you don't believe in magic, then you ain't giving the magician the right amount of respect. It is a town. Merlin lives in Nashville. And Solomon was a magician.

Did the magic of Nashville bring you back?

It's the only town I've ever moved back to. Yes. When we were in Louisiana, it was wonderful. It was eating gumbo every day. But if you were a songwriter in Lafayette, you were shit. If you were an oil man, you were somebody big. So I came back for the respect the songwriter has here. And for the music. And for the burn. There's just a burn here.

Nashville burns me. I can't stay in Nashville long. I find myself writing seven songs a day, like I used to. And you can only do that for a while until you got nervous and you have to quit. But it's on fire. It's different than any other place. Nashville is so on fire.

When you come here poor and you see how quickly you can get rich, Jesus, that lends itself to the heat, too.

Index

Song Index

Photo courtesy of John Briggs

ABOUT THE AUTHOR

Author **Philip Self,** left, pictured with legendary songwriter, **Eddie Snyder.** Mr. Snyder penned several American standards including **"A Time For Us,"** the theme from *Romeo and Juliet.*

In 1972, Self performed said composition rather poorly at the Plantation Park Elementary Talent Contest in Bossier City, Louisiana. The former pianist is now a drummer.

Philip Self is the author of **Yogi Bare.** He teaches yoga and meditation workshops across the country. The singer-songwriter lives in Nashville and can be reached at **pself@cypressmoon.com.**

The opinions expressed in Guitar Pull are solely those of the songerwriters interviewed, and do not necessarily reflect the opinions of Cypress Moon Press or the author.

For additional information regarding the legendary songwriters interviewed in *Guitar Pull*, please contact:

Cypress Moon Press
P.O. Box 210925 · Nashville, TN 37221

T: 615-496-4838 • F: 615-662-9385

e-mail: info@cypressmoon.com
www.cypressmoon.com